Gender, Discourse and Power in the Cameroonian Parliament

Lilian Lem Atanga

Langaa Research & Publishing CIG
Mankon, Bamenda

Publisher:
Langaa RPCIG
Langaa Research & Publishing Common Initiative Group
P.O. Box 902 Mankon
Bamenda
North West Region
Cameroon
Langaagrp@gmail.com
www.langaa-rpcig.net

Distributed outside N. America by African Books Collective
orders@africanbookscollective.com
www.africanbookscollective.com

Distributed in N. America by Michigan State University Press
msupress@msu.edu
www.msupress.msu.edu

ISBN: 9956-615-46-3

DISCLAIMER

All views expressed in this publication are those of the author
and do not necessarily reflect the views of Langaa RPCIG.

Other Titles by *Langaa* RPCIG

Francis B. Nyamnjoh
Stories from Abakwa
Mind Searching
The Disillusioned African
The Convert
Souls Forgotten
Married But Available

Dibussi Tande
No Turning Back. Poems of Freedom 1990-1993
Scribbles from the Den: Essays on Politics and Collective Memory in Cameroon

Kangsen Feka Wakai
Fragmented Melodies

Ntemfac Ofege
Namondo. Child of the Water Spirits
Hot Water for the Famous Seven

Emmanuel Fru Doh
Not Yet Damascus
The Fire Within
Africa's Political Wastelands: The Bastardization of Cameroon
Oriki'badan
Wading the Tide
Stereotyping Africa: Surprising Answers to Surprising Questions

Thomas Jing
Tale of an African Woman

Peter Wuteh Vakunta
Grassfields Stories from Cameroon
Green Rape: Poetry for the Environment
Majunga Tok: Poems in Pidgin English
Cry, My Beloved Africa
No Love Lost
Straddling The Mungo: A Book of Poems in English & French

Ba'bila Mutia
Coils of Mortal Flesh

Kehbuma Langmia
Titabet and the Takumbeng
An Evil Meal of Evil

Victor Elame Musinga
The Barn
The Tragedy of Mr. No Balance

Ngessimo Mathe Mutaka
Building Capacity: Using TEFL and African Languages as Development-oriented Literacy Tools

Milton Krieger
Cameroon's Social Democratic Front: Its History and Prospects as an Opposition Political Party, 1990-2011

Sammy Oke Akombi
The Raped Amulet
The Woman Who Ate Python
Beware the Drives: Book of Verse
The Wages of Corruption

Susan Nkwentie Nde
Precipice
Second Engagement

Francis B. Nyamnjoh & Richard Fonteh Akum
The Cameroon GCE Crisis: A Test of Anglophone Solidarity

Joyce Ashuntantang & Dibussi Tande
Their Champagne Party Will End! Poems in Honor of Bate Besong

Emmanuel Achu
Disturbing the Peace

Rosemary Ekosso
The House of Falling Women

Peterkins Manyong
God the Politician

George Ngwane
The Power in the Writer: Collected Essays on Culture, Democracy & Development in Africa

John Percival
The 1961 Cameroon Plebiscite: Choice or Betrayal

Albert Azeyeh
Réussite scolaire, faillite sociale : généalogie mentale de la crise de l'Afrique noire francophone

Aloysius Ajab Amin & Jean-Luc Dubois
Croissance et développement au Cameroun :
d'une croissance équilibrée à un développement équitable

Carlson Anyangwe
Imperialistic Politics in Cameroun:
Resistance & the Inception of the Restoration of the Statehood of Southern Cameroons
Betrayal of Too Trusting a People: The UN, the UK and the Trust Territory of the Southen Cameroons

Bill F. Ndi
K'Cracy, Trees in the Storm and Other Poems
Map: Musings On Ars Poetica
Thomas Lurting: The Fighting Sailor Turn'd Peaceable /Le marin combattant devenu paisible

Kathryn Toure, Therese Mungah Shalo Tchombe & Thierry Karsenti
ICT and Changing Mindsets in Education

Charles Alobwed'Epie
The Day God Blinked
The Bad Samaritan

G. D. Nyamndi
Babi Yar Symphony
Whether losing, Whether winning
Tussles: Collected Plays
Dogs in the Sun

Samuel Ebelle Kingue
Si Dieu était tout un chacun de nous ?

Ignasio Malizani Jimu
Urban Appropriation and Transformation: bicycle, taxi and handcart operators in Mzuzu, Malawi

Justice Nyo' Wakai
Under the Broken Scale of Justice: The Law and My Times

John Eyong Mengot
A Pact of Ages

Ignasio Malizani Jimu
Urban Appropriation and Transformation: Bicycle Taxi and Handcart Operators

Joyce B. Ashuntantang
Landscaping and Coloniality: The Dissemination of Cameroon Anglophone Literature

Jude Fokwang
Mediating Legitimacy: Chieftaincy and Democratisation in Two African Chiefdoms

Michael A. Yanou
Dispossession and Access to Land in South Africa: an African Perspevctive

Tikum Mbah Azonga
Cup Man and Other Stories
The Wooden Bicycle and Other Stories

John Nkemngong Nkengasong
Letters to Marions (And the Coming Generations)

Amady Aly Dieng
Les étudiants africains et la littérature négro-africaine d'expression
française

Tah Asongwed
Born to Rule: Autobiography of a life President

Frida Menkan Mbunda
Shadows From The Abyss

Bongasu Tanla Kishani
A Basket of Kola Nuts

Fo Angwafo III S.A.N of Mankon
Royalty and Politics: The Story of My Life

Basil Diki
The Lord of Anomy

Churchill Ewumbue-Monono
Youth and Nation-Building in Cameroon: A Study of National
Youth Day Messages and Leadership Discourse (1949-2009)

Emmanuel N. Chia, Joseph C. Suh & Alexandre Ndeffo Tene
Perspectives on Translation and Interpretation in Cameroon

Linus T. Asong
The Crown of Thorns
No Way to Die
A Legend of the Dead: Sequel of *The Crown of Thorns*
The Akroma File
Salvation Colony: Sequel to *No Way to Die*

Vivian Sihshu Yenika
Imitation Whiteman

Beatrice Fri Bime
Someplace, Somewhere
Mystique: A Collection of Lake Myths

Shadrach A. Ambanasom
Son of the Native Soil
The Cameroonian Novel of English Expression: An Introduction

Tangie Nsoh Fonchingong and Gemandze John Bobuin
Cameroon: The Stakes and Challenges of Governance and
Development

Tatah Mentan
Democratizing or Reconfiguring Predatory Autocracy? Myths and
Realities in Africa Today

Roselyne M. Jua & Bate Besong
To the Budding Creative Writer: A Handbook

Albert Mukong
Prisoner without a Crime: Disciplining Dissent in Ahidjo's
Cameroon

Mbuh Tennu Mbuh
In the Shadow of my Country

Bernard Nsokika Fonlon
Genuine Intellectuals: Academic and Social Responsibilities of
Universities in Africa

Lilian Lem Atanga
Gender, Discourse and Power in the Cameroonian Parliament

Content

Dedication vii

Acknowledgement ix

Preface xi

Transcription Conventions and Abbreviations xiii

Figures xv

Tables xvii

Chapter One
Introduction and Background 1

Chapter Two
Approaches To Gender, Power And Discourse Analysis 23

Chapter Three
Gender Differences in Parliamentary Talk 61

Chapter Four
'Traditional' Gendered Discourses Articulated in the
Cameroonian Parliament 93

Chapter Five
Legitimating 'A Model Traditional Cameroonian Woman' 121

Chapter Six
Modern 'Progressive' Gendered Discourses in the Cameroonian
Parliament 165

Chapter Seven
Discursive Strategies in Legitimating 'Positive Action
for Women' 191

Chapter Eight
Summary, Recommendations and Conclusion 215

References 229

Appendices 255

Dedication

TO MY SON, SUH ATANGA

Preface

With globalisation, traditional gendered practices in most, if not all post-colonial countries are changing. While what can be seen as male dominance is still very much in evidence, in many aspects of public and private life, masculine power continues to be challenged and even subverted in different ways. This book focuses on the role of *discourse* in the study of language and gender in the Cameroonian parliament.

The study is both quantitative and qualitative. Looking at Discussion and Question-and-Answer sessions in the parliament, I examined the amount of male and female talk and the gendered distribution of topics, as well as how female and male parliamentarians were addressed (i.e. titulation). Using Critical Discourse Analysis (the discourse-historical approach (e.g. Reisigl and Wodak 2001; Wodak 2009)), I continued by looking in depth at the available 'traditional' and modern, 'progressive' discourses articulated by MPs and how these were legitimated through different discursive strategies. Lastly, because I see power as contingent and not absolute, I explored gender, discourse and fluctuating power, using Feminist Post-Structuralist Discourse Analysis (Baxter, 2003) as a supplementary approach to Critical Discourse Analysis.

The quantitative analysis of talk in the parliament showed that 'traditional' discourse practices are evident in this 'modern' setting, evidenced by disproportionate masculine verbosity and feminine (relative) silence. Traditional differential constructions of gender identity were also evident in titulation.

Critical discourse analyses showed that 'traditional' gendered discourses tended to construct men and women in gender differentiated ways, legitimated discoursally in ways which included social, cultural and institutional discourses, and arguments for what I call 'the model traditional Cameroonian woman' macro-discourse as well as for maintenance of the status quo more widely. The 'traditional' gendered discourses were however also appropriated, even subverted, through the articulation and legitimation of counter modern and 'progressive' discourses which construct men and women in more equal ways, legitimating in particular positive action for women. Feminist post-structuralist discourse analysis showed how groups/individuals who were at some times and in some ways powerless (female MPs) could also be power*ful*, contingent upon the different subject positions made available to them through competing discourses, their own self- and other positioning, and the discourses they actively accessed (sometimes with institutional support). Similarly, a socially powerful male MP was shown to be relatively powerless at times (through his own self-positioning, and his positioning by a female Minister).

Through this combination of methodologies, this study illustrates the complexity of the nature of gender and institutional (parliamentary) discourse, and the provisional nature of power. While sexism in the wider Cameroonian society may not be as 'subtle' as is sometimes now claimed of 'western' societies, there is nevertheless evidence that gender relations in Cameroon are improving, supported by social and discoursal forces which are global, national and institutional.

Transcription Conventions and Abbreviations

[...]	Omitted portions
(...)	Unclear untranscribed utterances
...	(occupying a line) Large omitted portions of text
x ... x (where x is a word)	Long noticeable pauses
!	Statement understood to mean an exclamation or a rhetorical statement
?	Sentence understood to mean a question
CAPITAL LETTERS	High Pitch
Uhmm, ehm, you know, mhmm	Gap fillers
(sentences in italics in brackets)	Comments from audience or Speaker interrupting the person with the floor (overlaps) (field notes)
[sentences in English in brackets]	My comments (e.g. indicating non-verbal data, from field notes)
MQ	Male Question
MDQ	Male Discussion Question
FDQ	Female Discussion Question
FA	Female Minister's Answer
MA	Male Minister's Answer
Q & A	Question and Answer (Session, genre)

Figures

Figure 1.1
Traditional Political Set-Up Based on Bafut 6

Figure 3. 1
Talking Time by MPs in the June 2005 Session 73

Figure 3. 2
Percentage of Total Talking Time in June 2005
(male and female MPs) 74

Figure 3. 3
Total Talking Time MPs November 2005 Session 74

Figure 3. 4
Total Talking Time by MPs for November 25th
Q & A session 77

Figure 3. 5
Average MP Talking Time Nov 25th Session in Minutes 77

Figure 3. 6
Percentage of Talking Time by MPs and Ministers
in the November 2005 Session 78

Figure 3. 7
Plenary Seating Arrangement, Cameroonian Parliament 86

Figure 5. 1
Regions of Cameroon Showing Sangmelima 148

Figure 5. 2
Geographical Representation of Cameroonian Women 149

Figure 5. 3
(World) Geographical Discursive Construction of Social
Practices 150

Tables

Table 3. 1
Plenary Sessions (analysed) with Female Participation 66

Table 3. 2
Titles used to Address MPs 69

Table 3. 3
Titulation 70

Table 3. 4
Talking Time by Male and Female MPs in the June 2005
  Plenary Sessions 72

Table 3. 5
Summary of Talk in the Parliament, June 2005 73

Table 3. 6
General Average talking time during the June Discussion
  session 74

Table 3. 7
MPs' Talking Time, 25th November 2005 Q & A Session 76

Table 3. 8
Key Findings 79

Table 3. 9
Topic Choice during Discussion Session, June 2005 89

Table 5. 1
Regional and Ethnic Representation 126

Table 5. 2
Agency in Speech by Male MP, Honourable Etame 131

Table 5. 3
Argumentation Strategies 135

Table 5. 4
Summary of Discursive Strategies for the Legitimation of 'A
  Model Traditional Cameroonian Woman' 159

Table 6. 1
Percentage of Women in the National Assembly
since 1960 171

Table 7. 1
Mitigation Strategies 200

Table 7. 2
Argumentation Strategies to Legitimate 'Positive Action
for Women' 204

Table 7. 3
Discursive Legitimation Strategies for the Discourses
of 'Positive Action for Women' 212

Chapter One

Introduction and Background

A learned woman is a lost woman (Portuguese proverb, Schipper 2003)

Introduction

Cameroon is in many ways a modern, fast-developing African nation. It has indeed been referred to as 'Africa in Miniature' due to its cultural, ethnic, linguistic and geographical diversity. It has two main religions – Christians about 40%, Muslims about 20% and other indigenous religions about 40%[1]. It is currently one of the sub-Saharan countries with the highest literacy rates (15 years and over) of 84.4% for men and 73.4% for women making an average of about 79%. It is a democratic country with a multiparty system of government with a functioning unicameral (one chamber) National Assembly (Assemblée Nationale) with 180 seats; members are elected by direct popular vote to serve five-year terms.

However, although Cameroon can be considered a modern African country, traditional indigenous practices still prevail and are, in fact, a part of the daily lives of the people. Cameroonian women, for example, generally expect their husbands, fathers or male members of the family to speak for them (or for a member of the family) in public functions and generally perceive men as the head of the family. Such traditional gender-differential practices perpetuate assumptions about the 'naturalness' and desirability of gender differences. This makes gender relations in Cameroon quite complicated and problematic since some (educated) Cameroonian women often have to negotiate their identities as 'traditional' Cameroonian women who are expected to preserve their culture, and 'modern' educated Cameroonian women fighting against discrimination and seeking equal opportunities within the society.

Cameroonian women in parliament then face such particular challenges in negotiating these different identities in a society that constructs them both as traditional women with expectations to fulfil their traditional gender roles, and modern women who should perform their roles as educated female parliamentarians within a modern Cameroonian context.

A socio-historical perspective of this context will give a useful background to the study and will also provide part of the historical analysis of this study, a tenet of the discourse-historical approach to Critical Discourse Analysis. In the following sections, I therefore present the linguistic, political and gender background of the study.

Linguistic Studies and Gender in Africa

The continent of Africa is said to be home to more than a third of the world's languages. Ethnologue puts it at 2000 languages (Grimes, 2000). Greenberg classifies these languages into four main groups: Niger-Congo, Afro-Asiatic, Nilo-Saharan, and Khoisan (Greenberg, 1963). Cameroon is host to three of these main groups: Niger-Congo, Afro-Asiatic, and Nilo-Saharan with a complex linguistic history. It has over two hundred indigenous languages. Although Ethnologue (15th Edition - Gordon 2005) puts the figure at 279, some linguists (Breton & Fohtung, 1991; Ndongo-Semengue & Sadembouo, 1999; Wolf, 2001) challenge this claiming some dialects have been classified as languages while some languages are not classified at all. Breton and Fohtung put the figure at 247 languages.

Cameroon also has two colonial cum official languages: French and English. These official languages came onto the Cameroon linguistic scene in 1916 after the French and the British defeated Germany in World War 1.

Cameroon also has a (main) lingua franca, Cameroon Pidgin English (CPE), used by some as their first language, 13% as a second language and more than 50% of the population as a lingua franca (Dutcher, 2004). It is used most widely in the Northwest and Southwest Provinces but also generally in the rest of the country.

Linguistic studies in Africa and Cameroon in particular have to date primarily focused on the development of African languages and the linguistic description of these languages. The Summer Institute of Linguistics (SIL Cameroon) has been very instrumental in this process. Despite the numerous linguistic studies and linguists, there however has been little work in the area of language and gender.

A few studies especially in southern Africa have however been dedicated to language and gender, e.g. the *Southern African Linguistics and Applied Language Studies* (SALALS) journal has dedicated two

2

volumes: 20(3) and 24(4)-(2002, 2006) to papers on language and gender in (southern) Africa. The 2006 volume of SALALS was dedicated to reviewing the historical and theoretical development of gender and language studies in southern Africa.

Africa Today has also dedicated volume 49/1 (2002) of its journal to articles on language, gender and the law in Africa. Wanitzek (2002) for example examines how legal language reflects and reinforces male dominance over women and, more generally, gender bias.

None of these studies have focused on language and gender studies in Cameroon. Little has been done in Cameroon in the area of gender, language and politics— the topic of this book. Some exemptions are Mbangwana (1996) for example who investigated married career women in Cameroon, especially high profile women and Nzesse (2008) who, in an edited collection examined the language of politics in Cameroon. Mbangwana's investigation for example revealed that women as expected by traditional western culture (in contrast to traditional Cameroonian culture)[2] take the names of their husbands after marriage. The colonial legacy (though not institutionalised by law) required women to drop their maiden names after marriage.

In contrast to the paucity of research on gender and language, there has been a considerable amount of research in Cameroon (as well as Africa) in the areas of gender and development (e.g Endeley & Ardener 2004; Fonchingong, 2005) and gender and politics (Konde 2005, Ngwang 2004). In the following sub-sections, I draw on relevant literature and my own experience and insights as a female Cameroonian, to discuss the politico-linguistic background to this study of gender and language within a political set-up - the parliament in Cameroon.

Politico-Linguistic Background of Cameroon

In most traditional Cameroonian communities, women's linguistic practices are generally different from those of men, for example, because of women's expected (relative) silence in public, women are not expected to challenge men in public, and not allowed by custom to use certain taboo words e.g. sex terms (see also *hlonipha* in southern Africa - Thetela 2002; Rudwick and Shange 2006). Women are absent from most traditional 'secret societies'[3] which

3

constitute the ruling bodies of Cameroonian villages (Aletum, 1990). The gross absence of women in these decision-making bodies prompted me to investigate women and their linguistic practices in a 'modern' set-up which incorporates them into the political scene. The salience of men in the traditional political (public) scene means they have built up a legacy of linguistic capital (Bourdieu, 1991) in the modern public sphere, and may also mean they are generally seen as more suitable for public discourse and political participation. Correspondingly, women's relative absence in the traditional political scene may mean a near absence of linguistic capital in modern public settings especially since they are also *latecomers* as well as a minority in this community of practice (Eckert & McConnell-Ginet 1992, 1999, 2007).

Cameroon thus has two kinds of functional political systems: the traditional political system based on traditional government and the modern political system based on western style politics, introduced during the colonial era (Adams, 2006). These two systems operate side by side within the country, although at different levels. The traditional political systems operate at village (tribal) levels. Each village is headed by a chief. These chiefs are paramount rulers especially with regard to the customs and traditions of the people and have a great deal of power over the social life of their subjects (Aletum 1990, 2001; Niba 1995; Nkwi and Warnier 1982). However, their powers are superseded by that of the state of Cameroon. That is, they and their subjects adhere to the laws of the country. This is however a two-way relationship where the national institutions recognise the power and sovereignty of the traditional rulers and the traditional rulers also do the same.

The Traditional Political Structure

Indigenous languages demarcate different traditional political units (villages and tribes)[4] within the country. Each is headed by a chief. Chiefs are known by different appellations depending on the region of the country. For example, in the Grassfield area of the country (the Northwest and West provinces), the chiefs are called *Nfor* (or Fon in Cameroon English), *Lamidos* in the Grand North and *Sultan* in the Muslim west.

4

I draw on the political structure of one of the Grassfield regions (Bafut) to exemplify this. In this region, the Fon has multifarious functions: he controls internal laws, and justice is done in his name. He is the final court of appeal (of his village). The Fon is also viewed as possessing sacred attributes necessary for this office. As a 'chief priest', he offers sacrifices to the ancestors, intercedes with them for the welfare of the people and also presides over important festivals (Aletum 2001; Niba 1995). He occupies the highest executive seat in the community. He is referred to as *Tala'a* - 'father of the land' (Niba 1995). He is assisted by the *Mamfor* - the queen mother[5], the *Ndimfor* (the Fon's older brother), and the *Muma* (the Fon's younger brother). The *Mamfor,* that is, the queen mother title, could be held by either the mother of the *Fon* or a princess in the event that the *Fon's* mother is no longer alive. This position according to custom can never be vacant, the reason why a princess can inherit it. The positions of the *Fon*, *Mamfor*, *Ndimfor* and *Muma* are inherited.

Although the Fon is 'king', there are a number of checks and balances to control the absolute power of these rulers. This is achieved through secret societies and military associations which, in combination with the Fon's primary councillors and various lineage heads, provide the balance to his traditional power.

There is a great deal of mysticism and ritual surrounding the secret palace societies. Among these is the *Kwifor*[6] (literally the bearer of the chief) which is the strongest ruling body (Niba 1995). It is responsible for enthroning the chief and can be considered the local 'national assembly', for it conceives and executes policies. Decisions affecting the villagers are taken by the members of this 'house'. Figure 1.1 shows a typical administrative hierarchy in a Grassfield village, including its gender dimensions – see below on the women's 'Takumbeng'. Positions in the *kwifor* can be earned through valiant deeds or inheritance from one's father. If a member of the village is deemed worthy enough by the chief and the committee of notables, that person can be co-opted into this society.

However, no woman can become a member of this society either through inheritance or through achievement (Aletum 2001).

Figure 1. 1 Traditional Political Set-Up Based on Bafut

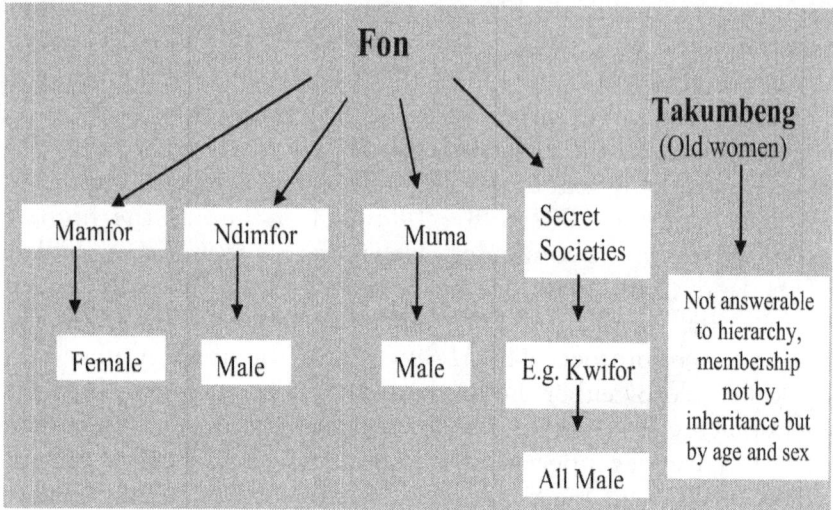

The *Takumbeng*[7], a women only group, although considered a secret society is not a constituted group but a form of occasional female political mobilisation with limited functions. Membership is not by inheritance or valiant achievements (as is the case of the Kwifor), but by age and sex. As Takougang and Krieger (1998) observe, membership of the *Takumbeng* group is open to all post-menopausal women. Generally, it functions as 'the power of powers' (Ngwang 2004), using maternal power (see also Stevens 2006), when all other methods of checks on power have failed (see Fombe 2005).

Women in Traditional Cameroonian Politics

A good dog keeps its tail tucked in; a good woman remains in the background
(*Burmese Proverb*)

For a woman, display is dishonour (Swahili)
(*Schipper 2003*)

Women's groups existed before and during colonial times which have had an impact on political activities, and the activities themselves which I suggest are indicative of the type of political involvement Cameroonian women had.

6

Women's Groups

There are traditional female-only 'secret' societies in Cameroon which included (and still include) the *Takumbeng* of the Ngemba[8] people (Takougang and Krieger 1998, Awasom 2002, Ngwang 2004, Konde 2005), the *Anlu* of Kom (Takougang and Krieger 1998, Ngwang 2004, Konde 2005), the *Liengu* of the Bakweri (Tande 2006) and the *Koo* of the Bassa (Nyeck & Mbide, 1989). These groups are only constituted in case of emergency remonstration against ruling bodies, to check the excesses of men in the society (especially in case of extreme human rights violation). They are made up of old (post-menopausal) women within the society. They are considered 'the power of powers' (Ngwang 2004) since they use 'genital power' (Stevens 2006) but generally have no say in the day to day running of the villages. According to Fombe (2005), it traditionally performs the function of checks and balances and moderates the activities of the *kwifor* (all-male society) in the village. These Communities of Practice (Eckert & McConnell-Ginet, 1999) have their own social practices which are different from those of men. The public participation is generally non-verbal, although they may have representatives who talk on their behalf. They present their discussions and petitions not in a general assembly of men and women but in protest forms in open spaces[9].

According to Konde (2005), Christian movements such as the 'Catholic Women Association' and 'Christian Women Fellowship' have also served (albeit apolitically) as powerful political support units. Konde notes that such women's groups served (mostly) the interests of women politicians (Konde 2005) and the first female MP was supported by one such group – the Catholic Women's Association. Some groups, e.g. the *Takumbeng* and the Christian ones, continue to serve as women's support groups in contemporary Cameroon.

Women's Activities

Awasom (2002) and Adams (2006) argue that Cameroonian women were involved in politics before and during colonial times. This is indeed true although I argue that this (un-constituted) involvement was minimal and peripheral since they did not take part in the day-to-day running of their communities. Female

7

traditional political positions such as the *Mamfor* existed (and still do) but were few. Women had few opportunities of actively partaking in decision-making process.

The *Anlu* (see above) for example, was constituted when attempts were made by the British colonial administration in 1958 to introduce far-reaching modern reforms in the agricultural sector (taxes and laws regulating farming techniques). This frightened women and the impromptu group (as is its nature) constituted itself and took to the streets during the Endeley[10] government. This sort of movement was replicated in the 1990s by women in the Bamenda central area with the *Takumbeng*.

In the 1990s, in the North West Province of Cameroon, women were mobilized into action by what they perceived as the economic hardship and suffering imposed on their children by the current Biya government. They also went out to protect the main opposition leader of the regime, Ni John Fru Ndi, from being taken to prison by the government. These post-menopausal women circulated nude in public spaces, their grey hair uncovered, teeth clenched with a large blade of grass gripped in between their mouth symbolizing 'no talk but action' (Cohen 2001). Their success was achieved through silence and nakedness, what Stevens (2006) describes as 'genital power' (the power of women's nudity).

In such events, these women do not usually have a face-to-face debate with the chief of the village or other men. Their protest could be described as self-imposed silence. The women position themselves strategically such that men cannot circulate without having to face them and thus confront their nakedness, a spectacle men cannot afford since the belief holds that seeing an old woman's nakedness is a curse, a belief Cameroonian men hold on to. Women's public political participation has thus been silent, albeit often effective within the context. It is not verbal participation as will be the focus of this study.

Women's participation in the public[11] sphere in the past was thus generally delegated to very elderly women. Other women were respected if they stayed quiet or spoke little in public settings. Women were therefore generally seen in public but not heard. Such practices may have had an impact on the public discourse of and discourses about Cameroonian women today.

Cameroonian Women in Modern Politics

Women achieved suffrage in colonial times, that is, in 1946, but, in practice, all they could do in politics was vote men into power. The first women stood in constituent National Assembly elections in 1952 but without success. In 1957, Cameroon had its first female parliamentarian from French Cameroon and 1959 in British Cameroon. Both candidates were co-opted into the parliament. During the post-colonial years, the government also co-opted women into political positions (Konde 2005). The first female to contest and win an election in Cameroon was in 1960 and the first Muslim woman in 1973. Until the 1980s, the percentage of women in the National Assembly however remained below 5%. After the 1980s, this rose to more than 10% reaching 14% between 1988 and 1992. Between 1990 and 2007, the number of women in the National Assembly dropped to 11%.

During this study (2004-2005), Cameroon had five political parties represented in the parliament: the Cameroon People's Democratic Movement (CPDM) - 82%, the Social Democratic Front (SDF) - 12%, the Union Démocratique Camerounaise (UDC) – 2.7%, Union du Peuple Camerounaise (UPC) – 1.6%, and the National Union for Democracy and Progress (UNDP) - 0.5%. The manifestos of the different parties all include reference to female participation in politics. The ruling Cameroon People's Democratic Party (CPDM) has a women's wing. As stipulated by the CPDM manifesto, this wing is in charge of organising women's and social affairs of the party, and also helps the smooth running of party affairs. Article 47/48 of the constitution of the CPDM party indicates that the women's wing, WCPDM, is in charge of 'the mobilisation of Cameroonian women with a goal to publicizing the party and their *full participation in the pursuit and realisation of the objectives of the party*' (my translation from French and my emphasis) and also of 'assuring their entire integration in national life' (my translation). To this effect, the WCPDM *'conceives and puts in place programmes with a social, cultural and political character'* (my translation and emphasis). The manifesto also notes 'The organisation of *this wing will be under the political tutelage of the party*' (my translation and emphasis).

The CPDM's manifesto is therefore contradictory as it asks for 'full participation' of women but limits it to participation *'under the*

9

... *tutelage of the party'*. Such a manifesto may suggest that women are subordinate in the party and their activities are only in support of the *main* party. It also focuses on women's activities in the social and cultural spheres. Such stipulations are indicative of how women are constructed within the wider Cameroonian society. Also, this construction can be perceived in the kind of ministries women tend to occupy. Since 1975, only women have occupied the Ministry of Social Affairs (5 women in all) and the Ministry of Women's Affairs and Family Matters (5 women in all). No male has been appointed to these ministries. Other ministries women have held are Health (2), Primary Education (1) and Scientific Research (1). They have served as deputy ministers in education and health but have never held positions in key ministries such as Economy and Finance, Defence or Justice.

The Social Democratic Front party is not forthright in its manifesto about female participation. It is silent on gender quotas and only stipulates that women *must* constitute at least a third of advisory positions in the party (see section 9:5 of the SDF Constitution). This party has little or no female representation in the parliament. The organisation of both this party and the ruling CPDM may be indicative of the entrenched male dominated political system within the country.

The situation has however doubtless improved as regards public participation. Cameroonian women's participation in formal political/public life during colonial times was even lower as a result of the western style of education which generally did not encourage women to attend mainstream schools and participate in public life (see Adams 2006; Endeley et al 2004; Nkwi and Warnier 1982). (However, women were active in other settings such as the economic sphere - production and sales of farm produce.) Colonial trends in female political participation persisted after colonisation. Fewer women than men went to mainstream schools and also into government.

With improved female literacy rates and programmes on gender equality and women's empowerment, those trends are being reversed. Women currently participate more in public professional domains, with female-led organisations and institutions including schools, NGOs, female lawyers, teachers, and directors of

10

companies. However, there are still very few women in *political* decision-making positions. There are many reasons for this, some of which this book explores. Although, as shown, pre-colonial public discourse required women to stay quiet in public (see Takougang and Krieger 1998, Ngwang 2004), and have representative (and delegated) speakers, modern political discourse, for example parliamentary discourse, requires participants to be verbally active, taking it upon themselves to contribute to ongoing debates. Parliament for example, demands of its members (representative and delegated) to speak out on issues without fear or favour. Modern political structures may thus still work in favour of men (see Walsh 2001, Cameron 2006) if we see these structures as in some ways extensions of (dominantly male) traditional political systems, and modern political structures as extensions of traditional male spaces within the wider society. The modern political systems require participants to be educated and this limits many women greatly considering the relative lack of education of many when young. Most women in the early years of independence (1960-1970s) had limited education and mostly went to *homecraft* schools. It is possible that with more women completing higher education in recent times, the nature of the parliamentary system will change.

Men thus still dominate politics and public administration while women, although more visible in the public sphere than in the past, continue to be responsible for domestic and child care tasks (Nsamenang 2000). As Konde (2005) points out, men during the post-independent era used women's votes and participation in political rallies for political gain but considered the political sphere itself a masculine domain (Awasom 2002). He also observes that men also considered women to be intellectually and politically unfit. Women's public appearance therefore consisted of supporting and cheering men, and women constructed as voters, but not to be voted for.

With all these conservative practices, there have however been some positive influences on gender relations especially within the public and political sphere as I show in the next section.

Political and other Influences on Gender Relations

Even after ratifying the 1979 United Nations Convention to Eliminate all Forms of Discrimination against Women (CEDAW), the Cameroon government did not take any serious measures and the Convention hardly benefited women in actual fact. Equal access to jobs and positions of responsibility by women was not achieved by this convention, for example, access to leadership positions such as provincial governors[12]. This convention had little impact on the number of women represented in key political circles and in the parliament. The UN Conference on Women in Beijing in 1995[13] in contrast had a lot more impact on gender relations in Cameroon. It served as a turning point for attitudes on gender issues. The years following the conference saw a form of feminist revolution in Cameroon and an upsurge of Women's movements[14]such as the International Federation of Female Lawyers (FIDA) and Association of Women's Information and Coordination Offices (AWICO). Women began to be more active in civil society and political parties, creating non-governmental associations for the promotion and active involvement of women in their daily lives. The government, through its Ministry of Women's Affairs, was also involved in activities for the promotion of women. Training workshops on female participation in politics were for example organised and run by international organisations such as the Commonwealth, World Bank and UNICEF (see e.g. www.britishcouncil.org/Cameroon-governance). Greater awareness of gender equality and women's empowerment also resulted from it (see also Endeley 2004, Fonchingong 2005; 2006). The increase of gender awareness did not however translate into the government legislating for positive change for Cameroonian women. Discriminatory laws still exist and gender quotas have not been institutionalised in public administration. Women's organisations such as FIDA Cameroon (International Federation of Female Lawyers) are more active than the government in promoting women's participation in public spheres.

Western feminism has had its own influence as it has affected Cameroonian women's views on gender equality and equal opportunity. Although the term 'feminism' in Cameroon remains problematic[15], Cameroonian women have learnt from western feminists that there is no biological gender division of labour (housework and paid work) and that they too have rights like western women and should fight to empower themselves. The advent of new technologies of information and communication has made information on gender equality and opportunities for women more available than it was before. This however is also problematic to many in the society and women tend to be criticised (by men and even some women) for copying practices that are foreign to their culture (see Chapters 4 and 5). Many educated Cameroonian women face the dilemma of acting as 'Cameroonian women', respecting the traditional expectations of women, and challenging conservative practices while actively participating in hitherto male dominated domains such as political spheres.

The increase in adult literacy among Cameroonian women within the last decades of the 20th century has also had a positive impact on the political participation of women in that they may become aware of the need for female participation in the public sphere through education. Previously, girls were not being sent to school because girls were constructed as housewives (a colonial concept), and Cameroon parents were interested in bride price (thus marrying off girls at young ages). Education for the girl-child was therefore very low. However, current trends are reversing the situation (especially in the southern parts of the country) as there are many (more) girls in school now, both at the primary and tertiary levels.

To conclude this section, although there are few women in decision making positions and the parliament, there are a lot more in the informal sector and they are more economically empowered than in the previous century. This may be considered in part the fallout of the UN Conference on women in Beijing, other international women's movements, 'western' feminism and in part a maturing of the Cameroonian democracy. It is hoped that this empowerment may translate to political participation and representation in decision making positions. In this study, I examine how all these shape the discourses and the discursive construction of women in the Cameroonian parliament.

Rationale for and Theoretical Framework of this Study

As shown above and indicated in the literature, Cameroonian women have in the past actively participated within the social, cultural and agro-economic domains but marginally in the public/political sphere (Goheen 1996). Also observed is the fact that women's political participation in Cameroon is shaped by the way women are constructed within the society and the political structures in place (see Awasom 2005; CPDM Manifesto). Such constructions tend to relegate women to subordinate positions in the political sphere (like voting but not being voted for).

Research on gender issues in Cameroon has focused inter alia on discrimination against women, and the contribution of Cameroonian women to the economy and development of the country (e.g. Fonchingong 2005, Endeley et al 2004). It has also focused on women's political participation (Konde 2005). However, there is no literature in the field linking discourse and the discursive construction of women in Cameroon to political participation and in particular verbal participation within the parliament. In carrying out this study, I hope to fill this gap by looking at women's political/ verbal participation in the parliament, and the discursive construction of gender through women's and men's articulation of gendered discourses in the parliament.

Also observed earlier, there are very few studies in Cameroon in the area of language and gender, and none specifically in the area of gender and political discourse. This book therefore presents the opportunity to investigate the relationship between language, gender, and politics (power) in Cameroon. It also hopes to investigate the way men and women are discursively constructed within the parliament and its possible effects on gendered participation in the parliament. To achieve this, a Critical Discourse Analytical approach (CDA) is used.

Beyond Cameroon, there have been studies in political linguistics using CDA (e.g. Chilton 2002, 2004; van Dijk 1997, 2006), and even more specifically in parliamentary discourse (e.g. van Dijk and Wodak 2000; Ilie 2003, 2006). Gender and discourse in the parliament has also been a focus of study (e.g. Wodak 2003, 2005; Walsh 2001; Shaw 2001; Christie 2003). Most research on gender and discourse within parliament has employed CDA and/or Conversational Analysis.

CDA views discourse as a 'social practice' and as 'constitutive' implying 'a dialectal relationship between a particular discursive event and situation(s), institutions(s) and social structure(s) which frame it' (Fairclough and Wodak 1997: 55). For Fairclough, and other CDA writers would probably agree, CDA has as a starting point 'social issues and problems' (Fairclough 2001: 229, see also

Wodak 2001, van Dijk 2001, Lazar 2005) and 'does not begin with texts and interactions; it begins with issues, which preoccupy sociologists, political scientists, or educationalists' (2001: 230). The issue in this book is *gender* (discrimination) (Sunderland 2004), and CDA is thus theoretically well placed to seek, identify and explain the workings of gendered discourse. The discourse-historical approach to CDA developed by Wodak and fellow researchers (see e.g. Wodak 2001, Reisigl and Wodak 2001) proves particularly useful as it acknowledges the importance of the historical context of the discourses articulated. I explore this theoretically framework in detail in chapter 2.

The Cameroonian Parliament and Parliamentary Discourse

The word *parliament*, as defined in the *Encyclopaedia of Languages and Linguistics* (2006), is derived from the French *parlement*, from *parler,* 'to speak'. It thus refers not only to the building that hosts such an institution, but to a particular kind of talk. Ilie (2006:189) observes that the parliament has different appellations in different countries - Legislative Assembly, Congress, Diet and National Assembly. In Cameroon, the parliament is called The National Assembly (*Assemblée Nationale* in French). Parliaments can be unicameral (one chamber) or bicameral (two chambers). Bicameral parliaments have an upper house (less powerful and advisory) and a lower house. Ilie also distinguishes between a parliamentary state and a presidential state, Britain being an example of a parliamentary state. Cameroon is a presidential state with a constitutional bi-cameral assembly but a functioning unicameral one.

Parliamentary discourse as defined by Ilie (2006:190) is discourse in which 'institutional face-work, political meaning negotiation, and power management are being articulated and publicly displayed'. Parliamentary discourse belongs to the genre of 'Political discourse' (see van Dijk 1997a, 1997b; Chilton 2004, Chilton and Schaffner 2002). As Swales (1998: 45/58) observes, a genre is a class of communicative events in which language (and/or paralanguage) plays both a significant and an indispensable role ... and the members of which share some set of communicative purposes ... these purposes are recognised by members of the parent discourse community, and thereby constitutive to the rationale for the genre.

15

Parliamentary discourse thus has specific features that make it so, for example, addressing an MP as the 'Honourable Gentleman' is peculiar to this genre, and as are arguments and counter-arguments. The linguistic characteristics of a text may situate it in a specific genre. Fairclough (2003: 65) sees genres as the specifically discoursal aspect of ways of acting and interacting in the course of social events. Genres have sub-genres. Question-and-Answer sessions, for example, may be characterised as a sub-genre of parliamentary discourse (as of other genres). Ilie (2006: 190) identifies sub-genres of parliamentary discourse which include *Debates, Question-and-Answer sessions, ministerial statements and speeches.* Speeches include motions moved and opening speeches. *Debates* within the British parliamentary system are called *Discussions* in the Cameroonian parliament (also 'Discussions' in French) and the British Question-and-Answer session or Prime Minister's Question Time is known as Oral Questions ('Questions Orales') in Cameroon. In this book, 'Discussion' and the 'Question-and-Answer' genres are examined.

The Cameroon National Assembly sits in the national capital, Yaoundé. Because it is housed in a glass building, Cameroonians fondly call it 'Maison de Verre (de Ngoa-Ekelle)' – *The Glass House.* The linguistic setting of this parliament is worth looking at as the country is officially bilingual. The languages of the parliament are officially French and English and deliberations are in these two official languages of the country, which coexist with the over 250 national indigenous languages. Code mixing and code switching abound in the parliament, sometimes with indigenous Cameroonian languages. Translations for the texts in French are provided and texts originally in English are indicated.

The physical structure of the National Assembly is worth mentioning as I believe it has an impact on gendered discourse within this parliamentary setting. The National Assembly consists of a plenary session hall. This hall is designed as a hemicycle (crescent shape). The Speaker of the House of Assembly (who presides over the proceedings) sits on an elevated stage at the centre of the hemicycle. Ministers sit to his right in a further row facing the parliamentarians and to his left are executive members of the parliament such as the Vice Presidents and the secretaries. MPs sit according to party affiliation. Plenary sessions are open to the public and although the public is not officially allowed to talk, they still do, with comments, laughter and even handclapping.

Another characteristic of the Cameroonian parliament is that ministers are not previously members of parliament as in the other parliaments, e.g. the British Parliament. Ministers in Cameroon are not elected MPs but are appointed to office by the ruling government. Also, ministers do not choose to talk but are solicited to do so through the questions asked by MPs. Thus, the motivations to talk for ministers and parliamentarians are different. Parliamentarians are limited to talk for 15 minutes (when asking a question) although this is often violated. Ministers can talk for longer periods of time. Thus there is an institutional imbalance in the sharing of talking time according to position. Deliberations in Q&A sessions are pre-planned and questions are submitted earlier to the Ministers by the parliamentarians through a bureau that selects them. The selection criteria for these questions are not known. MPs know in advance if their questions have been selected and the Ministers also know the questions in advance and prepare their answers. Both MPs and Ministers present their speeches from scripted (to be spoken) texts.

Talk in the Discussion genre is organised differently. A bill is tabled (from a script, usually a very long document taking several hours to read) by the Minister in charge and (unscripted) discussions about or surrounding the bill ensue. These discussions also take the form of questions and answers except that the Ministers do not know the questions beforehand as in the case of Question-and-Answer sessions. MPs must 'bid', competitively, to talk: they raise their hands and are selected by the Speaker of the House, apparently randomly. Not all MPs get a speaking turn as the number of solicits are generally high (at least during the sessions observed). There is thus the possibility of the Speaker favouring certain individuals or groups over others.

Issues in the Book

Focusing on women and men participating in Cameroonian parliamentary politics, I examine how gender is oriented to in the Cameroonian Parliament in the following ways:

Gender Differences in Talk

Considering that Cameroon is highly patriarchal, with social practices and laws overtly discriminating against women, a quantitative analysis of differences will be necessary to 'strategically' bring out differences (Holmes 2006) in order to address imbalances within parliamentary context. A quantitative analysis of talk allows explores how patriarchal ideologies and asymmetrical power relations are implicated in linguistic practices through *quantity* of talk and *quality* of contributions (through analysis of topics). It seeks to analyse *speech patterns* in terms of what is said (quality) and how much (quantity) (see Holmes 1995, 2003; Talbot 1998). It establishes in quantitative terms how gender ideology and power relations in discourse here do not assume 'more subtle forms' (Lazar 2005, Wodak 2003, Walsh 2001) but open discrimination. An analysis of difference will bring out some general trends within the parliament with implications for the society as a whole and give us a broader understanding of the discourse produced within these contexts, while giving us baseline statistics of gendered participation in the parliament.

This is done by examining *Titulation,* which looks at how identities of MPs are constructed through the way they are named in the parliament either by themselves or others. Verbosity and silence are some of the areas of focus in this book examining gendered difference in talk in the parliament. I examine *topics* drawn on by male and female MPs during Question-and-Answer and Discussion sessions in the parliament.

Gendered Discourses

Through time, some traditional practices have been maintained even when there has been a sort of feminist revolution in Cameroon. Because social practices are not stable but evolving, I examine how, through discourse, some *traditional* gendered practices are constituted, maintained and sustained, as are strategies used to justify the status quo, and how others are challenged and contested. I thus identify and examine *gendered discourses* and the *discursive construction* of women and men to observe how they are linked to political participation and even verbal participation within the Cameroonian parliament. Discourses can be seen to construct women and men in both what I call *traditional* and *'progressive'* ways.

18

Traditional gendered discourses, I suggest, are based on commonsense, taken-for-granted practices embedded in the society, historical beliefs and biological origins of human beings and are articulated in order to legitimate differential gendered practices within the Cameroonian society. On the other hand, *modern 'progressive'* gendered discourses tend to challenge and contest these discourses and advocate (positive) change and gender equality.

What traditional Gendered Discourses are Evident in the Cameroonian Parliament

Traditional discourses that construct women and men based on customary, naturalised and commonsensical ways are examined in this book. Such discourses focus on gender differentiation and construct men and women mostly in binary terms. Through *traditional* gendered discourses, a 'model traditional Cameroonian woman' is constructed. These discourses are articulated by both male and female MPs.

How are these legitimated? To legitimate the construction of 'a model traditional Cameroonian woman' based on the traditional gendered discourses, various discursive strategies are used (by men) and different arguments are put forth to maintain and reproduce the status quo of gender as difference, reinforcing asymmetrical relations of power.

What modern progressive discourses are evident in the Cameroonian parliament?

Although there is no clear cut binary between what is traditional and what is modern, or what is progressive and what is conservative, this book has tried to identify what it qualifies as modern discourses which are new discourses. These are generally 'new' counter discourses to the traditional and often conservative ones based on gender division of roles. These advocate affirmative action for women and gender sharing.

How are these discourses legitimated? Through different discursive strategies, modern progressive discourses (e.g. of positive action for women) are legitimated to counter male hegemony and patriarchal discriminatory practices against women within the society.

How are Gender and Power Relations Negotiated in the Cameroonian Parliament?

Women are dominated (and even absent) within many (traditional) institutional settings in Cameroon such as the parliament and power relations between men and women in such settings can often be seen to be asymmetrical. Although language and discourse play a role in constituting systematic gender discrimination (Walsh 2001, Lazar 2005), it is however important to consider its role in power relations (Fairclough 2001, Blommaert 2005). Power relations are sometimes challenged through contestation of another's talk to empower oneself or *dis*empower one's interlocutor. I therefore analyse different 'subject positions' (Baxter 2003) women and men in the National Assembly take up and the (competing) discourses they draw on to empower themselves or disempower others, and how they are in turn empowered or disempowered by these subject positions and discourses.

Analytical Methods

As observed by Wodak, CDA is a multi-method framework and requires different sorts of data (Wodak 2001, Reisigl and Wodak 2001). For this book, the data consists of audio recordings of parliamentary debates and field-notes collected during plenary sessions.

The data was analysed both quantitatively and qualitatively. The quantitative analysis was carried out in order to investigate the stark gender differences that still exist within the Cameroonian community. Quantitative analysis also served as a starting point for understanding gendered discourses within the parliamentary setting.

A qualitative discourse analysis of the data was carried out in order to investigate gendered discourses within the parliament and gendered relations of power within this context. Two analytical frameworks were employed - the Critical Discourse Analysis framework (and within this particularly the Discourse Historical Approach).

Organisation of the book

In this chapter (Chapter 1), I present the socio-historical background to the study and the rationale. I also identify the research questions I shall be addressing. Chapter 2 is devoted to a critical review of literature. I focus on literature on discourse analytical studies and gender and language. In Chapter 3, I carry out a quantitative analysis of the data, examining the gender differences which exist in the parliament, in amount of talk, topics and titulation - how members of parliament are differentially addressed by both government ministers, the Speaker of the House of Assembly and other MPs. In Chapter 4, I provisionally identify and analyse *traditional* gendered discourses within the parliament. The discursive strategies used in the legitimation of these 'traditional' discourses are analysed in Chapter 5. Chapter 6 focuses on the identification of *modern* *'progressive'* gendered discourses and analysis of the discursive and legitimating strategies for discourses of 'Positive Action for women' in the parliament is done in chapter 7. In Chapter 8, I discuss the contributions of the study, its limitations and recommendations for future research.

Notes

1. http://www.state.gov/g/drl/rls/irf/2005/51454.htm

2. By tradition, people from the Grassfield Bantu region (Northwest and West Provinces) have only one name which is their name, that is, their first name. They can only be referred to as' wife of X' but do not take the name of the husband. Only in the equatorial Bantu are girl-children referred to by the names of their fathers. Colonial practices made Cameroonian women take the names of their husbands, and children the names of their fathers.

3. They are termed 'secret societies' because membership is open only to a limited number of persons within the society and could either be all-male or all-female. These members of these societies are mainly responsible for village administration and the performance of certain traditional rites.

4. What some call villages today are actually cities as they have grown. These cities still retain those customs and political structures, and are still referred to by some as 'my village'. In such villages/cities, two

parallel political systems function, each respecting the other. The traditional one is more sexist in that, it still considers women cannot be chiefs and gender division of roles is instituted by tradition.

5. In the absence of the Fon's mother, the sister can be a Mamfor.

6. These serve as the legislating bodies in these communities. They make the laws and make sure that the village is well administered. However, with growing educated elite, this group does no longer have complete autonomy in making laws, but still serves as the executing body.

7. I distinguish between the Takumbeng in a village like Bafut, which is a male secret society and the Takumbeng described in this section. Takumbeng described in this section is a generic name used in the North West Region of Cameroon to represent the all female secret societies.

8. The Ngemba, Kom, Bakweri and Bassa are some of the tribal groupings in Cameroon and may constitute different villages.

9. Stevens (2006) observes that because these women are naked, men escape, so the audience is generally other women. Men are affected because they are obliged to address the problem in order to be free to circulate.

10. The then Prime Minister of the Southern Cameroons

11. I use 'public' here to mean the formal public domain.

12. These are appointed but there is no gender mainstreaming to ensure female appointments.

13. www.un.org/womenwatch/daw/beijing/platform/declar

14. There are 150 female NGOs working with the Ministry of Women's Affairs (Ministry of Women's Affairs 2000).

15. Popular interpretation of the concept of feminism in Cameroon refers to actions by women negatively directed against men, to challenge the 'legitimacy' of male dominance.

Chapter Two

Approaches To Gender, Power And Discourse Analysis

Introduction

In this chapter, I examine approaches to gender, power and discourse analysis and the different methods and theories employed in this field of study. I examine fruitful approaches employed in the book in the analysis of gendered discourse and power relations in Cameroonian political systems. I draw especially on Critical Discourse Analysis which looks at the relationship between language and social practices, and in particular, between language and power relations (Fairclough 1995, 2001; van Dijk 1996, 1998; Wodak and Meyer 2001). I also examine the different approaches to gender studies especially the social constructionist approaches.

In the next sections, I examine approaches to discourse analysis, with the different ways the term 'discourse' has been conceptualised.

Approaches to Discourse Analysis

I start this section by looking at different definitions of the term *discourse* as used by different discourse analysts. The word *discourse* has been used widely by linguists, discourse analysts, political analysts and other researchers, and has a multitude of definitions. The discourse-historical approach relates to the socio-cognitive theory of Teun van Dijk (1998) and views 'discourse' as structured forms of knowledge, whereas 'text' refers to concrete oral utterances or written documents (see Reisigl and Wodak 2009: 6). Some, like Fowler et al 1979) have used the term without defining it. Howarth (2000: 2) points out that *discourse* is a contested concept, which is defined, applied and analysed differently in each discipline that employs it,[1] and claims that the definition of discourse depends on the theoretical grounding of the researcher. The most basic definition of *discourse* is that of Schiffrin (1994) which sees discourse in its simplest form as both written and oral texts, that is, language beyond the sentence. Fairclough (2003:3) views discourse broadly as 'an element of social life which is closely interconnected with other elements. Sunderland (2004: 6) defines it as 'a broad stretch of written or spoken language'. She views discourse as both descriptive and interpretive. Descriptively, she observes that discourses are 'broad constitutive systems of meaning', for example, parliamentary discourse. I find this definition appealing and shall come back to it later.

Other researchers (Lemke 1995; Jäger 2001) see *discourse* as a form of *knowledge*. In this light, Lemke (1995) defines it as a 'concrete realisation of abstract forms of knowledge' while Jäger (2001: 34) sees it as 'the flow of knowledge - and/or all societal knowledge stored throughout time which determines individual and collective doing and/or formative action that shapes society, thus exercising power', thus seeing discourse as constitutive (see below). Fairclough (2003) as well as Litosseliti and Sunderland (2002) additionally view *discourse* from an additional perspective of 'practice'. They note that *discourse* is 'not only a form of knowledge about cultural ways of thinking and doing, but also a form of *practice* [their emphasis] (an 'event')'. Fairclough and Wodak (1997: 258) similarly see discourse as 'language use in speech and writing where discourse is a form of *social practice* rather than purely an individual activity or a reflex of situational variables, it represents things and positions people'. Their emphasis on the 'social' should be noted (as against the 'individual').

Blommaert's more recent definition of discourse also carries a semiotic aspect: he argues that *Discourse* includes concepts that are 'non-linguistic' (Blommaert 2005: 3). In his definition, *discourse* 'comprises of all forms of meaningful semiotic forms of human activity seen in connection with social, cultural and historical patterns and developments of use - language-in-action' (2005: 2). He argues that an analysis of discourse therefore needs to take into account all relevant semiotic aspects and could be fully 'non-linguistic'. Blommaert's view of discourse is not so distant from that of other Critical Discourse Analysts like Fairclough who also see a semiotic aspect in the definition of discourse. As Fairclough observes, ''Discourse' is used in a general sense for language (as well as, for instance, visual images) as an element of social life which is dialectically [see definition further below] related to other elements' (2003: 214; see also Fairclough and Wodak 1997). Sunderland (2004: 6) summarises definitions of discourse in four ways

1. a broad stretch of written or spoken language;
2. linguistic and accompanying paralinguistic interaction between people in a specific context;
3. broad constitutive systems of meaning
4. 'knowledge and practices generally associated with a particular institution' or 'different ways of structuring areas of knowledge and social practice' (Talbot 1995: 43).

Like Howarth (2000), Sunderland claims that these meanings do not only vary with discipline but also with intellectual persuasion. She also highlights the *constitutive* nature of discourse (what it *does*) in line with Blommaert (2005) and Fairclough and Wodak (1997).

In terms of what it does, discourse is seen to sustain and reproduce the status quo (Leeuwen and Wodak 1999: 93) and is *constitutive* of relations (social relations between people) (Wodak 2001: 66), *representations* (of the world) (Fairclough 2003: 124), and *identities* (people's social and personal identities):

a social practice [which] implies a dialectal relationship between a particular discursive event and situation(s), institutions(s) and social structure(s) which frame it. A dialectal relationship is a two way relation: the discursive event is shaped but situations, institutions, social structures, but it is also shaped by them. (Fairclough and Wodak 1997:55)

The above quote shows the dialectical nature of discourse as construed by CDA practitioners.

CDA researchers also see *discourse* not only as a social practice but also a *political* practice, which 'establishes, sustains and changes *power* relations and the collective entities … between which power relations obtain' (Fairclough 1992: 67, see also Foucault 1972, van Leeuwen 1996, van Dijk 1998, 2001, Wodak 2001). Through ideologies (see below), discourse thus serves certain ends, which are not only to sustain and reproduce the status quo, but also to resist and challenge it: in both cases power is exercised. As a political practice, it is not only a site of power struggle but also a stake in particular power struggles. Jaworski and Coupland's (1999: 3) similarly define discourse as 'language use relative to social, political and cultural formations […] reflecting social order and shaping individuals' and incorporates the notion of Parliamentary discourse.

Critical discourse analysts, following Foucault do not only talk of *discourse* but also of *discourses*. Fairclough distinguishes between the abstract noun, which he calls 'a domain of statements', and the count noun, 'discourses', for groups of statements (see Fairclough 2003: 124). He sees discours*es* as

> *ways of representing aspects of the world* (my emphasis) - the processes, relations and structures of the material world, the 'mental world' of thoughts, feelings, beliefs and so forth, and the social world.

And Sunderland as:

> 'ways of *seeing* the world' (where 'seeing' may extend beyond the receptive to actively 'thinking about it') (Sunderland (2004: 28, my emphasis).

We *see* the world through them and *represent* the world with them. Kress and van Leeuwen (2001) similarly regard discours*es* as 'socially constructed knowledges of (some aspect of) reality', claiming that different discourses contain different *perspectives* on the world, and are associated with different relations people have with the world. Importantly, all these researchers see discourses as *socially constitutive*. In this book, I use the term mainly in the sense of Fairclough (2001) and Sunderland (2004) as 'ways of seeing/representing the world', ways which are crucially constitutive. As regards the identification and analysis of discourses, Sunderland (2004: 7) notes that they are not in themselves visible but may be recognisable to language users through their manifestation in characteristic 'linguistic traces' (Fairclough 1989, Talbot 1998).

Discourse can be seen as synonymous to *text* within the English school of Critical Discourse Analysis (Wodak and Meyer 2009) although within other CDA approaches (e.g. the discourse historical approach), discourse relates to broad forms of knowledge. Halliday (2004, [1985, 1994]) for example does not distinguish between discourse and text. He uses the terms interchangeably. Fairclough (1992, 2001, 2003) however sees texts as the concrete material produced during discourse (e.g. words, spoken or on a page). Reisigl and Wodak (2001) also acknowledge texts as 'concrete' 'oral' and 'written' utterances. Hodge and Kress (1988: 6) distinguish between *text* and *discourse* claiming that 'Discourse [...] is the site where social forms of organization engage with systems of signs in the production of texts, thus reproducing or changing the sets of meanings and values which make up a culture', discourse thus referring here to social processes where texts are produced.

In this book, I use the term discourse in two ways following Fairclough (2003, 2007) and Sunderland (2004). I use discourse as an abstract noun, described by Fairclough (2007: 10) as 'a facet of social life', which appears neither with a definite or indefinite article. In this sense, I shall be referring for example to 'political discourse', 'parliamentary discourse' or 'developmental discourse'. I shall also be using the term discourse as a concrete count noun (Fairclough 2007:11) to mean 'ways of representing the world' (Fairclough 2003:124) or 'ways of seeing the world' (Sunderland 2004: 28). I shall also be drawing on van Leeuwen's definition which emphasises the notion of socially constructed knowledges. I shall thus be referring for example to a discourse of X as Y, or alternatively X discourse(s) (e.g. 'a discourse of women as domestic' or 'hegemonic discourse').

In the next section, I examine the main approaches to critical discourse analysis used in the book. The concepts of *critical, ideology* and *power* are the tenets of CDA.

Critical Discourse Analysis

Critical Discourse Analysis theory sees discourse as a social as well as linguistic practice that maintains social conditions which give rise to power relations aligned with race, class and gender ideologies, but which allows for resistance, contestation and subversion (Fairclough 2001; Walsh 2001; Van Dijk 1998, 2001; Weiss and Wodak 2003; Reisigl and Wodak 2001). CDA is based on the concepts of *critical, ideology* and *power* (Wodak and Meyer 2009: 6). Wodak and Meyer (2001: 9) see *critical* as 'having a distance to the data, embedding the data in the social, *taking a political stance explicitly*, and a focus on self-reflection as scholars doing research' (my emphasis). Wodak and Meyer (2009: 7) also note that CDA researchers have to be aware that their own work is driven by social, economic and political motives like any other academic work and that they are not in any privileged position. Naming oneself 'critical' only implies specific ethical standards: an intention to make their position, research interests and values explicit and their criteria as transparent as possible, without feeling the need to apologize for the critical stance of their work (Van Leeuwen, 2006: 293, see also van Dijk 2001, Wodak 2001,Krzyżanowskiand Wodak 2007). *Critical* has also been seen by Fairclough as essentially making visible the interconnectedness of language and other things. CDA is *critical*

> first, in the sense that it seeks to discern connections between language and other elements in the social life which are often opaque. These include: how language figures within social relations of power and domination; how language works ideologically; the negotiation of personal and social identities (pervasively problematized through the changes in social life) in its linguistic and semiotic aspect. *Second, it is critical in the sense that it is committed to progressive social change* (Fairclough 2001: 230 my emphasis).

In being *critical*, Fairclough (2003: 9) notes that 'we choose to ask certain questions about social events and texts, and not other possible questions'. We ask questions relating to issues of unequal power relations such as gender.

Ideology on the other hand, Fairclough notes, refers to 'representations of aspects of the world which can be shown to contribute to establishing, maintaining and changing of social relations of power, domination and exploitation' (Fairclough 2003: 9). *Ideology* looks at the more hidden and latent type of everyday beliefs, which often appear disguised as conceptual metaphors and analogies (Wodak and Meyer 2009: 8). Dominant ideologies appear as 'neutral', holding on to assumptions that stay largely unchallenged They do this very subtly, but sometimes overtly (van Dijk 1998, 2001; Reisigl and Wodak 2001; Fairclough 2001, 2003; Blommaert 2005). Weiss and Wodak observe that *ideology* relates to:

> social forms and processes within which, and by means of which, symbolic forms circulate in the social world. [It is] an important means of establishing and maintaining unequal power relations... there are specific historical reasons why people come to feel, reason, desire and imagine as they do' (Wodak and Weiss 2003: 14).

28

Ideologies function through discourse and serve as means of establishing and maintaining asymmetrical power relationships (Thompson 1984, 1990; van Dijk 1998; Mills 2000; Fairclough 2001, 2003; Vološinov 1973). Vološinov (1973) and Thompson (1990: 8) indicate that ideologies are 'complex ways in which meaning is mobilised for the maintenance of relations of dominion … This meaning is constructed and conveyed by symbolic forms of various kinds, from everyday linguistic utterances to complex images and texts'. Ideology and discourse are intricately linked since 'ideas' do not drift through the social world like clouds. Rather, ideas circulate in the social world as utterances, as expressions, as words which are spoken or inscribed' (Thompson 1984: 4). An analysis of discourse should therefore include 'interpretation', which is 'a form of discourse [analysis as] we may seek to move beyond the study of discursive structure and *construct* meaning which shows how discourse serves to sustain relations of domination' (Thompson 1984: 11, his emphasis). Although *discourse carries a stronger linguistic element,* Sunderland (2004: 6) points out that *a discourse* is sometimes used 'indistinguishably' from *an ideology* and notes that '*ideology* can, in fact, be seen as the cultural materialist antecedent of the post-structuralist use of *discourse,* and, for both post-structuralism and CDA, discourse can be seen as carrying ideology. Ideology establishes and maintains *power* through commonsense taken for granted assumptions (Blommaert 2005, Thompson 1990, Fairclough 2001, van Dijk 2001, Reisigl and Wodak 2001, Lazar 2005). Blommaert observes that when discourse is combined with power, the result is ideology. Ideologies are most effective when their workings are least visible (Fairclough 2001: 64), and when it penetrates the whole fabric of societies or communities and results in normalised, naturalised patterns (and become hegemonies) of thought and behaviour … that sustain social relation of power structures, and the patterns of power that enforce such common sense' (Blommaert 2005: 159).

Linking ideology to *power,* CDA as an approach to language study looks at the relationship between language and social practice, and in particular, between language and power (Fairclough 1995, 1997, 2001; Wodak and Meyer 1997; Weiss and Wodak 2003, Blommaert 2005). The exercise of power in modern society is increasingly achieved through ideology and more so through the ideological workings of *language*. Language is not powerful on its own but gains power by the use people make of it. Power 'does not derive from language but language can be used to challenge power, to subvert it, to alter distributions of power in the short and long term' (Weiss and Wodak, 2003: 15). Fairclough (2001: 3; 2003) distinguishes different kinds of power: coercion of various sorts including physical violence, and the manufacture of consent or acquiescence (which Gramsci calls hegemony). CDA is mainly interested in the second kind.

Blommaert (2005:1) argues that CDA should not be a discourse analysis that 'reacts against power *alone*' (his emphasis). He argues that 'critical approaches' should not be equated with 'approaches that criticise power' and suggests CDA should be 'about the analysis of power *effects*, of the outcome of power, of what power *does* to people, groups, societies, and *how* this impact comes about'. This is however not a very fair assessment of CDA. This is in part because what constitutes power is partly a matter of different readings, but also because power can be positive, that is, *empowerment* of marginalised groups.

CDA thus should not allow social phenomena and processes to be taken for granted, but also '*opening up* alternative options, and de-mystifying power relations... while de-constructing texts and discourses systematically and precisely in a retroductable way' (Wodak 2007). These 'alternative options' could be the perception of power as positive when it is contested, de-mystified and appropriated by a less powerful group or individuals, thus *empowering* themselves. Grillo (2005) also suggests that power must not always be equated to dominion (see also Hammersley 1997, Pennycook 2001, and Baxter 2003). It can take the form of mutual empowerment.

Different CDA practitioners use methodologies which are differently theoretically informed. Wodak and fellow researchers for example have developed the discourse–historical method (Wodak et al 1999, Wodak 2001, Wodak and Meyer 2001, Reisigl and Wodak 2001, Wodak 2003, Weiss and Wodak 2003) in analysing the socio-historical context and arguments by tracing the history of phrases and arguments for the discourse topics using original documents.

Kress and van Leeuwen (2001) and Kress (1997) emphasise the importance of incorporating visual images into concepts of discourse and thus of a move toward broader multi-modal conceptions of semiosis, that is, including a semiotic aspect in the analysis of discourse. Van Dijk (2001, 2006) uses a socio-cognitive approach which looks at mental structures, representations or processes and more abstract properties of societies and cultures involved in discourse and interaction. Fairclough's (e.g. 2001, 2003) framework is based on Hallidayan systemic functional linguistics as well as socio-semantic representation of 'social actors' (see especially van Leeuwen 1996 and Fairclough 2003).

I have chosen to use CDA for this study as it arguably provides a means to 'go beyond mere description and explanation, and pay more explicit attention to the socio-political and cultural presuppositions and implications of discourse' (Van Dijk 1993: 131), an important aspect for this study, as it draws on the traditional gender ideologies in Cameroon. Remlinger (1999: 5) also claims CDA can aid language and gender study through a critical examination of discourses and can provide it with a particularly developed understanding of the linguistic constitution of gender ideologies through 'a critical approach to examine more fully the interaction between language and social structures, to explain how social structures are constituted by elites' linguistic interaction' (see Remlinger 1999: 2-3). CDA methods provide a tool in the analysis of the social structures that underlie gender and power relations in Cameroon. Although CDA aims to show the 'non-obvious' ways (see Fairclough 2001: 229) in which language is involved in social relations of power and domination, I argue that it can also be useful in analysing even the *very obvious* ways language is used in political domination. As indicated, Fairclough (2001: 229) posits that 'the starting point for CDA is social issues and problems' (and that it does not begin with texts and interactions). Sunderland (2004: 10) notes that one such social issue is *gender*, which is 'often a problem for women and girls; in different ways, for men and boys; and accordingly for gender relations'. The social issue in this book relates to discoursal discrimination against women (in the society and parliament) and the perpetuation of traditional gendered practices on the one hand, and the challenge and resistance to these practices (by women and men) on the other.

CDA, especially in the discourse-historical approach (see Wodak 2001, Reisigl and Wodak 2001, Weiss and Wodak 2003), looks at discourses across different types of texts and allows for the analysis of similarities between different types of texts, hence bringing into the analysis the concepts of *intertextuality* and *interdiscursivity* (Bakhtin 1981, Kristeva 1986, Fairclough 1992, 2003). Cameroon is a hybrid society, made up of both traditional and modern social practices, and members of the public draw on discourses from both contexts. Secondly, the parliament is made up of MPs from other communities of practice (Eckert and McConnell-Ginet 1992, 1999, 2007) and is likely to draw on linguistic practices from other local or wider communities of practice. The main analytical framework for this book - the discourse-historical approach to CDA, advocates a socio-historical analysis which can only be achieved by drawing on other texts outside the data being analysed, thus the need to examine intertextuality and interdiscursivity in the sections below.

Intertextuality

I start this section by making reference to Foucault's claim that 'there can be no statement that in one way or another does not re-actualise others' (Foucault 1972: 98). This may imply that every statement made draws on others' words, either through quotations, or more indirect reference to what has been said or written before. Textual analysis therefore subsumes two complementary types of analysis: linguistic analysis (phonology, vocabulary, grammar up to the level of sentence semantics, textual organisation above the sentence) and *inter*textual analysis. *Intertextuality*, Kristeva states, refers to 'the insertion of history (society) into a text and of this text into history' (1986: 39). She notes that '...any text is constructed as a mosaic of quotations; any text is the absorption and transformation of another' (p. 37). In this light, in interaction, we draw on a bank of texts (knowledge) from the society, following Bakhtin's (1981: 89) assertion that 'our speech... is filled with others' words'. Fairclough (1992) thus views *intertextuality* as where a particular text may draw upon a plurality of genres, discourses, or narratives, for example, using direct quotes or reported speech. Fairclough extends his definition to include 'relations between one text and other texts which are external to it yet in some way brought into it' (Fairclough 2003: 39) including 'thoughts' from somewhere else – 'allusions or evocations'. Therefore, essentially, every text is informed by other texts, and indeed *anticipates* other texts.

Fairclough also uses the term *assumptions,* where 'what is 'said' in a text is 'said' against a background of what is 'unsaid', but taken as a 'given' (e.g. that women have domestic responsibilities when they are criticised for spending time in public). He notes that *assumptions* thus connect one text to the 'world of texts' (2003: 40) and indeed are linked to ideologies (Fairclough 2003, Thompson 1990, Eagleton 1991). The difference between assumptions and intertextuality is that intertextuality is usually attributable to *specific,* identifiable texts. In this study, I bring in the notion of *assumptions* to support that of intertextuality because much of the gendered discourse in the Cameroonian parliament is arguably brought in from the world of oral texts (from the traditional background). While this is still intertextuality, the notion of 'assumption' is particularly apt in what is said by the members of parliament, with what is not said.

Texts are 'open and hybrid' in that they are not closed systems: 'new sub-topics can be created and intertextuality allows for new fields of action' (Wodak 2001: 66). Analysis of intertextuality then looks at the links between one text and others. It is worth noting that differences in the understandings of the analysis of intertextuality by Fairclough and Wodak are slight, evident in the way they *use* the concept. Fairclough concentrates on *intra*-text intertextuality, looking at features of other texts (or assumptions) within the text (usually one) under analysis, whereas Wodak (see Wodak 2001, Reisigl and Wodak 2001) explores intertextuality *across different texts* looking at the intersection between different specific texts often from different genres. An example can be seen in her analysis of discourses of racism where she looks at racist discourse in presidential speeches, parliamentary speeches and newspaper publications. Texts can potentially draw on others either through direct quote and/or reference. Fairclough analyses traces of other texts in the same text through cues such as reported speech, allusions, e.g. to other texts or discourses from elsewhere.

I make use of both approaches to intertextuality (see Fairclough 1992, 2003; Wodak 2001, Reisigl and Wodak 2001) in this book for the following reasons. In a modern political system that is strongly embedded in a cultural context, where a traditional village system of governance still exists (chiefs and kings still have power and women marginally participate in politics), and where traditional beliefs are still held strongly, and traditional customs are still practiced by members of the parliament, and where at the same time globalisation is affecting societal values, elements of intertextuality can be expected to run through parliamentary discourse (see Fairclough 2003: 58 on assumptions and ideology). Members of Parliament, who are also active members in their own local communities, can be expected to continuously bring in texts associated with traditional systems and those associated with modern political systems.

In analysing the discursive construction of women within the parliament, I draw on party constitutions and also the millennium declaration (Millennium Development Goals). This constitutes cross-text intertextuality, as related documents are drawn on to support the data analysis.

Interdiscursivity

Intricately linked to intertextuality is *interdiscursivity*. Whereas intertextuality is the 'appropriation' of other's words, (i.e. overtly drawing upon other texts) *interdiscursivity* is a broader concept. For Fairclough, interdiscursivity is "constitutive intertextuality" (Fairclough 1992: 124), although manifest intertextuality may also be constitutive. Interdiscursivity allows for the co-existence of competing discourses. Wodak (2001: 37) defines interdiscursivity simply as 'the intersection between discourse A and discourse B'. Any stretch of language can be seen as containing more than one discourse (see e.g. Kress 1988: 134) and as Sunderland 2004 observes, the boundaries between one discourse and another are fuzzy. Interdiscursivity therefore means a macro-discourse of 'a model Cameroonian woman' can draw on another such as 'It's the culture', with related contents and themes, and oppositional and social actors can draw on conflicting discourses such as 'Gender equality' and 'Gender differentiation' to legitimate their arguments.

Interdiscursivity allows for the analysis of different but related discourses in different genres and texts that feature in parliamentary debates in Cameroon (Question-and-Answer sessions and Discussion sessions). It is a good conceptual tool in analysing gendered discourses, that is, 'traces' of the same discourses within the same and different texts.

Approaches to CDA Drawn on in this Book
Different theories of CDA are drawn on for different aspects they have focused on. I draw on Fairclough's definition of 'discourse' both as an abstract and as a count noun (see above), on van Dijk's 'political discourse analysis' (though not his analysis of 'discourse-society-cognition), van Leeuwen's 'representation of social actors' and Wodak's 'discourse historical approach'. Wodak's discourse historical approach is the main approach used in this book.

Political Discourse Analysis
Van Dijk (1997, 2006) in his 'political discourse analysis' (PDA), asserts that PDA is *critical* political discourse analysis. It deals with the reproduction of political power, power abuse, or domination through political discourse and manipulation (van Dijk 2006), but also includes various forms of resistance or 'counter power' against such forms of discursive dominance. Van Dijk analyses political structures and processes in terms of different categories. For example, in a parliamentary debate, there may be the following categories (with examples):
- Domain: politics
- System: democracy
- Institution: parliament
- Values and ideologies: democracy, group and party ideologies
- Organisation: political parties, lobbyists
- Political actors: members of parliament, cabinet ministers
- Political relations: legislative power
- Political process: legislation
- Political action: political decision making
- Political cognitions: attitudes about the relevant issue (e.g. about abortion, positive action (for women) or nuclear energy) (van Dijk 1997: 19).

35

Using these categories, van Dijk looks at the discourse structures in political discourse: the topic, textual 'schemata', semantics, lexicon, syntax, rhetoric, expression structures and speech acts.

PDA looks into issues of power and domination in institutional settings, and as such, some of it is relevant to my own study of gendered discourses in a political system.

Representation of Social Actors

Although not used in this book as a main approach in the analysis of data, van Leeuwen's 'representation of social actors' and 'social actions' framework (Van Leeuwen 1995, 1996; van Leeuwen and Wodak 1999) provides a useful contribution to the analysis of the data. The approach is not autonomous but based on Halliday's systemic functional linguistics (Halliday 2004; Martin 1992) and critical linguistics. Van Leeuwen analyzes representation as the recontextualization of social practices (Bernstein, 1990 and van Leeuwen and Wodak 1999:85). Its particular relevance to this book are the notions of 'exclusion' and 'inclusion' of social actions and actors in that the analysis of reference and nomination of social actors which I use in Chapters 5 and 7.

Discourse-Historical Approach to CDA

The Discourse - Historical approach to CDA (DH-CDA) has been used as the main analytical framework. Like other CDA, it assumes a dialectical relationship between particular discursive practices and specific fields of action. It draws on the representation of social actors (see above) in its analysis of 'positive self-presentation' and 'negative other-presentation'. This approach, developed by Wodak and associate researchers (van Leeuwen and Wodak 1999, Wodak 2001, 2004, Reisigl and Wodak 2001, Weiss and Wodak 2003, also Wodak and Meyer 2009) attempts to 'integrate much available knowledge about the historical sources and the background of the social and political fields in which 'discursive' events are embedded' (Wodak and Meyer 2001: 35). It makes great use of both sociological and historical context in its data analysis and seeks to identify the *contents* or *topics* of a discourse, investigate the discursive or argumentation strategies (see below) and looks at the linguistic means in the realisation of the above (Reisigl and Wodak 2001: 44).

To explore the interconnectedness of discursive and other social practices, the DH-CDA favours the concept of triangulation based on four different levels of context:

1. the immediate, language or text-internal co-text,
2. the intertextual and interdiscursive relationship between utterances, texts, genres and discourses,
3. the extra-linguistic social/sociological variables and institutional frames of a specific 'context of situation' and
4. the broader socio-political and historical context, which the discursive practices are embodied in and related to (Wodak 2001: 67; Weiss and Wodak 2004: 22).

An analysis of these different levels of context allows the analysis of texts to be intertextually connected to other related genres of discourse and strategies of argumentation. It thus incorporates large amounts of data from relevant historical and political background.

Within the approach, Reisigl and Wodak identify *discursive strategies* which are located within different levels of linguistic organisation and complexity. They define strategies as systematic ways of using language where 'a more or less accurate and more or less intentional plan of practices (including discursive practices) [are] adopted to achieve a particular social, political, psychological or linguistic aim' (Reisigl and Wodak 2001: 44). Such an aim could be to construct a social actor in positive or negative ways. Different strategies that could be used in analysing texts include:

1. Referential/nomination strategies by which one constructs and represents social actors (negatively positively). Referential/nomination strategies allow the examination of how in-groups and out-groups are constructed, for example through positive self- and/or negative other-presentation.
2. Predicational strategies: label social actors positively or negatively. Predicational strategies are closely related to referential strategies but focus on the labelling of social actors positively or negatively through stereotyping, evaluative attributes and implicit or explicit predicates.
3. Argumentation strategies: to legitimate inclusions or exclusions. Arguments are used to legitimate inclusions or

exclusions of social actors. In analyzing discursive strategies, different points of view are also taken into consideration, that is, perspectivation. They could function to legitimate, challenge or subvert other social practices.

4. Perspectivation (framing or discourse representation), by means of which speakers express their involvement in discourse and position their point of view and arguments expressed.

5. Intensification or mitigation e.g. of utterances (Wodak 2001: 72-73, Reisigl and Wodak 2001: 45). Arguments for the inclusion or exclusion of social actors could be mitigated or intensified depending on what is being said or highlighted.

The multiple perspectives of DH- CDA on context analysis gives the opportunity to explore the cultural, socio-political and historical context of the primary data and bring in other texts potentially useful in the analysis of this data. It also allows for the study of intertextuality in relation to the different texts and genres, and specifically to analyse assumptions based on 'common-sense' traditional beliefs and practices brought into (parliamentary) texts, while at the same time analysing discourses across different texts and genres in the parliament (cf. interdiscursivity). DH-CDA also allows for the identification of gendered 'traditional' and 'modern/ progressive' discourses and their legitimation within the Cameroonian parliament and strategies employed in legitimating traditional and conservative constructions of Cameroonian women.

Some of the discursive strategies (referential, argumentative and mitigation strategies) used in this book have been adopted from this approach and others developed in the analysis of how women and men use language and are constructed through discourse within the parliament. Although the approach is generally useful for analysis of data, it is adapted to the needs of this book.

CDA and this book

The question 'what type of CDA are you using?' is often asked of CDA analysts. I presented the different approaches to CDA in the sections above. These approaches differ from each other in subtle and less subtle ways as regards data analysis. The '*systemic functional linguistic*' approach used by Fairclough, the '*discourse historical*' approach of Wodak and the '*socio-cognitive*' approach of van Dijk nevertheless all have something to offer in this book. However, I use mainly Wodak's *discourse-historical* approach, given its emphasis on *historical context* which is central to this study, and the contextual analysis allows for focus on historical context, considering the all-important socio-historical background of Cameroon. The Discourse-historical approach's notion of 'discursive strategies' is also especially useful because it allows for the identification of (legitimating) strategies in the parliamentary talk used for perpetuating gender imbalance or for resisting change.

Van Dijk (2001) indicates that a critical analysis of discourse should be 'diverse', 'critical', 'with an attitude', focusing on 'a social problem'. CDA also focuses on the role of discourse in the production and reproduction of power abuse or domination' (van Dijk 2001:96). Using a critical approach to discourse is relevant to this study because an analysis of discursive practices brings to light the means through which power, domination and discrimination are legitimated within the Cameroonian parliament and by implication the wider Cameroonian society. I also draw on his framework of political discourse analysis since the data constitutes political texts.

Language and Power
In this section, I embark on reviewing literature on the concepts of power relations. The main mission of critical discourse is the analysis of discourse to make visible asymmetrical relations of power. This concept is important in this book as the study investigates unbalanced gender relations of power in institutional settings, and how MPs negotiate power in the parliament.

Beetham (1991:43) notes power also depends on certain preconditions: the presence of personal capacities or 'powers' such as health, strength, knowledge, skills; the possession of material resources; and space and scope, in the sense of freedom from control, obstruction or subservience to the purposes of others. The possession of material resources becomes a means of social power in so far as people can be systematically excluded from access to them. Equally, to have power is to control socially necessary activities and the skills associated with their performance. Power also consists of occupancy of positions, which carry with them the power of command over others. Such occupancy is accompanied by specific language use and this language is the language of power.

Different kinds of power in discourse have been identified. Gramsci (1971) talks of 'hegemony'. Theories of hegemony attempt to explain how dominant groups or individuals can maintain their power - the capacity of dominant classes to discoursally *persuade* subordinate ones to accept, adopt and internalize their values and norms.

Power in language use is *social* power, defined by van Dijk as 'a specific *relation between social groups* or institutions'. From a broad CDA perspective, Van Dijk (1997:18-21) identifies different kinds of power achieved using discourse:

- *Control of action and mind*: *control* here is the key word and could be force (using 'action') or control of the mind (social power). *Text* and *talk* are used to control the minds of people. People with access to special speech acts like religious leaders, judges, and police officers have such power.

- *Persuasive power*: such power is achieved through a kind of subtle control of the mind. It is based on compliance and argument and other forms of persuasion are used to get consent. The discourse of control is quite subtle and control here may come from people with symbolic capital like parents, teachers, bosses, and other superiors.

- *Hegemony and consensus:* hegemony is often used to refer to social power: hegemonic power makes people act as if it were natural, normal, or simply a consensus. No commands, requests or even suggestions are necessary. Here text and talk are used to manipulate people such that they do what the powerful group prefers. This is usually achieved through education, the media and other forms of public discourse.

- *Access:* in order to exercise hegemonic power, there is a need for *access* to scarce 'symbolic capital' such as knowledge, education, fame, respect, and indeed public discourse itself (see Chapter 4). One needs the above symbolic capital to have access to this kind of power.

In this book, I identify two main forms of power: power achieved through hegemony and consensus, and power achieved through access to scarce symbolic capital. Power achieved through hegemony makes use of taken-for-granted assumptions to dominate others, and, as shown in this book (see Chapters 5, 6 and 7) is evident in traditional gender ideologies and discourses (see Chapter 4) which function to dominate women in institutional settings. Most women do not have access to symbolic capital to actively and effectively participate in parliamentary debates and this lack thus constitutes a form of societal domination by those *with* this symbolic capital.

Also, Corson (1993:1) claims that all kinds of power including physical violence are directed, mediated, or resisted through language. People in positions of power can use 'discourse practices' that can routinely repress, dominate, and disempower language users whose practices differ from the norms that it establishes. Language then serves as an instrument of domination. Corson proposes four different relationships that exist between language and power. The first is that language is used as an instrument to wield power. The human ability to wield complex vocabulary (e.g. legal discourse) and the use of commanding language gives language a status and authority. The second sees language as a tool to shape thought and worldview (as in Sapir-Whorf hypothesis). The third relationship connects the instability of discourse within structures of power and meaning. Language is used not for the content of what is said but of who is saying it, (this relationship is connected to the first). The last links language to power by way of *ideology* (see Fairclough 2001). Corson's analysis of language and power is not unrelated to that of CDA as he also sees power operating through language use and ideology.

In analysing power through the notion of ideology, enacted through discourse Fairclough (2003: 10) observes that 'common-sense' is often involved in the service of power as 'ideologies are embedded in features of discourse which are taken for granted as matters of common sense' (Fairclough 2001: 66, see also Thompson 1990 and Eagleton 1991). Thus power achieved through ideology is most effective when unequal relations are sustained through common-sense taken-for-granted assumptions.

Although critical discourse analysts talk of *resisting* powerful discourses (see Fairclough 1992, Chouliaraki and Fairclough 1999, Lazar 2005), they however tend not to refer to strategies of empowerment of the dominated. Using Feminist Poststructuralist Discourse Analysis (FPDA), Baxter (2003) however observes that (marginalised) social actors can draw on empowering discourses to challenge dominant ones.

For poststructuralism, power cannot be held and kept or 'possessed' by a person: it is fluid and intangible, and keeps shifting. A person may thus be in a position of power for a period of time but never in possession of it all the time. Foucault (1980: 87) claims that power is never localised here or there, is never in anybody's hands, and is never appropriated as commodity or a piece of wealth. Power is exercised rather through a 'net-like organisation', and not only do individuals circulate between its 'threads', they are always in the position of simultaneously undergoing *and* exercising this power. They are not only its inert or consenting target, but are always also the elements of its articulation. An individual thus fluctuates between being powerful and powerless and is never permanently positioned as powerful or powerless.

Gender, Language, and Power

In studying language and power, I examine how language contributes to the domination of some people, (especially women) by others. Power is most effective in gender and power relations through the manufacture of consent, and according to Fairclough (2001: 3) by means of ideology. Power in gender and language relations is more than just an authoritative voice in decision-making but the ability to define social reality, Gal (1991:197). In traditional ritual ceremonies in Cameroon for example, men almost exclusively have the right to address crowds and carry out the (public) rituals. Such ceremonies include marriages, death ceremonies, religious sacrifices, incantations, and other power-related discourse. Power, according to Beetham, is used in modern times to mean 'societal control'.

This study concerns strategies employed by dominant groups (men) to maintain power within institutional settings (the parliament). Power can also be examined to show how both dominant and subordinate groups negotiate power and how both shift between positions of power and powerlessness (see Baxter 2003). Shaw (2000) defines such power as 'the extent to which a member of parliament (MP) controls the resource of debate floor 'as evidenced by linguistic exchanges' (Shaw 2000: 402), (what van Dijk 1997, 2001 refers to as *access*). As indicated, she argues that in the parliament, gender may be a more salient variable than occupational status in contributing to an individual's control of the floor.

Ideologies that either assume or assert that men should dominate women have been referred to by Phillips (2003: 255) as patriarchy. That is, to have authority over women, and tell them what to do, and that gender is more important than, say, class, in understanding human oppression. A male/female, public/private dichotomy which gave power to men, bolstered by a patriarchal gender ideology that found women lacking in whatever was required for public participation, maybe less important than the hitherto in feminist theory in social sciences, replaced by understanding of 'subtle sexism', but is arguably still very important in the African context.

Language, Gender and Power in Africa

There is a wide gap of knowledge on gender, language and power especially in the public sphere within the African context. Thetela (2002) however studied language and power relations in Southern African police interviews of rape victims. Relevant here is the phenomena of *hlonipha*, that is, the language of 'respect' among Southern Africans. *Hlonipha*, a culturally learnt linguistic code of 'politeness', however applies only to women, and provides unequal access to 'sex discourses'. Women are not allowed to (publicly) articulate certain lexical items especially those related to the sexual organs. Explicit reference to sexual acts is restricted to men. The public sphere is relevant here because; given *hlonipha* female victims cannot use certain 'adult' language in public.

Thetela looks at the issues of domination, power and disadvantage which all result from *hlonipha,* and which also constrain women's public discourse and in effect functions as a discursive strategy for constructing and maintaining dominant patriarchal hegemony in, inter alia, the socio-legal system. Thetela compares

43

cultural expectations of women's discourse on the one hand, especially in a public setting, which regard sex as a very private matter and thus a taboo subject for public (especially female) discussion, and the expectations of the legal system, which demands explicitness for the sake of precision of evidence. In relation to this, Sadiqi (2003), in a Moroccan context notes that language and gender interact in complex ways with power and power can thus only be interpreted through cultural norms and values. For this reason, the interpretation of power relations varies according to context. These are what I suppose Phillips (2003)sees as gender ideologies which tend to be context bound.

Kimenyi (1992) in studying the relationship between gender and power in Rwanda notes that in this society women are denied the role of agent as they are constructed to be in receipt of orders and advice from their fathers as parents and as wives from their husbands. As a daughter (before marriage), the male figure - the father, and after marriage, her husband are constructed as more powerful in gender and power relations within the culture. *Hlonipha* also applies in Rwanda where women are not allowed to pronounce the name of the in-laws. Through other linguistic means, from syntax to phonology and proverbs, women are constructed as subordinate and powerless within the Rwandan context. Kimenyi examined how power is reflected in language use through grammatical structures. Men appropriate power by positioning women constantly as patients. Women do not occupy subject positions in certain grammatical structures; if they did, the sentence would become meaningless. This is simply because they would be positioning themselves as actors in activities that give them power. If they are presented as agents, the sentence may not be contextually correct. Tellingly, these grammatical structures are especially associated with contexts dealing with male/female relationships e.g. verbs like 'gusaba' (to be engaged), 'kuroongora' (to marry), 'gutoongoza' (to seduce) and 'kweenda' (to have sex with) typically have masculine subjects: a woman does not marry a man but a man marries a woman. Taboos on certain other activities like climbing and building as well as wooing do not allow woman to occupy the subject position of a sentence of such activities. Kimenyi also notes that 'good objects', those associated with positive influence, have a masculine gender, while those associated with negative influence are associated with the feminine gender. Further, proverbs like 'the man has the final word' may, she claims, discourage women from taking decisions and help in degrading them. A woman is thus not allowed to show initiative or active participation.

Discourse is shaped by relations of power and ideology. Gender ideologies in the African context essentially construct women as subordinate, reinforcing and perpetuating male dominance. However, these ideologies are continuously being challenged and resisted as women try to empower themselves through articulating competing discourses. Power then is intricately connected to the study of gender and language. Although gender ideologies may position women as subordinate, they cannot be powerless all the time. In this book, I therefore explore the link between language, gender and power, with regard to the way men and women in the Cameroonian parliament negotiate relations of power and shift between positions of powerfulness and powerlessness.

Approaches to Gender Studies

Gender used to be solely seen as a grammatical, defined for example by Corbett (1991) syntactically as a form of classification of nominals (in the field of theoretical linguistics). It sometimes is still used in this way. However, to distinguish the social and the biological, feminists and others have made a distinction between *gender* and *sex*. Wodak (1997: 2) for example defines *sex* as 'biological or anatomical differences between men and women', whereas *gender* 'concerns the psychological, social, and cultural differences between males and females' (that is, masculinity and femininity). From a post-structuralist perspective, however, gender is fluid, continually being shaped and cannot be defined using binary terms. Poststructuralist researchers such as Butler (1999 [1990]) and Baxter (2003, 2006) posit that even sex, like gender, is a social construct and thus cannot be described as a dichotomy. Cameron (1997) considers the theoretical debates surrounding the question of sex and gender, working from three paradigms summarized by Mathieu (1989):

- *Homology*: "gender is seen as a socially mediated expression of the biological given, sex. Individuals learn 'feminine' or

45

'masculine' behaviour depending on their prior categorisation as biologically 'male' or 'female', with the social elaborating on the biological".

- *Analogy*: "gender *symbolises* sex. Gender identity in this paradigm is based on the collective social experience of living as a member of the group 'women' or 'men' – taking particular 'gender roles' in order to conform to cultural expectations. These roles and expectations may differ significantly in different societies and periods of history even though male and female biology *per se* shows no such variation." Gender roles are thus learnt but are crucially arbitrary. Conventional masculine and feminine behaviour varies from culture to culture (O'Barr and Atkins 1980:7). The main idea here is socialisation.

- *Heterogeneity*: "sex and gender are different in kind. The idea that their relationship is either homologous or analogous, or in other words that sex is in some sense the foundation for gender, is regarded within this approach as an ideological fiction. We should not take for granted that the world is 'naturally' divided into two groups, 'women' and 'men', but should see this division as something produced historically for the purpose of securing one group's domination over the other. In this paradigm, *gender constructs sex, not vice versa*".

Sex is not only a 'biological essentialism' casting people as boys or girls and men or women, but *also* socially constructed (Sunderland 2004: 14) or at least, its importance is. For this study, I choose to use a model which sees *gender* in the first two of these paradigms, that is, in terms of *differences* between males and females – *strategic essentialism* (see Holmes 2006; Spivak 1996, Stone 2004) and as *construction* (Meyerhoff 2003), (that is, as learned). I suggest that a *strategic* analysis of differences in language use of men and women, though problematic, is relevant in understanding the different ways (and means) they are discursively constructed through discourse *in a context where there is extreme disadvantage* (e.g. discrimination against men or women), for example, in many African settings. This *combination* of paradigms also means that I am not conceptualising gender differences in any way *fixed*.

Sociolinguistic Approaches to Language and Gender

There have been many approaches to the study of language and gender, ranging from variationist studies to social constructionist approaches, associated with poststructuralism. Below, I explore and trace the course of development of these fields, in order to locate my study in a wider epistemological context.

Variationist Studies

Researchers tended to treat gender as 'fixed' and not dynamic, and variation as conditioned by differences such as sex which 'predicted' that males and females would speak in fairly predictable ways. Particularly, Trudgill (1972), Labov (1990) and Milroy (1980) treated sex as another variable in language study such as class and ethnicity. The research paradigm here was one of 'gender differences' (see Romaine 2003). Swann (2002: 227) notes that 'variationist studies have [...] been concerned with statistical tendencies - the tendency of women to speak in one way and men in another.' Researchers have turned away from the quest for universal generalizations about men's or women's speech, and focused instead on the particular conditions shaping the behaviour of men and women in specific locales (Cameron 2003: 189). Here we talk of social constructionist approaches.

Social Constructionist Approach

Qualitative social constructionist approaches in language and gender studies examine not what differences exist, but the 'difference gender makes' in language use (Cameron 1992), for example, in different contexts. They conceive of social identity including gender identity as 'social construct[s] rather than a "given" social category to which people are assigned' (Cameron 2003: 11). Gender is thus treated as the accomplishment and product of social interaction, emerging over time in interaction with others. Holmes and Meyerhoff indicate that the social constructionist approach more comfortably accommodates the analysis of communities, cultures, and linguistic behaviours that do not fit the standard gender dichotomy. The focus is on the way individuals 'do' or 'perform' gender identity (see Butler 1999) in interaction. McElhinny (2003: 27) observes that

47

to suggest that gender is something one continually does is to challenge the idea that gender is something one has. A variety of metaphors have arisen to capture this idea: gender as activity, gender as performance, gender as accomplishment. As a group they can be understood as embodying a practice-based approach to gender.

A focus on such activities suggests that individuals have access to *different* activities, and thus *different* cultures and *different* social identities, including a range of 'different genders' (McElhinny 2003: 28). Social constructionism is compatible with critical discourse analysis, which also sees language as constitutive. Although Holmes and Meyerhoff endorse social constructionism, which is of course anti-essentialist, they however observe that,

> If we truly believed a radical version of the anti-essentialism that has recently become an axiom of the field, then we would put away our pens, our tape-recorders, and our notebooks, and the field of language and gender research would disappear … gender would have become such an idiosyncratic quality that it would be non-existent as a category across individuals (Holmes and Meyerhoff 2003:10).

Such a position entails that although we may not want to study language and gender in *fixed* binary terms. The category 'woman' cannot be ignored completely. Cameron (2006) and Holmes (2007) also acknowledge the position that we cannot completely ignore the question of difference, which would indeed be tantamount to stopping research on gender and language. In this book, I accordingly *do* look at gender differences (in parliamentary talk), as well as looking at how 'women' are conceptualised in parliamentary discourse.

Due to the (gendered) expectations and conventions of different social contexts, people speak differently (including, sometimes, in gendered ways) in different contexts, where they perform actions as well as speak. This recognition gave rise to the Community of Practice (CofP) theory. I examine this below, not because it is the only model social constructionists use, but because I draw on it in this book, where I see the Cameroonian parliament as one such CofP.

Communities of Practice

A group constitutes a 'community of practice' (CofP) if it has a sub-culture that identifies its members as members of a *community* and marks that culture as different from other cultures in the macro community. Being members of a sub-culture with its own range of activities builds a social identity shared only by members of that sub-culture.

Lave and Wenger (1991) and Wenger (1998) were the first to develop the concept of communities of practice, which goes beyond 'speech communities'. Eckert and McConnell-Ginet in (1992, 1999) took this up as they thought it could provide valuable insights into the study of language and gender. The Communities of Practice approach to language and gender studies addresses some criticisms of the previous language and gender models, as it assumes language *based on shared linguistic norms and values* within a community that distinguishes itself from other communities. As such, it is context-specific. Wenger, McDermott, and Snyder (2002:4) define communities of practice as

> groups of people who share a concern, a set of problems, or a passion about a topic, and who deepen their knowledge and expertise in this area by interacting on an ongoing basis. These people don't necessarily work together every day, but they meet because they find value in their interactions.

Interactions normally, of course involve *discourse*. Wenger et al. (2002) explain that 'members of these communities accumulate knowledge; they become informally bound by the value that they find in learning together'. Over time, they develop a body of common knowledge, practices, and approaches. They also develop personal relationships and establish ways of interacting and may even develop a common sense of identity. As a community of practice they 'shar[e] tacit knowledge [which] requires interaction and informal learning processes such as storytelling, conversation, coaching, and apprenticeship of the kind that communities of practice provide' (Wenger et al 2002:9), again, language is important. Wenger (1998:76) identifies three crucial dimensions of a CofP:

1. Mutual engagement, which typically involves regular interaction,

49

2. A joint negotiated enterprise where members of the policy units are engaged in an ongoing process of negotiating and building their contributions toward the larger enterprise, and

3. A shared repertoire of negotiable resources accumulated over time which *includes linguistic resources such as specialized terminology and linguistic routines* (my emphasis).

Following these dimensions, public settings such as a parliament may constitute a community of practice. Members of parliament are constantly in 'mutual engagement' in that they meet at regular and specific intervals for 'a joint enterprise'. During parliamentary sessions, a 'joint negotiated enterprise', interaction of members is marked by a 'shared repertoire' (referred to elsewhere in this book as parliamentary discourse), for example, the members use specialised terminology.

Wenger's notion of the Communities of Practice was intended for education, rather than linguistic study, but linguists, especially feminist linguists have found it valuable in the study of gender identity and gendered discourses. Eckert and McConnell-Ginet (1992, 1999, 2007) adapted Wenger's notion of Communities of Practice to the study of language and gender, redefining the CofP as:

an aggregate of people who come together around mutual engagement in an endeavour. Ways of doing things, ways of talking, beliefs, values, power relations – in short, practices – emerge in the course of this mutual endeavour. As a social construct, a CofP is different from the traditional community, primarily because it is defined simultaneously by its membership and by the practice in which that membership engages. (1992: 464, 2007: 155)

Holmes and Meyerhoff (2003) underline that becoming a member of a CofP involves learning, that is, learning to perform appropriately in the CofP, in large part the acquisition of 'sociolinguistic competence'. The practices or activities of members of a CofP typically involve many different linguistic aspects of behaviour, including global and specific aspects of language, discourse and interaction patterns like use of riddles, proverbs and other special registers. Bucholtz (1999) for example analyses the linguistic practices associated with a previously unexamined social identity, the 'nerd community', and illustrates how members of a local community of female 'nerds' at a US high school negotiate gender and other aspects of their identities through linguistic and other practice. In her study, Bucholtz shows how members of a CofP perform their group identity, yet a peripheral member of the nerd community, while performing the group identity, also subverts it through language. Through language, she challenges the 'hegemonic femininity' of the society.

A CofP approach emphasizes the acts of becoming (say) gendered, of moving from 'peripheral' or 'novice' participation in linguistic action within the community to a central or more experienced enactment, with a 'shared repertoire of linguistic resources' (Wenger 1998). Female parliamentarians in Cameroon can for example be considered *novices* or *peripheral members* in their professional 'community of practice' since they are 'new' to public speaking. A CofP approach thus presupposes that members all *belong* to the CofP, Eckert and McConnell-Ginet emphasizing 'shared ways' (1999: 109). Nevertheless, these shared linguistic practices may still be gendered! A community of people who agree on ways of doing *and* saying things may order their linguistic behaviours in a given community of practice in a specific and perhaps gendered way, in that males and females (tend to) speak, say, in different ways. The approach of CofP explores why this is.

Gender and Discourse in the Public Sphere

Defining the public sphere, Walsh (2001:67) observes that it subsumes both institutions of the state and what some social theorists have referred to as 'civil' sphere domains, for example the church, parliament, and board meetings. The public sphere constitutes not only formal but also informal interaction, for example work-places (which 'host' informal chat) are also public spaces (Holmes 2006). Freed (1996) observes that certain spaces, settings and domains may be gendered as either masculine or feminine. Public and private spaces have traditionally been viewed as gendered with men occupying public spaces and women occupying private ones.

Cameron (2006:4) traces the historical dichotomous distinction between *public* and *private*. She observes that the binary distinction between *public* and *private* usually went alongside that of *male and female* - parliament for example has been considered a public space and therefore a male dominated one. She quotes from an anonymous writer:

> Women have no voyse in the parliament. They make no lawes, they consent to none, they abrogate them. All of them are understood married or to be married and their desires or [are] subject to their husbands... Cameron (2006: 4)

Historically, then, there has been a gendered division of space into *public* and *private*. This division of space has extended to division of jobs where jobs such as Law, politics and commerce have been traditionally 'masculine'. Certainly law, politics and commerce in the past have been dominated by men. Historically in Cameroon there was no parliament, but there were (and still are) traditional councils which functioned as parliaments. These were exclusively male set-ups. The *male/female, public/private* distinctions were thus and still are evident in Cameroonian society (Abdela 2000).

Marra, Schnurr and Holmes (2006: 255) distinguish between *private* and *public*, looking at *private* as home and *public* as workplaces. Although they see workplaces as public, they however acknowledge the fact that there could be private domains within workplaces and more public ones such as formal public meetings. Private informal one-to-one chats in public workplaces may be informal although the discourse in such interactions would not be the same as in formal public interactions in workplaces. Cameron (2006) also distinguishes between the *public setting* and the *public sphere,* where the latter may involve more formal political and legal discourse. The data of this study is conducted in a public sphere - the parliament. Although this public sphere may also have informal talk, it does not constitute part of my data. I focus mainly more on formal public talk in the parliament. Kendall (2006) distinguishes between *ordinary* talk in a public sphere and *institutional* talk, bordering on distinguishing between formal and non-formal workplace language.

Gender and public talk is in fact a relatively new concern in language and gender studies. Early studies had looked mainly at the private domain, for example DeFrancisco's 'Sounds of silence' (1998 [1991]) which looks at the power of silence, that is, how men dominate women in marital relationships through silence. Later work on gender and language investigated the public setting and the public sphere e.g. Walsh (2001), Wodak (2003) and Christie (2003) on language and gender in the parliament; Sunderland (2002) and Baxter (2002) on Classroom discourse; Baxter (2003) and Holmes (2003, 2005, 2006) on workplace discourse.

Holmes (2006: 33) observes that there has also been a tremendous increase in the number of women in actual positions of public responsibility in the past few years (in a New Zealand context) whereas previously there were few models for women in such positions. She examines ways in which gendered norms of workplace talk can however *subtly* contribute to excluding women from positions of power and influence, and suggests that patterns of workplace talk are very important in systematically discriminating against women in leadership roles.

Studies on language, gender and the public sphere have now been brought to the forefront with a recently edited volume by Judith Baxter (2006): *Speaking out: the female voice in public contexts*. Baxter defines *institutional* talk as 'having an orientation to a goal or task, and as entailing an identity associated with an institution' (2006: 180). Institutional talk could therefore be legal, medical or political language for example. Different public spheres are investigated in this volume including Susan Ehrlich's study investigating gendered identities in courtroom discourse, Silvia Shaw looking at political debates, Claire Walsh's of media discourse and Sara Mills' of gender and academic discourse in conference presentations.

In the past, the public sphere was formally dominated and monopolised by males and is still predominantly male especially in domains like the parliament (Walsh 2001, Wodak 2003, 2005), managerial positions (Baxter 2003) and the church hierarchy (Walsh 2001, Jule 2006). This goes a long way back into history as the public sphere has long been associated with masculinity (Cameron 2006). Martin Rojo (2006: 747) observes that within the public sphere, reference to women generally

> 'place[s] emphasis on their physical and emotional qualities
> [...] and when they do evaluate their moral worth, they usually
> refer to traditionally imposed traits (fidelity, resignation, care
> for other) or their traditionally disdained traits (domineering,
> masculine in style, wielding of 'female weapons).

Discourse patterns of male speakers have thus become the established norm in public life. Access to the public sphere by women is relatively difficult in Cameroon, as the relevant 'symbolic capital' (Bourdieu 1991) is not available to most women. Education, knowledge and public discourse was mostly available to men and women and women were generally trained for homecraft[2].

The public sphere can thus be considered a domain of power struggle: public spaces may of course put women off entering them not because they are public but because they are male dominated. The situation is a complex one. Spertus (1991) claims that women's under-representation in the public sphere is not primarily due to direct discrimination but to subconscious behaviour that tends to perpetuate the status quo, which is furthered by subtle use of sexually biased language.

Language and Gender in Parliament

Recently, there has been a lot of interest in parliamentary discourse, including the aspect of gender, especially critical discourse analysis. Walsh (2001), Christie (2003), Shaw (2000) and (Wodak 2003, 2005) have researched issues of gender and language within European parliaments. Parliamentary discourse is however a hitherto un-researched area within African linguistics.

Walsh (2001) focuses on social struggle in the production, maintenance and transformation of gendered identities and relations in the UK parliament. Taking a feminist approach to CDA, Walsh (2001:30) states she 'aims to offer readers the analytical tools to recognise the subtler and hence more insidious discriminatory and exclusionary discourses that abound'. She combines CDA and a range of feminist perspectives on discourse as social practice. In particular, she seeks to examine 'whether women [in parliament] uncritically accept pre-existing discursive practices, [or] whether they shift strategically between these positions, depending upon what is perceived to be appropriate at any given time' (Walsh 2001:1).

Walsh uses Fairclough's model of CDA (Walsh 2001: 39) in her parliamentary study, Walsh observes that previously, in the UK parliament, being seen but rarely heard was the norm for women (p. 68) and that although men and women belong to the same CofP, they do so on unequal terms, with men being more powerful participants. Linguistic practices differ as the culture of bullying persists emphasised by the physical layout of the parliament which encourages (face-to-face) confrontation (p. 69). She also noted that sexism persists in the House of Commons albeit in covert forms as there is parliamentary intolerance of overt sexism. Quoting Margaret Beckett, a female British parliamentarian, Walsh (2001) indicates that women's personal identities are brought into professional life (p. 78) and their personal accomplishments are minimised (see section on titulation). Women are rarely given agency and are usually discursively constructed (in the media) as interlopers. She looks in particular at how women's presence in male dominated public spheres affects the construction of gender roles and identities and men's exaggerated performance of 'macho masculinity' (Walsh 2001:40). I examine such 'performances' in the Cameroonian parliament in the later chapters.

In another study on gender and discourse in the parliament, Shaw (2000) looks at language and 'floor apportionment' in political debates in the British House of Commons using Ethnography of Speaking and Conversational Analysis. The study gives an insight into gender relations in the House of Commons. Shaw looks at the extent to which Members of Parliament control the resources of the debate floor as evidenced by linguistic exchanges, these contributing to the extent to which an MP has power in this sense. She suggests that gender may be a more salient variable than occupational status in contributing to an individual's control of the floor. This, she claims, may be attributed to the fact that the parliament has traditionally been a male domain and the norms of participation and discourse styles are organised to define, demonstrate and enforce the legitimacy and authority of linguistic strategies used by men - while denying power to others (Shaw 2000: 402, see also Gal 1991: 188). Shaw looks at 'illegal turns' and how they may be used as a strategy to disempower social actors during parliamentary debates. This is particularly effective when these 'illegal turns' or interruptions are meant to discourage, insult, or criticise female MPs with regard to their linguistic style or content of their contributions if they find these do not meet their expected feminine linguistic norms.

Christie (2003) similarly explores gender in the UK parliamentary discourse using a 'Communities of Practice' perspective. She argues that gender identity within the practice of parliamentary debate is best seen as an effect of the way in which male and female MPs negotiate the institutional constraints on linguistic behaviour they are subject to in the performance of their role. She argues that gender identities in the parliament may be realised through apologies and transgressions.

In her study of elite women, Wodak (2003) examines multiple identities in the European Union parliament. She starts by acknowledging patriarchy and inequality in professional and public life and observes that the political world is dominated by men, especially white men. In the European Union, in spite of gender mainstreaming, the trends have not changed much. Unequal treatment of men and women in the public context is manifest in language use.

Wodak in this study examines how women establish themselves in such complex settings such as the parliament, and the strategies they employ to present and promote themselves and guarantee that they are taken seriously. She uses the discourse-historical approach to CDA, to analyse these multiple identities and subject positions and the different discursive strategies employed. She observes that female EU MPs sometimes tend to draw more on their national identities than their gender identities and at other times on their party affiliations more than their gender identity. They use different referential strategies sometimes highlighting their gender status and at other times their national identities (see Wodak 2003: 689).

Wodak's study is very relevant to my study in answering Research Question B - *'What gendered discourses are evident in the Cameroonian parliament and how are they legitimated?'* I examine how female Cameroonian MPs construct themselves and legitimate 'progressive' gendered discourse within this parliament and how they position themselves and are positioned by different discourses circulating within this setting. And like Wodak, I also use a discourse-historical approach in the analysis of argumentation and legitimating strategies within parliamentary Discussions and Questions-and-Answers.

Still, other researchers have examined strategies of political empowerment and access to public and institutional discourse with a focus on gender (see e.g. Wagner and Wodak 2006). Geisler (2000) examines discourses of women's struggle in new South African Parliament. She examines the role of women's movements in the inclusion of women in the parliament and how these women negotiated their new roles as decision makers and struggle to integrate in this new community of practice and take up different linguistic norms. The legitimation of women's place in the parliament went across party lines and Geisler observes that even though the ANC entered parliament with an understanding of changing it,

> men had "no understanding of parliament as a gender-friendly institution". One of the problems was that men tended to draw an artificial line between public and private spheres, because they had wives who looked after the domestic side of life (2000: 617).

We observe here that women had to legitimate multiple gender identities in the South African parliament as mothers and parliamentarians, and through this, men sometimes felt disempowered within the discourse of 'parliament as a gender-friendly institution'.

While women in the South African parliament may have been empowered by such discourses as 'parliament as a gender-friendly institution', Cameroonian MPs potentially face a counter discourse to this. Abdela (2000) notes that, in Cameroon, there is a perception amongst men and some women that command posts (governors, secretary-generals, senior divisional officers etc.) can only be handled by males, which some leaders justify as a consequence of the men receiving appropriate training for these, and also arguing that the community does not have enough educated women to handle these positions.

Gender and Silence in Public discourse

As shown above, public speech generally, and political debates in particular are traditionally seen as a 'masculine' genre; there are thus likely to be differences in the way male and the female speakers take part in public speech genres[3]. One of the forms in which such masculine power is realised in language use is to silence the dominated group. On a socio-political level, silencing of women as a group has been very successful. Jaworski (1992) observes that the silencing of a group may take very subtle but equally very effective forms: brainwashing, indoctrination, and negative stereotyping, which all lead to the creation of a group's self image as powerless, submissive, inferior and with nothing relevant to offer. Rich (1978:18) also indicates that silencing of women can take the form of namelessness, denial, secrets, taboo subjects, erasure, false-naming, non-naming, encoding, omission, veiling, fragmentation, and lying.

Cameron (1990, 2006) addresses the themes of silence and exclusion in relation to male dominance and female culture. Women's silence does not however mean they are silent everywhere, or that they lack that ability to use language. Women's traditional linguistic activities, which include gossip, diaries, and letters, are all either private or not for public consumption. Silence, Cameron says, is an absence of female voices from the *high culture* e.g. religious ceremonies, legal discourse, science, poetry, and political rhetoric (see Cameron 2006). Women are explicitly prevented from speaking either by social taboos and restrictions, or tyrannies of custom and practice. The causes of silence, Cameron notes, vary from illiteracy, economic dependence, practical and psychological barriers. Even when it seems that women could speak if they chose to, the conditions imposed on their lives by the society may make this a difficult or dangerous choice. For example, silence can mean censoring oneself for fear of being ridiculed, attacked or even ignored.

As regards women's silence in Africa, Mukama (1994) exposes the fact that women do not participate in or are part of decision-making positions in East Africa and that even when they are members of the parliament, they remain mute. Other evidence of women's silence in East Africa is that women do not express themselves in writing: men dominate the literary scene. Women's invisibility and silence is enforced with them underrating themselves with expressions such as 'I'm only just a woman', a phrase which stems from their cultural background. Mukama identifies different methods used in silencing women: proverbs to discourage women from positions of responsibility (Mukama (1994: 554), threats (of husbands and fathers) of disinheriting their children if they talk a lot, and of not appointing them to higher administrative positions if they are professional women. Mukama claims that silence, inertia and diffidence on the part of the women are a *universal* [?] phenomenon imposed on them in different ways or forms. Mukama (1994:5 52) also posits that 'culture' is what men revert to when they want to win an argument and keep their privileged positions. She claims that governments in East Africa regard women who want to press their case as subversive, influenced by outsiders, and claims that they want to destroy the culture. In the Cameroonian parliament, men also revert to 'culture' to legitimate discriminatory practices against women.

Mukama's study presents a 'macro' picture of strategies used in silencing women. It could be criticised by post-structuralists on the score that it *generalises* the silencing of women in East Africa and essentialises them as silenced and dominated and does not look for pockets of power and verbal expression. However, in my study, I also use a 'gender difference' approach and find them relevant when disadvantage is *extreme*.

Conclusion

This chapter has explored the concept of CDA as the main theoretical and analytical framework for this book. I have also explored literature on approaches to language and gender; gender and parliamentary discourse; gender and silence; and gender and power. Although I have broken these down into different sub-topics, they are all intricately linked to each other, and to power. I therefore hope to show how marginal groups appropriate powerful positions by challenging the status quo and demystifying dominant gender ideologies (Lazar 2005).

Chapter Three

Gender Differences in Parliamentary Talk

Women are nine times more talkative than men
(Hebrew Proverb) (Schipper 2003)

Introduction

While there is anthropological and historical evidence that women do participate in important speech events and make good orators, the literature also suggests a more common pattern, that is, men dominate highly valued forms of public speech (see Kaplan 1998 [1986], Kennedy 1998; Cameron 1998, 2006). The absence of women's voices from 'high culture' may be a result of women's fear of being ridiculed, attacked or ignored (Kaplan 1998: 62 [1986]). Cameron observes that speech and silence are 'powerful metaphors in feminist discourse used to figure all the ways in which women are denied the right to or opportunity to express themselves freely'. She however also argues that, although women are frequently thus denied, 'they are not always and everywhere *literally* silent, nor lack the capacity to use language' (1998: 3).

Current research on gender and language has focused on women's linguistic practices in public contexts (Baxter's 2006 edited volume), and has also criticised older 'gender differences' research, claiming this highlights (especially) social essentialism (e.g. Holmes and Meyerhoff 2003), and does not allow for change, intra-group diversity or for different meanings of the same linguistic behaviour by men and women. These critics also claim that such research looks at the *how* (of talk) rather than the *what* (discourse) (see also McElhinny 2003: 24). Lazar (2005: 9) however observes that for more recent language and gender study, in particular feminist CDA, there has been a

> recognition of *difference* and *diversity* among 'women' ('men'), which has called for undertaking historically and culturally contingent analysis of gender and sexism; and the pervasiveness of the *subtle*, discursive working of modern power in many modern societies (my italics).

While I agree that pervasive and insidious in 'modern'[1] societies is the operation of 'subtle' sexism (Walsh 2001, Wodak 2003, Lazar 2005: 9) and what may seem trivial forms of power that are substantially *discursive* in nature, sexism and gender differential practices in Cameroon are however not subtle but very obvious and materially damaging. Although the Cameroonian parliament could be claimed to be a modern parliament, it is set against a cultural and historical background that is far from 'modern', where sexism and ideologies of *essential gender differences* are deeply entrenched in its traditional beliefs and practices and thus cannot be characterised as 'subtle'.

This chapter looks at whether differently gendered traditional practices such as expectations of women's silence (absolute or relative) and men's public verbosity within the traditional systems are reflected in the modern political domain through the amount and type of talk in parliament. It thus addresses the questions '*What gendered differences in speech patterns are evident in the Cameroonian parliament?'How are men and women MPs constructed in the Parliament through titulation? Are men more verbose than women in the Cameroonian parliament? Do women and men talk about different topics in the Cameroonian parliament?*

I analyse these gender differences quantitatively not in terms of 'how it is said' - hedges and interruptions - but 'what is said' in terms of *topics* and *titulation* (address forms) and 'how much is said,' that is, silence and *verbosity* through an analysis of volume of talk. A study of such differences in the parliament tells us about gendered value systems, that is, traditional vs. modern, and the contribution of these and the gendered talk itself to an understanding of gendered discourses within the parliament and ways they legitimate gender inequality. These differences in verbal participation in Cameroonian parliamentary sessions, may dialectically affect those gendered value systems.

Rationale for a Gender Differences Approach

Here, I look at gender differences in parliamentary text and talk and how power is manifested in this domain through the presence or absence of talk by men and women, and through an analysis of what is said. Although it cannot be claimed that there is essentialism or stagnation in gender relations in the Cameroonian community, the notions of 'post-equality' (Lazar 2005: 20) and 'post-patriarchy' (Walsh 2001) are not (yet) politically relevant within the Cameroonian context. The concept of post-equality cannot be claimed since male hegemony and patriarchy are still entrenched.

Walsh (2001:17) argues against 'patriarchy' claiming it implies a monolithic and totalising system of oppression in which all men dominate all women. This would indeed be a reductive view as even in the most 'patriarchal' societies, not all men dominate all women. This does not deny the fact that there are 'patriarchal' societies with gross and overt gender discriminations. Men's access to, and control over resources and rewards within the private and public sphere (Cameron 2006) derive their legitimacy from the patriarchal ideology of male dominance. Patriarchy varies in time and space, it changes over time, and varies according to class, race, ethnic, religious and global-imperial relationships and structures. Thus patriarchy in the West cannot be conceived to operate in the same way as patriarchy in African societies. The laws of Cameroon for example still recognise male supremacy and authority and are explicit about the man being the head of the family (see Fonchingong 2005). While western feminist researchers examine linguistic strategies employed in 'subtle-sexism' (Wodak 2005, 2003; Lazar 2005; Walsh 2001), African activists and researchers still have to deal with overt, crude sexism, which is often legitimated by the very laws of their countries, and seek for strategies to subvert patriarchy (e.g. female genital mutilation has not been legislated against in Cameroon and many other African countries, and education of the girl child is still very low in many regions).

With the background of African feminism (See Sunderland 2009), this book seeks to expose the gender gap through discourse to show how these dominant patriarchal discourses are legitimated even in parliament by men and even women, and how they are also challenged and resisted. While in the West there may only be 'residual aspects of paternalism' (Walsh 2001:17) and the West can be claimed to be a post-patriarchal society, in Cameroon, considering the overt discrimination women face and their 'pre-equality' status, what can be called a 'Non-equality discourse' is articulated and made relevant in the data itself. This however, as suggested above, is not to say that women do not contest and challenge these discriminatory and patriarchal practices.

International conventions such as 'Convention of the Elimination of all Forms of Discrimination against Women' (1979 ratified in 1994) and the 'Equal Opportunities Act' are dutifully signed by governments including the Cameroonian government, but have minimal effects on gendered practices within the society. Traditional practices and gendered division of labour are entrenched, based on the traditional beliefs of gender differentiation (as beneficial).

Against such a background, although women's emancipation and gender equality are argued for by some, lack of access to *basic* issues such as guaranteed civil, (women's) rights and equal access to decision-making positions have also led to the articulation of alternative (new) discourses. A study of the basic gender differences in speech styles (at least as exemplified in parliament) is necessary as they constitute traces of these (as well as more traditional) discourses.

As observed (see Chapter 2), there has been a shift in gender and language studies from difference and dominance models to models of construction and performance (Butler 1999; Holmes and Meyerhoff 2003). However, this shift does not exclude the fact that overt gender disadvantage remains characteristic of Africa, and that even overt, crude (not subtle) discrimination is neglected. Gender *difference* (material and discoursal) should thus not be ignored. While in the West, extensive literature on differences in men and women's language (second wave feminism) in the 1970s and 80s gave way to third wave feminism (see Mills 2002) and even 'post feminism' (Stone 2004, Lazar 2005), it should be recognised that the ideological changes these notions conceptualise are not universal and vary in time and space, inter alia relating to culture, race and religion. The African perspective in some ways is unique. In Cameroon, for example, 'naturalised androcentric' assumptions (Lazar 2005) are overt and discrimination between the sexes is seen (by many) not as problematic but as a legitimate part of the culture. Gender differentiated roles are seen as the norm (and even celebrated) (see Kitetu and Sunderland 2000), thus the need to research difference where there is clear gender *disadvantage* — both material differences and differences in discourse. Analysis of difference in this chapter is therefore *not* to *reflect* 'inherent' gender identity or gendered language, but gender relations of *power* and related gendered constructions of women (and men) in discourse within the Cameroonian parliament.

Quantitative Analysis of Gender Differences

Quantitative analysis shows how unequal social arrangements are sustained through language use. Using quantitative analysis as a starting point within this geographical context, differences in talk may construct and reflect the impact of gendered constructions (within parliament and beyond). This may also go some way to show that, contrary to the situation elsewhere (see Lazar 2005), gender ideology and asymmetrical power relations in discourse do not always assume 'subtle forms'. Assumptions and linguistic practices are implicated in loosely 'patriarchal' ideologies and forms of oppression could be constructed through the amount of talk and topics of male and female speakers. We do not therefore seek to celebrate or negate gender difference but rather to *expose* it with a view to seeking ways to tackle issues (gender discrimination and exclusion) and achieve concrete political goals.

Quantitative analysis therefore seeks to investigate whether the parliament can be seen as an extension of traditional male domains of power and responsibility. The small number of women participating in decision making in Cameroon tends to mean they are rarely 'core' members of key prestigious Communities of Practice (CofP) (Wenger 1998; Eckert and McConnell-Ginet 1999), in particular, political circles like the government and parliament. I wanted to find out whether men in the CofP of the Cameroonian parliament 'legitimate' the gender division of verbal space by making it difficult (intentionally or unintentionally) for women to participate fully in these domains of power (see Walsh 2001, Cameron 2006), thus reinforcing and perpetuating exclusionary politics through language use. One 'indicator' of such exclusion and influence in public (as well as private spheres) is *speech patterns* in terms of what and how much is said (see Holmes 1995, 2003; Talbot 1998).

In this chapter, from a 'strategic essentialist' standpoint (see Holmes 2006; Stone 2004; McElhinny 1996; Spivak 1996), gender differences are analysed in language use in the parliament. Within such a position, gender differences are generalisable to all Cameroonian women. Actual essentialism is not suggested but rather we seek to *highlight* differences in talk and how women and men are constructed through discourse (e.g. titulation) in the parliament. Such differences are a consequence of many factors including access to knowledge, power, and even physical space, and male dominance and oppression of women legitimated through political, social, economic, legal, cultural, religious and military institutions.

Data

The data for this chapter (as well as for this book) was collected during the June and November 2005 Parliamentary sessions (from 7 plenary sessions of June 2005 and 3 plenary sessions of November 2005. These sessions include 1 Discussion and 9 Question–and–Answer 'sub-sessions'. Included in the Discussion genre is the 'tabling' of bills. The tabling of bills itself is not included in the analysis as the process is generally a long monologue often lasting several hours. However, 'discussions' that ensue *from* the tabling of these bills are analysed, noting talking time by each MP.

In the 10 sessions recorded and analysed in this chapter[2], women spoke in only two (MPs or as Ministers): 3 women in a Discussion during the June 2005 session and 1 in a Q & A session during the November 2005 session. The analysis is in two layers: general female participation (in the 10 sessions recorded) and female participation in the two sessions in which women spoke. As such, a general result of women's participation in recorded parliamentary sessions and more narrowly, women's participation in *specific* parliamentary sessions. The table below presents the parliamentary session dates[3] and genres in which women participated, and also the time taken.

Table 3. 1   Plenary Sessions (analysed) with Female Participation

Session Date	Genre	Number of female MPs	Total time in Minutes
12th July 2005	Discussion	3 MPs	9 (2, 3, and 4 minutes respectively)
25th November 2005	Q and A	1 MP	3

In the two sessions analysed, more women participated during the discussion genre than during the Q & A genre. Table 3:1 shows all four women took less than their allocated time of 15 minutes.

Gender Differences and Party Politics: Political Parties

In this section, I re-address the role of different political parties to examine whether some are more progressive in gender issues than others.

As observed in Chapter 1, there are five political parties in the parliament: The longest ruling party - Cameroon People's Democratic Movement (CPDM), had 149 seats in the 2005 parliamentary session; the main opposition party - the Social Democratic Front (SDF), 23 seats; Union Democratic du Cameroun (UDC), 5 seats; Union du Peuple Camerounaise (UPC), 3 seats, and Union Nationale de Démocratie et du Progrès (UNDP) with 1 seat. Only *one* of the five parties had female MPs, that is, the ruling party, CPDM. It had a total of 20 women, that is, 13% of CPDM MPs, and 11.11% of the National Assembly. The party manifestos of both the ruling CPDM party *and* the main opposition party, the SDF, however indicate the importance of the inclusion of women in decision-making.

The CPDM has a unit to foster women's affairs, the 'Women's Cameroon People's Democratic Party' (WCPDM) (in French 'Organisation des Femmes du Rassemblement Democratique du Peuple Camerounais' - OFRDPC). This 'wing' is charged with promoting the social and the cultural affairs of the party (see article 47 and 48 of the CPDM constitution). Female participation in this party is in practice open mostly to 'elite' women (see Nyamnjoh and Rowlands 1998.

The SDF does not have a women's wing like the ruling party, the CPDM, although within the SDF party, women generally massively participate in political rallies and tend to be more militant than men in opposing the government through strike actions (organised by men). The manifesto and the constitution of the SDF party carefully chooses the terminology *persons* and *chairpersons* instead of men and chairmen, but choose not to highlight gender. In some contexts, the absence of a women's wing or mention of women could be indicative of gender equality having been achieved within the party, but not in this case here. The party however does openly advocate female inclusion in its activities (in advisory positions but not key leadership positions), and stipulates at least a one-in-three representation (although there are in practice no female

MPs). Considering the complete absence of women MPs, it may be claimed that this party (like the other opposition parties) does not prioritise gender parity in its actual political mission.

This minimal female representation within the parties in parliament can be argued to be indicative of gender relations within the wider society. The quantitative analysis seeks to substantiate this fact and show that although the ruling party, the CPDM, does encourage and promote women to participate in political (parliamentary) activities, and has 20 women MPs, their actual verbal participation is still very minimal even compared to their representation within the party and the parliament as a whole (see further below).

Titulation

Titulation here refers to how both male and female parliamentarians are addressed (titulated or not titulated) by both the Speaker of the House of Assembly and the other members present at the House of Assembly (ministers and parliamentarians). Specifically, it examines how the use of *titles* in the parliament. Titulation, as indicated by van Leeuwen (1996: 53), is an aspect of nomination, where nomination relates to how individuals are identified and named through their unique identities. Members of Parliament may be titulated through the honorific title – 'Honourable' or 'Honorable' (French) depending on the language. Other possible address forms are 'Honorable' or alternatively 'Monsieur/Madame (le/la Député(e))', in French while ministers are addressed as either 'Monsieur/Madame le/la Ministre –Mr Minister, 'Madam Minister' or 'Your Excellency'. This can be seen as identity construction through *ascription* (of someone by someone else).

Female parliamentarians are always addressed as 'Madame', omitting their political title of 'Honourable', while a majority of the male parliamentarians are addressed using titles 'Honourable/ Honorable'. Table 3. 2 shows examples of how male and female MPs are addressed by the Speaker of the House of Assembly, other MPs and ministers.

In being addressed as 'Madame', (only) female MPs (not males) are thus ascribed a personal (social) identity at the expense of their available professional and political identities.

As the Speaker of the House of Assembly, the President of the National Assembly calls on the parliamentarians to talk as Table 3. 2 illustrates the range of title use for MPs by him and other MPs and ministers.

The use of 'Monsieur' or 'Madame' to address the ministers is fairly consistent as there is little choice in the address form. In contrast, the Speaker of the House chooses to address male *MPs* as 'Monsieur X (Surname)' e.g. Monsieur Ndinda Ndinda, Monsieur Yoyo, interchangeably with 'Honorable X (surname)' e.g. Honorable Adamu Ndam Njoya, Monsieur Honorable Awoudou, Député Ndinda Ndinda or even 'Monsieur le Député' or 'Messieurs les Députés' or Honorable Député. There is no reason why the Speaker of the House should not similarly address women as 'Honorable' or 'Madame la Députée'. The Speaker seems to be consciously or unconsciously resorting to social relations *outside* the House of Assembly when addressing these women, constructing their identities more in social terms as wives rather than as MPs. The systematic use of 'Madame' in addressing these women functions to downgrade their positions as parliamentarians, which may in a small way contribute to their relative silence and few contributions to parliamentary debates. Such titulation may also serve as a trace of and basis for the articulation of 'conservative' discourses.

Table 3. 2   Titles used to Address MPs

Female MP Titles	Male MP Titles
	No Prefix
(Self-titulated) Honorable[4]	Honorable _
	Honorable X
	Député X
	Honorable Député X
	Monsieur le Député X
	Monsieur Honorable X
	Monsieur et Honorable X
Madame X	Monsieur X

Table 3. 3   Titulation

Female MPs and Ministers Addressed	By	Titulation (Appendix 4)	Male MPs Addressed	By	Titulation
Honorable Ndoh Evina	Speaker	La Parole est à **Madame** Ndoh	Honorable Fouda Fouda Frederick	Speaker of the House	No prefix
Honorable Mebanda Rose	Speaker / Herself	**Madame** Mebanda, vous avez la parole / Honorable	Honourable Ndinda Ndinda	Speaker of the House	• Depute Ndinda Ndinda • Honorable Depute
Honorable Njini Ekwa	Speaker	**Madame** Njini, vous avez la parole		Minister of Youth and Sports	• Honorable Ndinda
Minister of Women's Affairs	Speaker	la parole à **madame** la ministre	Honorable Awoudou	Speaker of the House	• Honorable Awoudou • Monsieur Awoudou • Monsieur Honorable …
Secretary of State, Commerce	Honorable Ndi	Madame Le[5] Ministre	Ndongo Ndjemba	Honorable Njini	• Honorable Ndjemba
Honourable Emilia Monjowa	Speaker	Madame Monjowa vous avez la parole		Speaker of the House	Honorable Ndjemba
			Honourable Etame	Speaker of the House	• Monsieur le Député • Honorable Etame
				Minister of Sports	• HonorableEtame
				Minister of Women's Affairs	• Honorable Etame
			Honorable Ndam Njoya	Speaker of the House / Prime Minister	• Honorable Adamu Ndam • Monsieur et l'Honorable Adamu • L'Honorable Député

The range of titles especially by the Speaker, for men, shows multiple identity construction of these men and their 'recognised' multiple identities (*including* the professional). For example, nominating a male MP as 'Honorable' or 'Monsieur le Député' may point to his identity as a Member of Parliament while addressing an MP without a title as 'Fouda Fouda' may suggest familiarity and peer membership. In contrast, the Speaker sometimes emphasises their titles' as in 'Monsieur et l'Honorable', or 'Honorable Député', giving the MPs 'double titles'.

Gendered Differences in Language Use
Verbosity: Gender Differences in Talking Time in the Parliament

An analysis of 'talking time' was carried out to examine verbosity in parliamentary session(s) in both Q & A sessions and Discussion sessions.

Below, the percentage of women's and men's verbal participation in relation to the number of women in the national assembly in both parliamentary genres is analysed. The time used by the Speaker of the House is not included as he is the (male) moderator. His status in the parliament is unique. If included, it would only widen the gender gap. Talking time is counted to the nearest minute. Only actual 'talking time' is measured. Gaps such as time used to move to the rostrum are also not included.

Differences in Talking Time June 2005 Session

The data analysed here consists of plenary sessions[6] from the June 2005 session from both Question-and-Answer and Discussion genres. Female parliamentarians did not ask (nor answer) any questions at all during these sessions and therefore talking time during these Q and A sessions is not analysed. Women did however talk during the Discussion session. Total talking time during this session[7] was 191 minutes. MPs used only 49 minutes[8]. Of these 49 minutes, female MPs used only 9. Only three female MPs spoke, once each, taking 2, 3, and 4 minutes respectively (as shown above). Thus in analysing talking time in the June session, I single out this Discussion session since both male and female MPs participated.

71

Table 3. 4 Talking Time by Male and Female MPs in the June 2005 Plenary Sessions

Speaker	Number of Speaking Turns	Sex	Q and A Time in Mins. (6 sessions)	Discussion Time in Mins. (1 session)	Total talking time in minutes
Honourable Etame	2	M	7		
Honourable Ndi	1	M	8		
Honourable Sani	1	M	2		
Hon Ndong Ndjemba	2	M	2	10	
Honourable Yoyo	2	M	6		
Honourable Owona	1	M	6		
Honorable Ndinda Ndinda	2	M	13	7	
Honourable Fosso	1	M	15		
Ndam Njoya	1	M	6		
Awoudou Mbaya	1	M	4		
Honourable Sundjock Sundjock	1	M	21		
Honorable K. Sama	1	M	11		
Honourable Fouda Fouda	1	M	5		
Honourable Sonkeng	1	M	15		
Honourable Ayafor	1	M		10	166
Honourable Ndebi Yembe	1	M		6	
Honourable Ndinda Ndinda	1	M		7	
Hon Angeline Ndoh	1	F		2	
Honourable Njini Ekwa	1	F		3	
Honourable Mebanda	1	F		4	9
Total Men			126	40	
Total Women				9	
General Talking Time					175

Table 3. 4 shows talking time recorded and analysed in the June Discussion session, and is indicative of verbal trends in the parliament. From the **Table 3. 5** we observe that women did not ask questions during Q and A sessions in the June 2005 Parliamentary sessions.

Table 3. 5   Summary of Talk in the Parliament, June 2005

Parliamentarians	Question-and-Answer in minutes	Discussion in minutes	Total Talking time in minutes
Male	126	40	166
Female	-	9	9
All	126	49	175

Presented graphically by gender, genre and percentage of talking time, Figure 3. 1 shows that women speak for 0% of the time during 6 Q and A sessions. This is quite shocking given that women still make up 11 % of MPs. Given this, their 18% of talking time during the Discussion session is relatively encouraging. However, given that we are looking at only three women, little can be generalised.

Figure 3. 1   Talking Time by MPs in the June 2005 Session

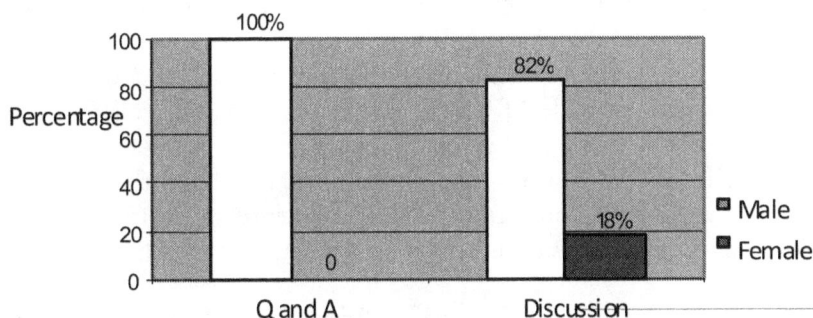

When we consider the *total* talking time during the June session (see Figure 3. 2), which includes 6 sessions in which *no* female MP spoke, the 18% female verbal participation during the entire June sessions then is reduced to 5%, as women spoke only for 9 of the total 175 minutes talking time by MPs.

73

Figure 3. 2   Percentage of Total Talking Time in June 2005 (male and female MPs)

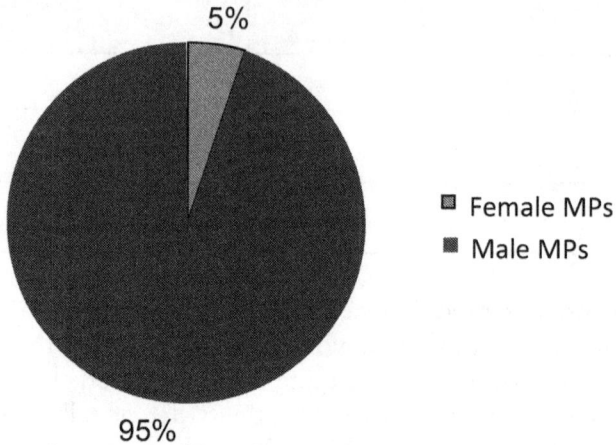

One reason why men thus disproportionately dominated the total verbal space (over the seven plenary sessions) is that four men and no women had more than one speaking turn during this June session (in both genres). This table also shows the number of minutes each MP used. During the Discussion session where women participated, the total *average* talking time (male and female MPs) was 6 minutes. However, that of male MPs ranged from 6-10 minutes and that of female MPs only ranged from 2 to 4 minutes. So even the *most* verbose female MP during this session talked for less than the *least* verbose male MP. These female MPs therefore speak for only half of the average talking time by parliamentarians in the June session.

Table 3. 6   General Average talking time during the June Discussion session

Average talking time by male MPs	Average talking time by female MPs	General Average talking time of MPs
8	3	6

The data above is very small and therefore cannot be *statistically significant*, but as Cameron (2001: 138) observes, such results are *indicative* here of the trends in the parliament. One may question why more women talk in 'spontaneous' than organised pre-planned questions. Has this to do with the selection procedure by the speaker? The way they 'bid' for question turns? These are questions that should be addressed in further research.

Differences in Talking Time (November 2005 Session)

The second phase of the main data collection process took place in November 2005. This was the session immediately following the June session and consisted of the same group of parliamentarians. The proportion of women MPs in parliament remained the same (11%). Of the three plenary sessions my assistant was able to record, one was Prime Ministerial presentation of the budget, the two others were Question-and-Answer sessions[9] in which women did not talk. No Discussion session was recorded during this phase, and for this reason, data from different genres, recorded at different times could not be analysed together (recall that in the June Q & A session, no women talked). Carrying out a quantitative analysis of the 2 November Q & A sessions served to find out if the gender trends in verbal participation were similar to those of June (although in June women spoke rather in Discussion sessions). This in itself would prove little but large differences would highlight atypicality.

Figure 3. 3   Total Talking Time MPs November 2005 Session

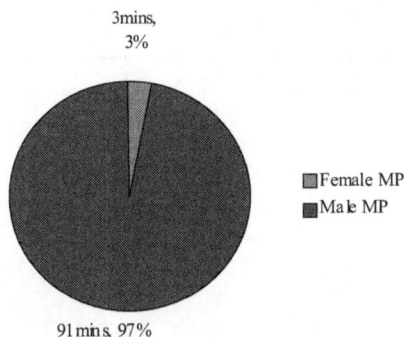

3mins,
3%

☐ Female MP
■ Male MP

91 mins, 97%

75

Of the three plenary sessions recorded during the November Parliamentary session, men *and* women spoke only in one (the November 25th Question-and Answer session). During this session, a total of 8 MPs spoke, taking a total of 42 minutes. Of these 8 MPs, only one was a female, who talked for 3 minutes.

The one woman who spoke during this November 25th session represented 13% of all the MPs who spoke. However, the amount of time she took up (3 minutes out of 42) constitutes only 7% of the verbal space (the average verbal space per MP during this particular session was 13% (Figure 3. 4). Of the 42 minutes used by MPs during this session, an MP who spoke would on average have taken 5 minutes (more than the female MP's 3 minutes).

Table 3. 7   MPs' Talking Time, 25th November 2005
Q & A Session

Male MPs	Female MP	Time Taken in Minutes
Honourable[10] Tasi Ntang		6
Honourable Tasi Tasi Ntang[11]		10
Hon Limi		2
Honourable Jua		8
Honorable Ndi Francois		3
	Honourable Monjowa Lifaka	3
Honorable Sende Pierre		2
Honourable Ndinda Ndinda		8
Total		**42**

Figure 3. 4   Total Talking Time by MPs for November 25th Q & A session

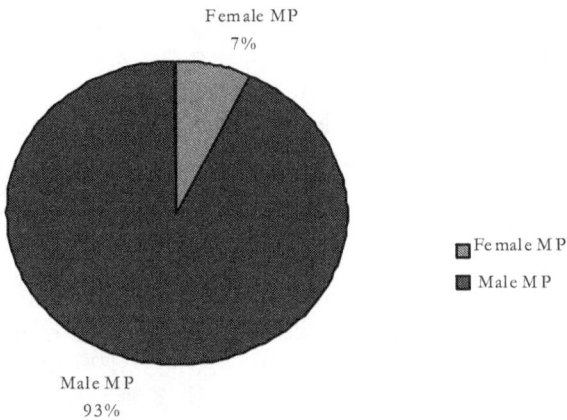

The male range was 2 – 10 minutes, so partly because of the relative verbosity of 3 male MPs (6, 8, and 10 minutes); the *male* average was 6 minutes, indicating they took up more time than the general average of the session. The only female MP who spoke took up only 3 minutes; half of the average time taken by male MPs (see **Figure 3. 5**).

Figure 3. 5   Average MP Talking Time Nov 25th Session in Minutes

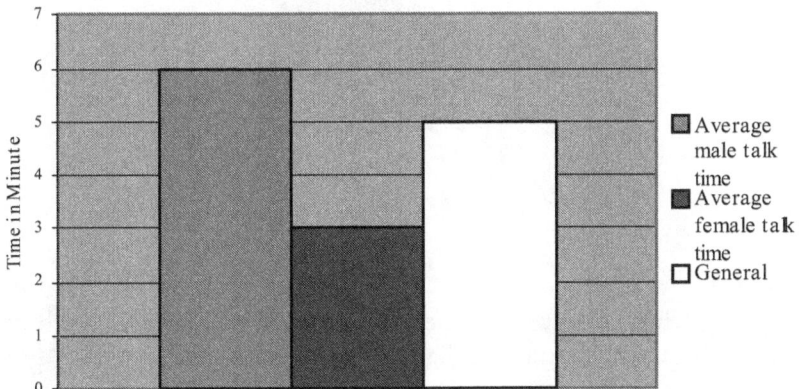

77

If we take these figures above to be indicative of the talk patterns of men and women MPs more widely, we may conclude that individual men talk for longer than women in this public, institutional setting.

Figure 3. 6 shows that male ministers spoke for 102 minutes consisting (about 50% of the talking time), a female minister spoke for 11 minutes (5%), 7 male MPs spoke for 91 minutes (44%), and a female MP for 3 minutes (1%). If we look at the total verbal representation of women in the Cameroonian parliament during the November session, this is even worse than to that of the June session. One further observation is that, as with the June session, although men tend to talk for most of the time, only a few (men) actually talk. 15 male MPs spoke (9% of the total number of male MPs), while 5% of women spoke (1 female MP out of 20).

Figure 3. 6   Percentage of Talking Time by MPs and Ministers in the November 2005 Session

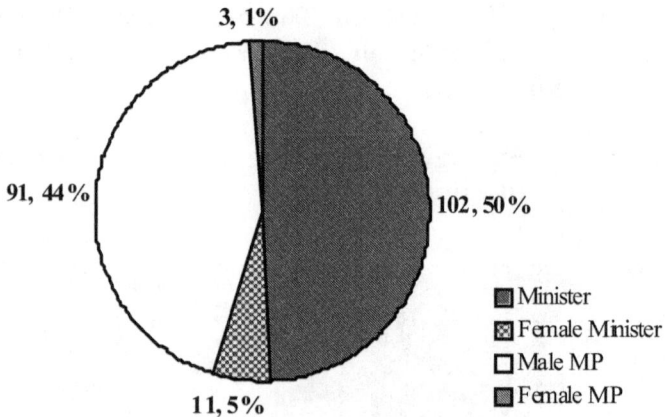

This is however yet another example of *relative* male verbosity within the Cameroonian parliament.

Summary of Talking Time in the Parliament (June and November Sessions)

The analysis in the previous sections point to the general claim that not only do men occupy more verbal space than women, they also participate numerically more than women in parliamentary talk. Below, I present some key findings relating to gendered participation of male and female MPs during the two sessions.

- General average female MPs verbal participation of all parliamentary talk 4%
- General average male MPs verbal participation of all parliamentary talk 94%
- General average females MPs talking time of all parliamentary talk 3 minutes
- General average male MP talking time of all parliamentary talk 7 minutes
- General average talking time by all MPs in Parliament (male and female in both sessions) 6.5 minutes.

Table 3. 8   Key Findings

Verbal participation	Female MPs	Male MPs	All MPs
General average percentage verbal space occupied in the parliament	4%	96%	
Total talk time female June	5%		
Total talk time female November	3%		
Average talk time June	3 mins	8 mins	
Average talk time Nov	3 mins	6 mins	
General average talk time June			8 mins
General average talking time Nov			5 mins
Average Talking time in Minutes	**3 mins**	**7 mins**	**6.5 mins**

It is thus evident that male MPs generally dominate the verbal parliamentary space, in terms of:

a the proportion of men who speak relative to the proportion of women

b how much talking time they use

c how many contributions they make

These results thus lead us to answer the question 'Are men more verbose than women in the Cameroonian parliament?' The answer is 'Yes, in several ways!' In the next session, I look at possible explanations for this.

Understanding Masculine Verbosity

The above quantitative analysis suggests that it is associated with *masculinity*. Folk-linguistic beliefs hold that women generally talk more than men (see Cameron 1992). This may however only be true when women are alone *together*, often in private contexts and not the public sphere (Cameron 1992, 2006) or mixed sex domestic settings (see Fishman 1983). James and Drakich (1993), in a critical review of gender and language research, observe that men generally speak more than women in most circumstances and especially in public institutional settings (see Holmes and Stubbe 2003, 2005, and also Lazar 2005, Baxter 2003). Holmes and Stubbe (2003:575) argue that organisational role and status are most influential in amount of talk, but these of course *intersect* with gender. The analysis suggests that women are silenced by the very factors that influence the amount of talk in public spheres which include being in influential and power (decision-making) positions.

Men in most societies and Cameroon in particular have a historical legacy and 'cultural capital' (Bourdieu 1991) which legitimates their verbosity in public. I examine below two factors that may influence male verbosity in this case: the genre of 'parliamentary discourse' within a particular CofP and 'socio-cultural background'.

Parliamentary discourse could be looked at as a 'discourse of verbosity' as MPs are expected to be the mouthpieces of their constituencies. The role of parliamentary sessions is to enable talk and the election MPs assumes the very capacity to talk (Shaw 2006). Parliamentary discourse, including in the Cameroonian context, can be seen as a discourse of attacks and counter-attacks, legitimation and counter-legitimation. As noted by Chilton (2004), parliamentary question time is mainly adversarial and 'questions are weapons in the party battle' (p. 92). Parliamentary discourse may thus warrant a certain degree of verbosity (Walsh 2001) and point scoring (Labov 1966). However, this is not gender-blind. In many cultures, women, unlike men, are not *expected* to be verbose, adversarial or competitive in public discourse (Christie 2003). Shaw (2006: 82) observes that women in the British House of Commons indicate feelings of 'terror' speaking in the parliament, and notes that 'particular settings can be the domain of some groups and not others', thus following Bourdieu's *habitus* of linguistic sense of place that

> governs the degree of constraint which a given field will bring to bear in the production of discourse, imposing silence or hyper-controlled language of some people while allowing others the liberties of a language that is securely established (Bourdieu 1991:82).

Such a 'field', here, parliamentary discourse, constrains female verbal participation by 'imposing silence' (in a relative sense) and enabling male verbal participation. Using the Communities of Practice notion, Eckert and McConnell-Ginet (2007: 28) observe that 'practices articulate the wider world' and that

> it is through the articulation of the local, the extra-local and the global, that we can understand how gender is produced and reproduced, that we can make a principled connection between our observation of people on the ground and the gender order.

Gendered practices within the parliament may therefore be explained by the articulation of 'local' practices (outside the parliament), with those of this specific, parliamentary setting. If women are not 'core' members (Lave and Wenger 1991) of ('local' public) CofPs that legitimate talk in the public sphere, they may thus remain (relatively silent) peripheral members of the parliamentary CofP, and, accordingly, generally occupy what Shaw (2006: 98) calls 'an interloper status'.

Relatedly, the **s*ocio-cultural background*** of the parliamentarians may also have made it possible for male MPs to speak more. Cameroonian men are socialised from a young age to talk in public through membership of various (public) communities of practice (e.g. drinking together in a public hall or bar, or having a public meeting together). One associated social practice is male 'homosociality' (Kiesling 2005; Cameron 1997; Cameron and Kulick 2003, Walsh 2001) where men tend to spend time together in public places. Walsh (2001: 18) refers to this as 'homosocial bonding' with power flowing horizontally (among men) and being maintained through 'masculinist' discursive practices. Cameroonian men are therefore traditionally seen in public, talk in public and are used to being with other men; women were expected not to be *seen* much in *public formal* meetings, (but rather to be concerned with *domestic* affairs. Although women may tend to talk more together in private spaces (see Coates 1996), their public talk in mixed sex contexts is not characteristic. Most parliamentarians have grown up in rural (thus traditional) settings, absorbing the culture, only going to cities for education. Even with such education, the bond with traditional practices still appears evident in the discourses they draw on. The traditional culture is asserting oneself as a 'man' (through verbal participation in public). Because of such backgrounds, people's (women and men's) *experience* of men and women speaking in public places is different. Men may then extend these social (including discourse) practices and expectations into institutional settings such as the parliament, as indeed may women as seen in the finding.

Silence
'If who speaks signals who is significant, who has status, then the men's roles position them into power' (Jule 2006: 115). In this section, I examine *silence* from the perspective of presence or absence of the female voice in the public sphere, and in particular, the Cameroonian parliament, as shown indicatively earlier in this chapter. Women's exclusion (silence) and marginalisation from linguistic practices and contexts to which society accords particular value (generally the public sphere) is widely attested (Cameron 2006: 3) and, as shown above, men rather than women tend to dominate highly valued public speech (Walsh 2001, Holmes and Stubbe 2003, Cameron 2006). Analysing women's *silence* is accordingly salient in understanding male verbosity.

Silence has been studied from different perspectives and can in fact be looked at as a power*ful* tool of linguistic communication (Jarwoski 1993, Stevens 2006), including to suppress the marginalised (Tannen and Saville-Troike 1985, De Francisco (1998 [1991]), Thiesmeyer 2003). De Francisco (1998 [1991]) for example, observes that in domestic spheres, men can and do exert power through silence. Men's silence in the domestic sphere therefore serves as a powerful tool. Silence thus has different effects depending on the context, including *who* is silent and the power they already possess.

'Silence' can be looked at both as a verb, 'to silence', and as a noun, 'silence'. The noun is seen as not necessarily problematic in gender and discourse studies as it describes a situation of being quiet which may be from 'personal choice' (Eades 2000), a sign of agency (as well as powerlessness). On the other hand, 'Silenc*ing*' and 'being silenced' include 'choices made by other people as well as by the potential speaker' (Thiesmeyer 2003: 2), and 'being silenced' cannot be a choice at all. Thiesmeyer points out that 'silencing [may] result from an act of language where language is used in order to enable some kinds of expressions and to disenable others' (2003: 11). It is thus not necessarily *total,* but limiting in relation to, say, topic, discourse, or, as here, 'some kinds of expressions' (cf. *Hlonipha).* 'Silencing' is thus 'a way of using language to limit, remove or undermine the legitimacy of another's use of language' (Thiesmeyer 2003:2) – for example, women's talk on economic (or other focussed non-gender) topics in the parliament.

Silence (and silencing) is discussed in this section from a public (institutional) perspective. Silencing does not take place in a void but in part in and through (institutional) discourse. I suggest that silencing is also related to specific genres. Silence and silencing in parliamentary discourse may, for example, as I have suggested above, be indicative of particular traditional, institutional and gendered discourse practices, and may indeed further *construct* these.

Institutions promote certain kinds of knowledge and discourage others and knowledge that is discursively promoted accompanies behaviour in personal interactions (see van Dijk 2001) – and, we can add, professional and public ones too. This implies that members of institutions can institutionally silence in order to 'enable certain kinds of expressions' and disable others, and to enable/disenable certain *people*. Looking at the genre of parliamentary debates (in Cameroon), abuse, heckling, accusations and discrediting others are part of the discourse (but are institutionally not allowed). There is also no regard for age or status. This is contrary to wider social practices in Cameroon where age and status do affect speech styles[12]. Gender is also an important variable in this. From my personal observation, women, by tradition and culture, for example, are not expected to use abusive or assertive language (towards men) in public nor accuse a man in public, in particular if the man is older. However, in parliament, they may need to do precisely this. In practice, women in public settings (here the parliament) tend to generally use face saving strategies[13] (see also Brown and Levinson 1987), which may include silence (for example, not verbally reacting as expected). All these factors may affect institutional discourse where gender equality is statutory but (expected) traditional gender (differential) practices remain.

MPs choose to be MPs and the presupposition is that they will represent their constituencies in the House of Assembly. This representation includes asking and answering questions or discussing issues relating to the problems affecting these constituencies. They are *expected* to talk to do their job, so are unlikely to be comfortable with their own silence, if this is continuous. The disproportionately small amount of talk by women in the parliament shown in this chapter could in part thus be a result of (self) silencing due to the historical, traditional background. Different 'traditional' *discourses* available to both men and women articulated outside parliament may play a role in this silencing process, 'traditional' discourses whose traces include proverbs such as 'good women stay silent in public', 'a good woman remains in the background' or 'good women do not challenge/criticise (older)[14] men in public' (see also Schipper 2003).

The small quantity of talk by women in the parliament can itself be seen as a factor in further silencing of women. Because so few women (a number disproportionate to their presence) mount the rostrum and talk, this may discourage other women MPs who are not bold enough to do so. They have few role models to copy from,

84

resulting in a vicious circle. Gendered discourses may also reinforce the stereotypes about women's silence in public. Thus discourses that circulate in the parliament may thus be additionally silencing and restricting for women (see Leander 2002).

Silence and Access

> *For a woman, display is dishonour Fulani (Cameroon) proverb.*

Van Dijk (1996:86) observes that access to discourse and communicative events may be one major element in the discursive reproduction of power and dominance. Not everyone has access to political text or talk, certainly not historically. Access can also be looked at in terms of 'setting', that is, physical space, and its organisation, its effects on different speakers (members of parliament). Does this have an effect on the speech styles of the others and even their quantity of talk? I look at these below to explore the role of access and setting could be factors in these women's silence in the Cameroonian parliament.

Access to scarce 'symbolic capital' (Bourdieu 1991), such as knowledge, education, fame, respect, status and indeed public discourse itself, could affect differences in speech patterns in terms of quantity (and quality) of contributions in the parliament (van Dijk 1996). Although I am not claiming that the literacy level of women in Cameroon has a significant impact on amount of talk by women MPs, their level of education (as well as gendered social status) may well have such an impact. This is because, on the whole, women are less educated than men (and some women MPs are 'barely' literate. In an early informal interview, a male MP observed that most women in the parliament are there not in their own right but because they are 'forced into the parliament because of one reason or another' (see Nyamnjoh and Rowlands 1998 on elite associations and the politics of belonging). This MP may have based his claim on male stereotypes that women are incompetent in public roles and cannot attain such positions in their own right, but he may also have identified (unintentionally) a barrier to women's participation.

The parliamentary institutional *setting,* as van (Dijk 1996: 87) observes, may also affect talk in the parliament. Setting, in this way, is looked at in terms of the organisation of space (seating arrangements, structure of the building, and even geographical setting). Geisler (2000) observes that, after apartheid, South African female freedom fighters suddenly found themselves in the parliament (voted in of course), and in their private narratives observed that they were awed by the structures, and felt they did not know what they were doing there. These women had been quite vocal outside parliament, but the new physical space affected their newly required discursive practices within the parliament. And, as observed previously, Freed (1996: 67) notes, public 'meeting rooms' are predominantly male spaces, as is also the case in Cameroon.

Figure 3. 7   Plenary Seating Arrangement, Cameroonian Parliament

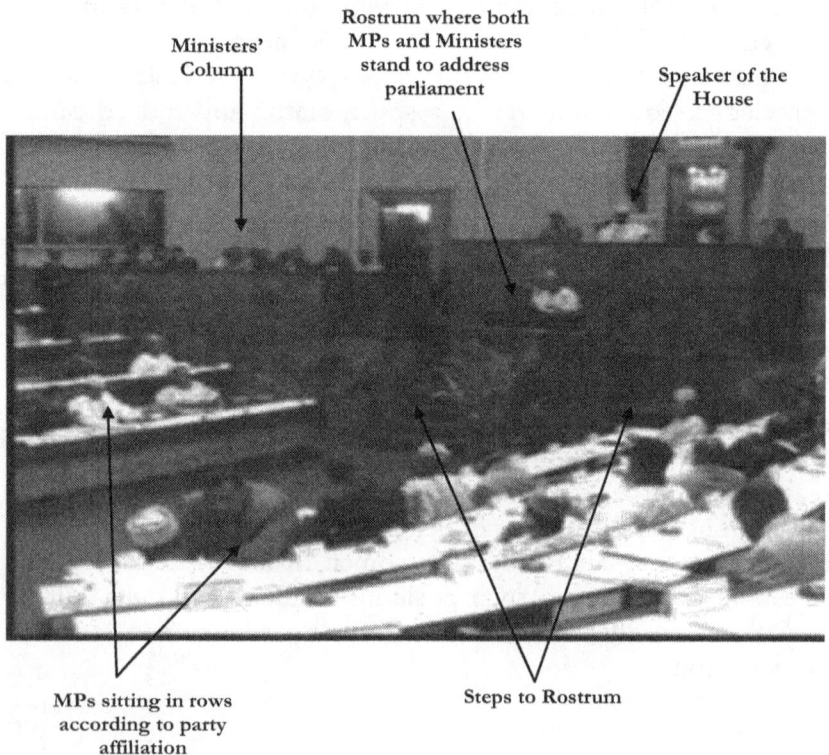

The arrangement of seating in the parliament could also be a factor in influencing the amount of talk by different MPs. The parliamentarians sit in a hemicycle (a semi-circular form) according to their political parties without any gender segregation. This hemicycle is arranged in three columns with several rows. The President (Speaker) of the National Assembly sits at the head in an elevated position in front of the hemicycle on a raised podium flanked on both sides by two columns occupied by Ministers on one side and parliamentary administrative staff on the other. The Ministers' column is thus adjacent to that of the Speaker of the House although not as elevated. Directly below the Speaker is the rostrum where parliamentarians and ministers stand to ask or answer questions (see Figure 3.7). Because the rostrum is higher than the hemicycle and faces it, it may be quite daunting to climb it to ask or answer questions from there. As parliamentarians sit in rows, to ask questions, they have to 'shuffle' themselves out of their row to mount the rostrum (unlike the British Parliament where parliamentarians generally stand up to ask questions without having to move from their seats) and this shuffling inevitably attracts attention. This arrangement in the parliament could be seen as *additionally* 'silencing' for a social group that has been socialised to be (sometimes) seen but not to be heard[15] in public, especially in this formal mixed-sex gathering because of this extra attention and 'male gaze'. Self-consciousness thus may prevent a lot of MPs, particularly women, from taking the floor during parliamentary debates. Being quiet in the Assembly may thus be in large part a result of these social structures.

Silence and Topic Choice

In addition to the problem of *physical* access to the rostrum in the parliament, I look at silence (and access) in terms of knowledge and *topic choice*, that is, *issues* under discussion in the parliament. I ask the following question:

♦ *Do women and men talk about different topics in the Cameroonian parliament?'*

I look at women's participation with reference to *topics*, which could be silencing in themselves – because they are not seen as women's concerns or are taboo, for example.

87

I identify topics from the different 'themes' raised within a speakers' text. I choose to analyse topics only in the June 2005 parliamentary sessions as it was the only session with more than one female MP participating. In the data collected, female parliamentarians did not participate at all during the Q & A sessions. As such, I analyse the one Discussion session where more than one woman verbally participated. Analysis of the content of female MPs' contributions during this session shows that topics generally consisted of praising of the incumbent government (all female MPs are members of the ruling party) or were on social issues (generally family or gender issues). This contrasted with contributions of male MPs which were varied and ranged from economic problems to political and scientific ones (men however sometimes focused on gendered topics). Men's contributions in the parliament were either to explore problems, criticise current solutions and propose 'better' possible solutions or put the government to task of seeking better options. A comparison of the topics presented by male and female MPs is presented in Table 3. 9.

Although almost all the MPs (from the ruling party) congratulated the government on the bill on the new Penal Code, only female MPs (Honourable Mebanda and Honourable Njini) raised issues in the bill that were related to the welfare of women and the law. The male MPs spoke more generally. None of them evoked an overtly gendered topic during this particular session even though there were gender-specific laws. These women may thus *identify* with Cameroonian women in general, or may see it as their role to represent women in particular, as a consequence of the overt gender imbalance in the parliament and discrimination in the society as a whole.

Table 3. 9   Topic Choice during Discussion Session, June 2005

Male MP	Female MP	Topic
Sonkeng		Presentation of proposal for Penal code
Ayafor		<ul><li>Bill of human rights,</li><li>Aspects of bail, limitations of powers of the magistrate,</li><li>Other loopholes in the law.</li></ul>
Ndebi Yembe		<ul><li>Government's efforts to institute this bill (Praise)</li><li>What the government has done (positive analysis)</li><li>Funds to disseminate new bill to the grassroots</li></ul>
Ndinda Ndinda		<ul><li>Praise of the government</li><li>Positive deeds of the government (analysis)</li></ul>
	Ndoh	<ul><li>Government's good deeds (praise)</li><li>Calls on the other MPs to vote the bill</li></ul>
Ndongo		<ul><li>Penal Code (Praise critique of Minister)</li><li>Lack of lawyers to deal with issues stipulated by the law</li><li>Lack of medical doctors are available</li><li>Magistrates' safety</li></ul>
	Njini Ekwa	<ul><li>Penal code (praise)</li><li>Distinction between family visits and professional visits to prisoners</li><li>Family Code</li></ul>
	Mebanda	<ul><li>Women who get pregnant in prison despite article 583 which says pregnant women will not be sent to jail until after they have had their babies.</li><li>Women's security in prison (since they share prisons with men).</li><li>Separate prisons for women</li><li>Women's health and incidents of rape in prisons</li></ul>
Fouda		<ul><li>Availability of bailiffs</li></ul>

These male MPs may be more interested in maintaining and perpetuating the gendered status quo here for their own gains (see Chapter 5 on legitimating 'traditional' discourses), or may simply be unaware of the position of women (or think it unimportant), or, more likely, are not as aware of themselves 'as men' (as members of a majority powerful group, this is often the case). Women, on the other hand, may consider other 'non-gendered' topics to be 'masculine topics', not because they are not of interest to them (women), but because they are not as pressing to women as to men. Alternatively, the fact that women do not contribute to debates on general topics may be explained through the fact that they are less familiar with what happens out of the domestic sphere and in the wider world (as a consequence of lack of experience and education).

Conclusion

In this chapter, I have identified and systematically analysed some gender differences in parliamentary discourse in Cameroon. With regard to Titulation, female MPs in the National Assembly are generally referred to using their social titles rather than their (parliamentary) professional ones. Male MPs in contrast are referred to as a group in *various* ways, including both their social, (professional)[16], and parliamentary titles, indicating a multiple identity construction as opposed to women's limited identity construction of motherhood and wifehood.

The findings about differences in quantity of talk do not point in a different direction from previous research: men generally talk disproportionately more and for longer in this public institutional setting. In this study of the Cameroonian parliament, men in these sessions and across genres use more than double the time women use, with an average of 7 minutes per speaker, while women generally take less, with an average of 3 minutes. This points to male verbosity and women's silence. Also, this analysis shows that women tend to take up only about 5% of the 'verbal space' in the parliament, which is disproportionate considering they occupy more than double that (11%) in terms of representation in the parliament.

As regards the topics discussed in the parliament, in June 2005 Discussion session genre examined, women's contributions generally related to gender and social issues,[17] as the primary focus of their questions. Male MPs did not generally focus on gender issues. Gender issues may be central to the contributions of female MPs because of the blatant gender discrimination in the society (affecting mostly women), and perhaps because of their 'minority group' status in the parliament. Geisler (2000) similarly found that in the new post-apartheid South African parliament, women mainly raised issues specific to gender relations both in the parliament and in the society.

It is my hope that these differences will serve as a basis for an understanding of gendered discourses and the discursive legitimation of these, as documented and discussed in the following chapters. The gender differences I have identified here can be seen as 'traces' of these.

Notes

1. Although I use modern above to refer to western – e.g. European and American, modern in the quote can however be seen as contemporary.

2. The 2004 parliamentary session, which includes the texts APP 1and FA1 used in Chapters 6 – 9, is not included in the analysis in this chapter. In that data only, one Female minister spoke and no female MPs.

3. These are dates recorded by the researcher and do not include dates in which the researcher might have been absent. However, this represents more than 80% of the total plenary session.

4. She quotes somebody addressing her 'On me dit 'honourable…'' (I am told 'honourable…')

5. Note masculine pronoun even when she is a woman. This particular data was not coded and was used only in this chapter.

6. MPs did not talk in all the sessions as some were opening sessions and others only to ratify bills.

7. Only one plenary session was thus analysed during this June parliamentary session.

8. The rest of the time was taken by Ministers, and by the presentation of a bill which took several hours.

9. One of the two Question-and-Answer sessions was spent quarrelling over English speaking Cameroonians being referred to as Biafras, a slang meaning Nigerians. There was no speaking order here and everyone spoke at the same time. Norms were not respected here as it was not even part of the day's business.

10. I use titles in English and French to indicate the OL1 (first official language) of the speaker.

11. This male MP asked two questions to different ministers.

12. In most cultures in Cameroon, there are address terms for older persons e.g. the prefix 'ndi' in Grassfield Cameroon is indicated of the fact that the addressee is older. There are translated into French and English 'Uncle' or 'Auntie'. Thus people are addressed thus even when there is no blood relation as a mark of respect for the age.

13. Here, not saving their face but that of their male (elderly) interlocutors.

14. Popular proverbs in Cameroon.

15. E.g. For a woman, display is dishonour - Swahili/Fulani (Cameroon) proverb.

16. Not shown in the analysis is titulation of a male MP as 'Honorable Dr Pierre Sende', a double professional emphasis.

17. The lone female speaker during the November session spoke on students' (whom she called 'children') welfare in the universities.

Chapter Four

'Traditional' Gendered Discourses Articulated in the Cameroonian Parliament

Introduction

Cameroon, a fast changing country, can be claimed in many respects to be a modern African state. It is experiencing a cultural, economic and political transformation triggered by influence from more developed countries. The World Bank, International Monetary Fund and other international organisations such as the United Nations and the Commonwealth of Nations have helped shape the economic, cultural and political life of the country. Programmes such as the Structural Adjustment Programme have practically forced women into the economic and public sphere since a second pay cheque is necessary for many families. However, I suggest that these innovations have had minimal impact on the way men and women are constructed in a society still based on patriarchal values. As Fonjong (2001) observes, Cameroonian women are still generally discursively constructed as subordinate, incapable, consumers, uneducated, and this is inherent in both traditional and state institutions. Their place is generally seen to be in the kitchen[1] (see also Abdela 2000).

In this chapter, I look at what I call 'traditional' gendered discourses drawing on overt gendered differences. These are discourses based on long-standing practices and beliefs. 'Traditional' is viewed here as relating to a mode of thought or behaviour of a people from generation to generation, leading to 'a custom'. Traditional can also be taken as a given, that is, what is generally acceptable in a particular society. This includes the different acceptable ways members of that society construct themselves and are constructed by others through discourse. Any 'transgressions' may be judged negatively or even punished in some way[2]. Common-sense, taken for granted notions and practices and ideologies (Thompson 1990; Eagleton 1991; Fairclough 2001, 2003) are based on such modes of thought. 'Traditional' then is used as opposed to modern (sometimes synonymous to progressive)which relates to *new* (socio-cultural and political) practices.

'Traditional' gendered discourse can thus be seen as generally 'conservative' although one may not neatly equate gendered 'traditional' or 'conservative' discourses to discriminatory ones. It is my opinion that a parliament with an overt gender imbalance is a fertile ground for 'traditional' gendered discourses. A dominant 'gender differentiation' discourse (Baxter 2003; Sunderland 2004) is logically intrinsic to societies where women and men have segregated, 'homosocial' practices (Cameron 1997; Walsh 2001, Cameron and Kulick 2003; Kiesling 2005). Tannen & Saville-Troike (1985) similarly affirm that discourses on 'gender differentiation' are more dominant in patriarchal societies (such as Cameroon) where stereotypes regarding gender divisions of labour are prevalent (Goheen 1996; Kitetu and Sunderland 2000, Sunderland 2004). Such stereotypes are manifested within the discourses of these societies and including (as shown through this book) the proverbs used.

Society generally defines and redefines what is acceptable and what is not based on shared 'common ground knowledge'. *Common ground knowledge* depends on 'its truth criteria ... [being] taken for granted, undisputed and generally (discursively) presupposed'. Wodak and Meyer 2009) add that institutional practices which people draw upon without thinking often embody assumptions which directly or indirectly legitimate existing power relations and are 'commonsensical'. To *project* practices as universal and commonsensical leads to *ideological power*. This chapter shows how commonsense, taken-for-granted traditional practices embedded in the society are used to control and legitimate gendered practices within the Cameroonian society. Discourses relating to these (socially) acceptable norms and practices within a given society are based on historical beliefs in particular about the biological 'givens' of male and female human beings which are extended to beliefs about corresponding social roles (cf Mathieu 1989's first meaning of 'gender' in chapter 2). Kitetu and Sunderland (2000) regard this as 'a gender fixity discourse'.

What a community may perceive and articulate as *'traditional'*, can be seen as reinforcing dominant discourses. In such a 'traditional' discourse, *gender differentiation* is dominant and therefore largely perceived as positive (including the dominated group); the marginal alternative, what we might call 'gender comparability' as negative. It must be pointed out here that social differentiation does not *entail* social dominance or disadvantage, but does tend to be associated with it.

In this chapter, 'traditional' gendered discourses which are often 'conservative' and discriminatory are examined as they tend to construct men and women differently, and emphasise a gendered, limiting division of roles within the society. 'Traditional' discourses articulated in the parliament are intertextually drawn from this traditional background and arguably act to sustain conservative practices which are based on a gender division of labour (in particular, men being involved in public roles, and women in domestic ones). Analysis in this chapter therefore addresses empirical question:

♦ *What traditional gendered discourses are evident in the Cameroonian parliament?*

'Traditional' is put in single quotes to indicate that such discourses are not fixed *and* that they have been *interpreted* as such (they may be interpreted differently). In the course of the chapter, intertextuality and interdiscursivity are also shown to be relevant to the production of these (and related) discourses.

'Traditional' Gendered Discourses

The workings of 'traditional' gendered discourses (as opposed to new, contemporary ones are identified and analysed. A macro-discourse of *'A Model Traditional Cameroonian Woman'* is identified here. It is named as such following the construction of Cameroonian women based on traditionally accepted practices and perceptions of women who fit into these representations as *model*. These constructions are seen in everyday talk in Cameroon as Cameroonians tend to say, for example, 'she is not acting as a (Cameroonian) woman'. *Model* here is used to indicate an *ideal* to be copied by those represented as *deviant*. 'Model' and 'traditional' are associated because speakers within the Cameroonian parliament emphasise tradition, implicitly (I argue) prescribes what can be seen as a 'model', and emphasise that there are deviations.

Within this macro discourse, different realisations call discourses - the count noun, are identified following Fairclough (2003, 2007), for example, 'Women as domestic'. It can be identified within this macro-discourse in part through the way gendered characteristics and practices are often attributed to 'culture'. Cameroonian (and African) women and men are traditionally represented within this macro-discourse as different from western (European and American) women and men and so are expected to behave, dress and act differently from them. The 'warrant' (Swann 2002) of 'culture' is used to identify discourses and I suggest that 'ordinary' speakers (members of this community) also use such a warrant to justify claims that gender differences (for example, in labour) are natural (and indeed desirable).

The notion of women's empowerment is contemporary and relates to women being able to do what was previously exclusively reserved for men. Discourse surrounding empowerment and gender equality therefore does not conform to traditional ideologies as Cameroonian women have never had equality with men (in all domains) nor have they articulated publicly and explicitly that they needed to be empowered. Women then, *to an extent*, can do what they could not before. Nevertheless, Cameroonian women and men were, and still are viewed through a lens of *gender as difference* and any ideologies and practices relating to equality and empowerment of women were (are) seen as deviant by conservatives.

Traditional Gender Ideologies - a Clash of Cultures: Ancient vs. Contemporary Voices

Cameroon is a country caught between two civilisations with competing ideologies: 'traditional' vs. contemporary ('progressive'); pre-colonial vs. colonial and post-colonial (Said 1985). As a post-colonial country, it is caught between two major civilisations and thus suffers from a 'clash of civilisations' (Huntington 1993), trying to preserve its ancient traditional cultural practices while accommodating new and modern ones, against a background of globalisation. It is caught in a dilemma of national identity, trying to accommodate globalisation and at the same time celebrating its cultural (traditional) identity. With the advent of free flows of information through books, seminars, training, and information and communication technology, the government has limited control over the population copying modern (western) practices (especially socio-cultural practices). Members of the community gain access to information on new lifestyles (e.g. from America and Europe) which implicitly challenge traditional practices of the society: e.g. gender roles, fashion, and accordingly the general mentality of the society. The older generation of Cameroonians have to deal for example with younger people and women who may have, in the past, accepted traditional practices (even when they were repressive) but now question such values orchestrated by a fast-changing world. With globalisation, new discourses emerge.

In this section, I present 'ancient voices' as widely held beliefs relating to traditional gendered practices of a particular society. These 'ancient voices' articulate discourses such as 'you are a woman, you have to get married', 'you are a woman, you have to bear *many* children[3]', 'you are a woman, you have to listen to your husband', 'you are a woman, you have to cook for your family', 'you are a woman, you have to be modest in dressing', and 'do not show yourself off in public' (e.g. by talking loudly or drinking in bars with men). These traditional ideas are summed up by a cliché in Cameroon: 'weti bicycle di do for petrol station' – *what is a bicycle doing in a petrol station?* Such a cliché positions men as public and women as domestic, and implicitly challenges the very presence of women in the National Assembly, a supposedly male space. Traditional gendered discourses produced within the society today can be seen as drawing on these 'ancient voices' which also construct *men* in particular ways: 'husbands', 'fathers', 'independent', 'public' (free to drink, talk and do many other things in public women shouldn't do), 'leaders and family heads' who are 'decision makers' both for their families and for the society (with women having the same subordinate position and equal status as children (Konde 2005)). Listening to these 'ancient voices', women and men are 'subject' to the roles traditional society ascribes to them (or are 'subject positioned' *by* them). The marriage institution and children are highly valued and respected by both men and women. Men however are not directly involved in child care (Chungong 2007 and Nsamenang 2000). In a society with a traditional gender division of labour, men *marry* women, house them and have children with

97

them. It is women's duty to care for children and run the home. Women within this sociological context are thus perceived as crucially *domestic*. Although their main duties include farming (which is not domestic!), this is not however a *public* domain. Women's public participation and activities are therefore still very limited, both in practice and in discourse.

The 'Model Traditional Cameroonian Woman': Her Construction and Representation in the Cameroonian Parliament

This section focuses on the macro-discourse of *a model traditional Cameroonian woman* in parliamentary debates. Within this macro-discourse, other discourses such as *women as domestic, women as preservers of culture* and carers' are identified. This macro-discourse multiply constructs women as domestic with roles such as *mothers, wives, carers, family cooks,* and also as a minimal participator in public events. The discourses surrounding the construction of 'a model traditional Cameroonian woman' are examined within the broad genre of parliamentary discourse and the sub-genres of Question-and-Answer and Discussions sessions.

During parliamentary sessions, political elites, in this case MPs and government ministers, talk about political, social, cultural, scientific and economic issues affecting the society as a whole. I show that talk produced during these debates manifests conflicting positions and ideologies by MPs and ministers collectively advocating 'traditionally' accepted behavioural patterns within the society while at the same time evoking competing ideologies which legitimate change, progress and evolution of new practices that give women more freedom and power within the society.

One key 'site' of debate was women's social practices during the 2004 Women's Day celebrations, which were criticised and represented as deviant. This traditional discourse, evident as such within a modern political context, is analysed *intertextually* below. As observed by Bakhtin (1986: 89), 'our speech... is filled with other's words'. As such, intertextuality indicates 'relations between one text and other texts which are external to it yet in some way brought into it' (Fairclough 2003: 39). Fairclough (2003) also notes that in representing a social event, one is always incorporating it within the context of another social event (thus re-contextualisation). I look at how different arguments for and against both emerging practices and conservative beliefs are re-contextualised through and in parliamentary debates to bring out traditional gendered discourses of a 'model Cameroonian woman'. Such re-contextualisation selectively filters social events, with some excluded, others included (Van Leeuwen, 1996) and still others given more or less prominence. Here, discourses on *deviant* women are *highlighted* and women's negative social practices *included*. Men's negative actions are selectively filtered and suppressed as are traces of 'progressive' discourses (see Chapter 6 and 7).

As explained earlier, the complete data-set for this book consists of transcripts of audio-recordings from the June 2004 (3 plenary sessions), June 2005 (7 plenary sessions) and November 2005 (3 plenary sessions) parliamentary sessions. These constitute two main genres of parliamentary discourse: Q & A and Discussion. The transcripts of the audio-recordings constitute vast amounts of text and I chose to focus on explicitly gendered texts. I have selected one key text (Appendix 1) as primary data for this chapter. This text constitutes an extract from a parliamentary session of June 2004. I chose this indicative 394 word text for its overt gendered nature and also for its critique of women's social practices. The extract is the speech of an Honourable MP of the Cameroon People's Democratic Movement (CPDM), Honourable Etame François of the ruling party in Cameroon - an educated professional, born during the colonial period and fairly well placed on the economic ladder. He is an MP from a constituency in a rural equatorial forest village in the southern part of the country with its nearest town being Sangmelima. Geographically, this area is set in a tropical forest, and several hundred kilometres from the capital city, Yaoundé. Although economically and politically not one of the most important towns in Cameroon, it however developed its importance from the fact that it is the Divisional capital of the Head of State's village. The Cameroon map below shows Sangmelima, Foumban, the West (Ouest), and the North (Nord) - geographical areas mentioned in the text.

The text is a 'question' addressed to the Minister of Women's Affairs and focuses on issues relating to women's activities during International Women's Day celebration – March 8th 2004. This would have been *scripted* to be read aloud. The text is a critique of these activities and an appeal to the Minister of Women's Affairs to 'do something' about Cameroonian women's public behaviour.

As indicated, I have identified a macro-discourse of 'a model traditional Cameroonian woman'. As these 'model' characteristics do not apply to men, this draws on the wider, underlying discourse of 'Gender difference', which, as I have shown, and as Sunderland (2004: 44) observes is an '"overarching', 'common-sense' 'dominant' discourse. '[I]t dovetails with popular and [...] widely *enjoyed* understandings of gender as *difference'* (her emphasis). Logically, the different constructions of Cameroonian women implicitly indicate the representation and construction of men within that society. For example, if a woman is expected to stay at home, then it must be men who go out (and hence who have a *public* role in society).

The discourse-historical approach does not explicitly indicate how *discourse, macro-topics* and *sub-topics* can be identified although reference to 'establishing their specific content' with 'ingredients' of the discourse is mentioned (Wodak 2001: 72). However, drawing on Sunderland's (2004) approach to discourse identification, I proceed with the identification of discourse*s* through a close reading of culturally familiar texts. For example, a prescriptive discourse of 'women as silent in public' is culturally familiar for me as a Cameroonian woman. However, discourses are also identified through particular linguistic traces. These include lexical and collocational patterns such as words and phrases or even sentences, which are often repeated (see Sunderland 2004). Further linguistic and semiotic traces (achieved through linguistic realisations) are:
- Pronominal choices
- Naming practices (Titulation)
- Themes (content)
- Syntactic forms e.g. adverbs, imperatives, interrogatives, modality, transitivity, phrasal structures
- Adjectives

Map of Cameroon Showing Sangmelima

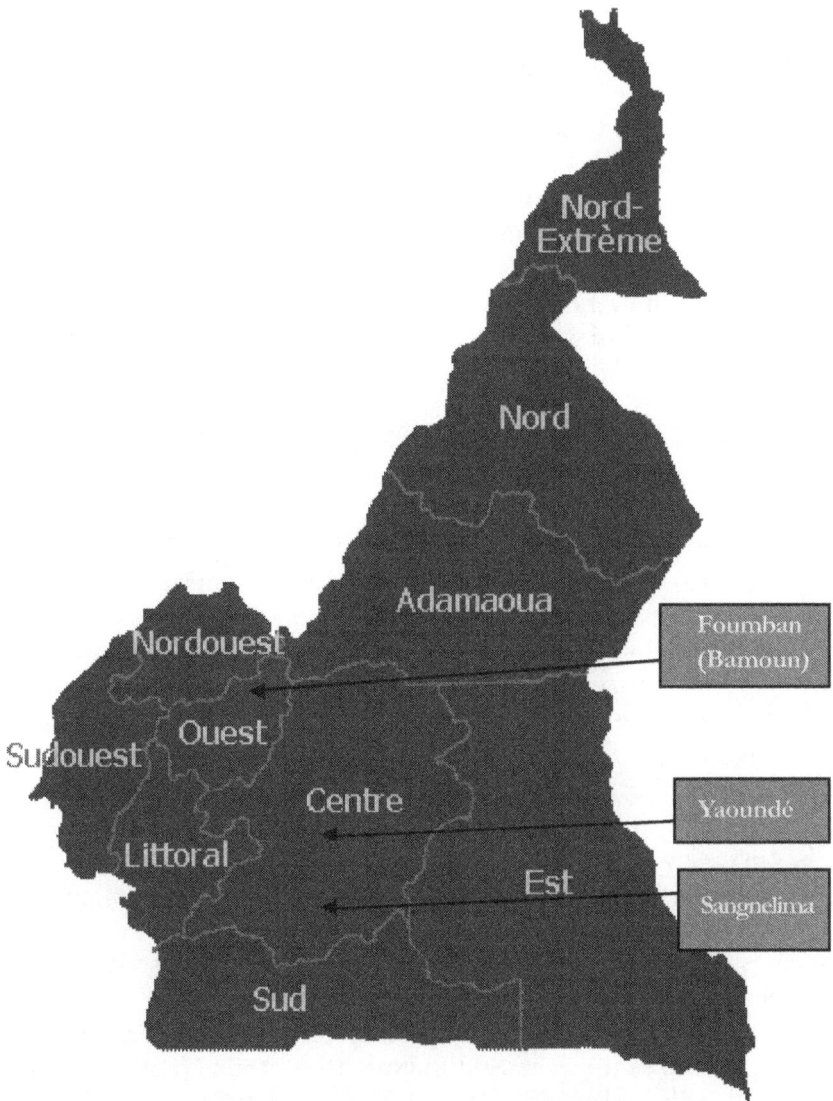

Nord-Extrême

Nord

Adamaoua

Nordouest

Foumban (Bamoun)

Ouest

Sudouest

Centre

Yaoundé

Littoral

Est

Sangnelima

Sud

www.world-gazetteer.com

Mills (2000: 17) observes that we can 'detect a discursive structure' because of the 'systematicity of ideas, opinions, concepts, ways of thinking and behaving which are formed in a particular context'. This *systematicity of ideas* may be manifested through repetition of words or phrases.

For Sunderland (2004: 47) discourse[4] naming is not a 'neutral' activity but says something about the namer. Researching gendered discourses from a feminist point of view and being an educated African will necessarily influence the way I name these discourses and analyse how men and women are constructed within and through them. Adopting the approach to the naming of discourses by Sunderland includes both conceptual and linguistically formal considerations. As Walsh (2001) indicates, analysis of discourse can also be a macro-level analysis of texts and social contexts.

I name the material under analysis descriptively as 'parliamentary discourse', with the term *discourse* used here as an abstract, non-countable noun (see Fairclough 2003, 2007). This gives a description of the whole body of text produced within a *specific* institutional setting, that is, the parliament. I name and examine the specific macro-discourse within this chapter with regard to the general issue under discussion in the text, 'a model traditional Cameroonian woman', within the domains of political action and social action.

The discourses identified and named are mostly interpretively done with regard to their specific nature: a discourse of 'x as y', where typically the structure is: a discourse of + Noun + as + adjective, e.g. *a discourse of mother as carer*. In my discussion, other discourses are identified and named either through their *function* such as gender partnership discourse (abstract noun + discourse), or with regard to the intertextual relationship they have with other discourses such as *dominant* or *competing* discourses (adjective + discourse) (see Sunderland 2004 for a fuller discussion). Some of the discourses presented below have previously been identified and named in the literature, and in those cases, I indicate the author. In other cases, I newly identify and name them within this book.

In the following sections, I identify and name discourses that relate to the macro-discourse of 'model traditional Cameroonian women'.

'Woman as Domestic, Men as Public'

In Cameroon, women have generally been perceived as *domestic* and, as I have shown, even the law tends to reinforce this. I use *domestic* here to relate to activities in, around and about the home, and in opposition to *public*. The notion of *domestic* has however changed over time with regard to Cameroonian women who have gradually shifted from being *housewives only* to other public domain occupations. *Domestic* in the past meant not having paid jobs. Career women were greatly discouraged. With recent economic developments, (poverty, urbanisation and modernisation, and greater need for money, for example), families often need a second pay packet, and there has been a redefinition and reinterpretation of *domestic* within the Cameroonian context in relation to women, to include working women outside the home. The notion of 'primarily domestic' has involved *adding* the *public* (professional) domain to the *private* domain, with *public* relating to women's additional *limited* presence and participation in activities within the public sphere, but not subtracting from their traditional domestic chores (these are still expected to be carried out by women). This therefore meant their 'public' appearance was only limited by not being in certain 'male' spaces like bars. Although in contemporary Cameroon, women have constitutionally *unlimited* access to the public sphere, there are however also still legal[5] and traditional expectations of them to continue with their *expected* (traditional) roles within the domestic sphere.

My indicative text (Appendix 1) demonstrates this very well. The MP, Honourable Etame François criticises women who do not go home immediately after a public event - the 2004 March 8th International Women's Day celebrations which involve a march past. Honourable Etame observes that after the event, some women instead of going home immediately, remained behind (the bold font marks particular expectations or criticisms of social practices):

[...] **et dès que** le défilé est fini, **ces femmes sont rentrées** dans leurs maisons, **sauf** les femmes de Sangmélima ... **qui sont rentrées dans les bars** (14-16)

*[...] **as soon as** the march past finished, **these women returned** to their houses **except the women of Sangmelima ... who went into bars.***

103

The polarisation of women who went home and those who stayed behind is achieved by the use of the adverb 'sauf', *except*. He constructs those who stayed behind as 'bad' Cameroonian women by juxtaposing them with (good) women who *returned home* 'as soon as the march past finished'. (My cultural knowledge of the context of the text is essential in identifying such represented domesticity as, here, desirable.) Raising the issue in parliamentary question time is indicative of the MP's worry about the practice of women being (or becoming) less domestic. Possible reasons for his concern might be that women's presence in the public sphere may pose a challenge to the social order, and/or that their presence in the public sphere (formal and informal) might be perceived as encroaching into male territory. Women's absence from home may mean absence from child care, from cooking family meals and not being subordinate to men. It may spell equality and a balance of gendered power, a threat to men's independence and sovereignty in the social order. That could possibly be the main worry of the MP, and other men within the parliament and society, that is, that traditional social practices are changing *and* being subverted by women. Here, we can read that gender inequality is being made relevant by the MP and his emphasis – though this reading is unlikely to be his intention.

The use of the adverb of time 'dès que' (*as soon as*) in **'et dès que** le défilé est fini, ces femmes sont rentrées dans leurs maisons'- *as soon as the march past finished, these women returned to their houses,* also shows the construction of *model* Cameroonian women in the sense that, even if they have a public, officially approved function, they (must) go home immediately after, an indication that *outside* such a function, their activities are circumscribed.

Women staying in a public place may be seen as transgressive but being in bars (definitely not traditionally approved!) - a presumed exclusive domain for men is seen as worse. The MP explicitly refers to *drinking in public:* 'boire en publique'. It is not so much the act of drinking alcohol that is disapproved of but drinking *in a bar*, a public (gendered) space, traditionally a male domain, where women can only traditionally be brought by their husbands.

Through my *own knowledge* (as a Cameroonian), and supported intertextually (though indirectly) by the (Cameroonian) law, women are constructed within this context mainly as domestic[6]. A law on prostitution, enforced 1972[7], entails women's domesticity, and questions their presence in leisure spots (e.g. bars and night clubs) when not accompanied by a male. Such women are thus positioned as prostitutes, where prostitution is not only criminal but seen as immoral. It is therefore understandable when the MP questions women's presence (unaccompanied by their husbands) in bars: he sees this not only as a violation of the law, but also a collapse in the (moral) social system and 'loss of customs'. Good women, in principle, thus, do not go into bars, as their reputation (and that of their families) could be damaged, but normatively stay at home. Women's public presence, especially in bars could also be interpreted as a mark of independence - both financial independence and independence of men's control. For women to go into bars alone (unaccompanied by men, husbands or not) means they have financial independence to buy their own drinks. This too could be frowned at since in the Cameroonian society, women are known to be more responsible in spending – it is expected that only men will spend money on leisure (which includes spending on drinks).

The sub-sections below show different discoursal manifestations of the discourse of 'Women as Domestic', which I call discourse*s* following Sunderland 2004. All these presume the domesticity of women.

Women as Carers

Wagner and Wodak (2006: 390) observe that women are constructed as carers within society irrespective of their status. They further suggest that when women fail to fit these roles, they are criticised. This discourse of *women as carers* is articulated in this indicative text with different care roles ascribed to women. Within the Cameroonian traditional context, women are presumed carers of their families and especially of young children. This care is presumed to take place in a domestic, private context. Childcare then can be seen as women's responsibility. As the previous brief extract continues:

[L]es femmes de Sangmélima [...] **sont rentrées dans les bars**. Elles ont **abandonné les enfants** dans les bars... (7-9, 13-16)

The women of Sangmelima [...] **went** *into bars. They* **abandoned** *children in bars [i.e. by going to bars]*

105

Lexical traces 'rentrée dans les bars' (went (back) into bars), and in particular, the transitive verb 'abandon' are indicative of children lacking care and women as agents here. Childcare and women in bars are not reconcilable. Men go to bars; women look after the children. Also noteworthy are the 'compulsory heterosexual' (see Rich 1980) and 'fertility' discourses which represent all women by default as heterosexual and mothers and thus domestic.

Reference to motherhood in relation to children and childcare and responsibility can also be indicative of the care expected of mothers and thus women in general. In another extract from a different male MP, Honourable Tasi in a Discussion session (June 2005), in relation to the presentation of a bill on the modified Penal Code of Cameroon, he says,

> I am not a lawyer, but I can reason, by virtue of my age and my **experiences as a tutor**, and **vice principal**, and **principal**, and then **director**, and **conseiller technique of one minister** who is sitting here as a parliamentarians
> ...
> I crave the indulgence to listen to us as we take our responsibility, because you are like **a mother** who **has cooked food** for **the children**, and your anxiety mama, is **to see that they eat**. But my fear is that some of your children will eat and throw up, so you are better off accepting the situation as it is because when the children **say mama, let us go back to the kitchen**, willing to come and work with you, we do not want to eat and go behind and throw up, because some of us may, because some of us may vomit and die. And you will be **an unfortunate mother**.

This MP, Honourable Tasi, constructs two types of gender identities here. He constructs himself as a 'tutor' (secondary school), 'vice-principal', 'principal', 'director' and 'conseiller technique' (Technical adviser) which are all public functions. He juxtaposes such (masculine) experience and identity metaphorically with a woman's domestic and care roles of mother, cook, and responsibility towards the general welfare of the family. If her food (presumed unsuitable) is rejected, she is 'an unfortunate mother'. The essentialism of women's traditional social roles, contrasted with

106

men's, should be noted here. While women's expectations are domestic, men's are professional and public. A model Cameroonian woman then is first of all seen as a mother who has as one of her duties taking care of her family by being with them at home and also cooking for them.

A model Cameroonian woman in particular thus stays away from bars to care for the family. Sunderland (2004:51) refers to a related discourse of 'good mums stay at home with their children'. The construction of a model Cameroonian woman as *domestic* is based on the presupposition that childcare is a *natural* responsibility of women, and women *only*. This discourse allows the inference that if women are not to be at home to take care of their children, they (but not their husbands) should make alternative arrangements, which should not involve men. The presupposition in the excerpt is that children have been 'abandoned' *because* their mothers are not at home. There is no expectation of men being there when women are not, and no parallel discourse of men as fathers who should be responsible for taking care of the children in the absence of the women (even less that there should be equal responsibility in parenting – motherhood and fatherhood). Men as fathers are backgrounded (van Leeuwen 1996) in the domain of *childcare*. Fathers cannot 'abandon' children since it is not their duty to look after them in the first place. This 'logic' is made possible by a traditional discourse of 'woman as carer'. Sitting and having a drink in a bar is then a sign of neglect of this duty, and a woman who is a full time 'carer' is a 'good woman'. The juxtaposition of the phrases below further polarises 'good' and 'bad' women:

women went back to their homes	Good ones. Expected conduct
women... went into the bars and	Bad ones. Deviant
They abandoned children in the bars	Even worse conduct

'Women as carers' discourse echoes the 'Women as main parents' discourse identified by Sunderland (2004). In this discourse, the task of childcare is mainly that of the mother. In all of Appendix 1(the MP's question), there is no mention of the word 'father', signalling a 'missing discourse' of 'fathers as carers'. As van Leeuwen (1996) observes, certain exclusions could be political and intentional. Here, it could be seen as *intentional* to highlight the representation of a

107

model traditional Cameroonian *woman* since the text was produced shortly after the disturbing (for some) International Women's Day celebration.

In her scripted response to the MP, Honourable Etame, Catherine Bakang Mbock, the Minister of Women's Affairs, discoursally appropriates the role of the woman as *carer*. She is a member of the ruling party (Cameroon People's Democratic Movement), whose manifesto emphasises the role of the woman in uplifting the social and the cultural aspects of the party and the country. (The Minister is herself a wife and a mother as well as a career woman.) The connotative meaning of 'mère' (mother) in the context of the utterance below is 'carer'.

Woman as Wife/Mother/Madonna

In his 'question', I suggest that the Honourable Member of Parliament additionally constructs a model traditional woman as one who should marry and bear children, or at least bear children even if she cannot marry. The default Cameroonian woman is a mother. *Traditionally*, in Cameroon, children are seen as a reason for marriage. After marriage, the general expectation is for children to be born.

The construction of 'woman as mother/wife' within Cameroonian society is dominant. The MP represents women as 'mothers of the world'. He intertextually quotes an expression:

> On a toujours dit de la femme : **'ce que femme le veut, Dieu le veut'**. On a toujours dit que **'la femme est la mère du monde'**, **la femme accouche l'homme, la femme accouche la femme**... Nous sommes chrétiens, **la femme a accouché Jésus**. Nous avons perdu notre identité, nous avons perdu nos coutumes (25-27).

> *It has always been said: 'what a woman wants, God also wants'. It has always been said that* **'the woman is the mother of the world'**, *a woman gives birth to a man, a woman gives birth to a woman...We are Christians;* **a woman gave birth to Jesus**.

'What a woman wants, God wants' is not (despite the rhetorically telling 'always') in fact a familiar expression. Within the context of this speech, it may be read as women can safely do whatever they want - but that is not the rhetorical goal of the MP. What he insinuates here may relate to women's *relative* importance in the society (that is as wives and mothers (including of God)). However, womanhood and motherhood are emphasised by indicating that a woman (and not a man) is the mother to men, women, and Jesus: *'even a woman is the mother of Jesus'*, positioning women as mothers to show how important a mother is, but doing so in a very *conservative* way. What we might call a 'compulsory Christianity' (even 'Catholicism') discourse underlies this motherhood discourse: he underlines the importance of motherhood because *'we are Christians'*. The MP's implied reference to the Madonna could amount to a projection of the association of women with purity, modesty, self-respect and respect for others, and care (e.g. provided to Jesus), by using her as a model. We may also see these allusions and analogies to the mother of Jesus as discoursal strategies to construct a model of a traditional Cameroonian woman - even though the construction of the mother of Jesus is far from a *traditional* construction and representation of a model Cameroonian woman (as pre-colonial traditional 'dress' expose most of women's bodies).

The pure, caring Madonna image may also function as a contrast to women who drink in bars and 'abandon children in bars'. A possible reason why the speaker brings in these particular references, we may claim, is that they 'legitimate' his concerns about the conduct of women. A Madonna-like woman is his model of a Cameroonian woman. Women who went back home after the march past are represented as the *good* women and those who remained in the bars are the bad ones or, implicitly, 'whores' (since presumably, in this discourse, only prostitutes visit bars). This seems to be a 'divide and rule' strategy, constructing a dichotomy for types of women: either a 'whore' or a 'Madonna'. Such a strategy contributes to an oppositional, conservative discourse of women who transgress these values as 'bad women', a conservative discourse also available to women. Women themselves may thus help in reinforcing these stereotypes: it is beneficial for the maintenance of the traditional, conservative social when women see the world this way.

Other speakers in the parliament similarly articulate this discourse of motherhood: in particular, again, the Minister of Women's Affairs in her response to the MP's 'question' (our text). She also constructs women as wives and mothers (although with an educational brief). She articulates this 'traditional' discourse but in a less conservative way, thereby appropriating motherhood and even celebrating it in quite a modern way:

> Ces actions se matérialisent par l'éducation morale et physique aussi bien que les jeunes filles des systèmes scolaires que des femmes. L'éducation sexuel, la maîtrise de la procréation, l'éducation à la vie familiale, rôle de mère, très important, rôle d'épouse également, de gardienne des valeurs social positive et d'agent de développement.

These [positive] actions are materialised by physical and moral education, and also young girls and women in school systems. **Sexual education, the mastery of procreation, education in family life, the role of the mother, very important, and the role of the wife equally,** *the keeper of social positive values and agents of development…*

The 'primary role' of women as mothers and wives is thus emphasised by this female Minister. This may also be interpreted as her appealing to Cameroonian women's presumed belief in this traditional construction of women as mothers and wives as very important in their society. Since however this discourse is articulated within parliamentary genres, we can also see the speaker as strategically manipulating language so as not to alienate the 'questioner' and men (and other women) within her party, and indeed other female MPs and ministers.

It is of course possible to see this dominant 'traditional' discourse not just as a conservative or (and non-'progressive') discourse, but a positive discourse. Motherhood and wifehood have a prime place within this particular society but are also highly valued, seen as good and important within the society. Certainly, we can see this speaker as shifting between subject positions as a woman, a wife, and a minister, trying to negotiate her own different professional and personal identities by 'appropriating' this discourse and critically presenting it in a more progressive way by challenging the very notions of motherhood and wifehood as domestic (she being both mother and wife but *not domestic*). Certainly we should note that her representation of women in such roles is not *negative* at all and she does not ascribe any domestic or subservient duties such as cooking, but rather talks of women playing their roles responsibly. This contrasts with the male MP (Honourable Tasi, see above) who equated motherhood in a metaphorical manoeuvre with cooking and caring for her family. His 'Mother as Carer' discourse compares a minister to a mother (hence a cook) who must cook good food for the children:

> ... the Vice Prime Minister of Cameroon, a seasoned citizen who is holding an important place in this government, ... **you are like a mother** who has cooked food for the children

We see the analogy between 'minister ... holding an important place in this government' juxtaposed through the comparative 'like' with 'mother who has cooked food for the children' (holding an important place in the family). While it is true, in my experience, that most children's food is cooked by mothers (or female relative), what is significant here is that this male MP *selects* this gendered analogy to make his point.

I discuss this construction and representation of Cameroonian women as cooks in the section below.

Women as Family Cooks

Although I discuss this discourse of 'women as family cooks' differently from that of 'Woman as wife/mother/Madonna', it should be noted that these three are closely and intertextually related as seen by their shared linguistic traces. In our male MP's 'question', there are no lexical references to women as cooks (although this is implied in the expectations of women as child carers). However, in the wider data set, there are explicit lexical traces of this (one of the major expectations within the society). Generally, both women and men within the society acknowledge and do not contest these duties and take them as given, that is, there is a missing contrasting alternative discourse here. The speaker of the text is a male member of the main opposition party, the Social Democratic Front. Let us consider again the text repeated below referring to the Vice Prime Minister:

> I crave your indulgence to listen to us as *we take our responsibility*, because **you are like a mother who has cooked food for the children, and your anxiety mama, is to see that they eat.** But my fear is that some of your children will eat and throw up, so you are better off accepting the situation as it is because when the children say mama, let us go back to the kitchen, willing to come and work with you, we do not want to eat and go behind and throw up, because some of us may, because some of us may vomit and die. **And you will be an unfortunate mother.**

This text was produced during the presentation of a bill on the modification of the penal code in the Cameroonian parliament in June 2005. Although the discussion at hand was not 'about' women's duties in any way, the MP draws on this analogy 'you are like a mother' (whose duties are *to cook*) to make a political point. The point in question was diligence in preparing such an important document as the Penal Code. The analogy drawn between the preparation process of this 'important' document and 'cooking for the family' is presumably meant to show that the document does not only serve a few but the whole country, and positions the Minister/committee in charge of that as very 'important' in doing something also very important for the country. If this is not well done, the society, compared to 'children' in the text, will 'vomit', that is, will reject this document. So this minister and his team are positioned as 'mothers' in this context who have to 'cook' something for the country, their 'children': this something has to be palatable otherwise it will make the 'children' 'vomit'.

The extended analogy is very striking, comparing the importance and responsibility of a minister to its people to that of a mother to her children. This analogy is however effective only *because* the discourse 'Women as family cooks' is 'commonsensical and presumptuous' (Fairclough 2003). Again, it belies a missing discourse of family care as *shared* responsibility, with fathers also partaking in cooking family food (and, more widely, being responsible for family well-being, beyond the financial).

Women as Preservers of Culture

Many different MPs and ministers draw in both Q and A sessions and Discussions on the discourse of 'preservation of culture', a case of cross-textual interdiscursivity (Reisigl and Wodak 2001: 37), in line with the post-colonial concern to preserve tradition and culture (Huntington 1996). The discourse of 'preservation of culture' focuses on promotion and preservation of culture and [social and moral values]. Women are seen as guardians of these 'social positive values' in some of these texts.

Culture is very complex but large or small, can be broadly seen as 'shared' beliefs, values, customs, practices and normative 'rules' of social behaviour of a particular nation or people including ways of dressing, producing and also cooking food. Dahl (2006) notes that a culture is learned, shared, patterned, mutually constructed, symbolic, arbitrary and internalised. This therefore means that 'being a Cameroonian woman' is actually learned, shared and internalised and what is constructed as 'our culture' are our *learned* ways of doing things.

Evidence for this discourse is the articulation of an acceptance that although men may not conform to these 'rules of social behaviour', women *will* stick to and police them. Honourable Etame's bone of contention is accordingly (as we have seen) women's practices in public settings (and this implies their attitudes):

> Il apparaît de toute évidence que le premier et seul combat gagné jusqu'à lors par la femme camerounaise est le droit de se déshabiller et de marcher nu en public, le droit de boire en public … nous avons vu des exemples dans la fête du 08 mars. … dès que le défilé est fini, ces femmes sont rentrées dans leurs maisons… sauf les femmes de Sangmelima qui sont rentrées dans les bars. Elles ont abandonnées des enfants dans les bars de… [excerpts from text above]

> *It seems from all evidence that the one and only battle won so far by the Cameroonian woman is the right to* **undress and walk naked in public, the right to drink in public** *… we saw this during the March 8th celebrations…as soon as the march past finished, these women went back to their homes except the women of Sangmelima who* **went into bars**

and his juxtaposed claim that 'we have lost our customs':
  Je demande au MINCOF, est ce qu'il peut faire quelque chose
  pour amener la femme camerounaise à s'exhiber moins et à
  retrouver sa dignité... Nous avons perdu notre identité, nous
  avons perdu nos coutumes. [Excerpts from text above]

  I am asking the Minister of Women's Affairs if she **can do
  something** *to* **bring** *the Cameroonian woman to* **exhibit herself
  less and regain her dignity**...**We have lost our identity,
  we have lost our customs.**

In blaming women for the loss of culture, he puts them at the
forefront of the preservation of culture. He claims that
Cameroonian women essentialised through a singularising
synecdoche, 'la femme' – (the woman),[8] are changing as seen in
their non-conformist social practices. In so doing, he negatively
positions these women as agents of destruction of culture and
positively presents 'we' as the 'sufferers' or patients (van Leeuwen
1996) of women's practices, as in his phrase 'Nous avons perdu
notre identité, nous avons perdus nos coutumes'- *We have lost our
identity, we have lost our customs* (ln 28-29). The pronominal choice of
'we' can be inferred to mean other Cameroonians, perhaps especially
men, 'good women,' and children. In presenting women as destroyers
or preservers of culture, he attributes *'our* loss of culture' to *certain*
women's social practices: the fact that women can apparently
practise any activity implies they are challenging cultural norms. As
such, they are no longer guardians of cultural values.

In articulating the discourse of women as preservers of culture,
the MP is *resisting* what can be seen as a modern counter-discourse
of gender *equality*, dominant in both the UN and Commonwealth
Millennium Development Goals as he subverts it through ironic
use of active verbs such as 'conquerir' (roughly translated as *achieve*
since conquer is a transitive verb), collocating with nouns such as
'egalité (equality), 'l'abolition' (abolish) collocating with 'sévice' -
(violence), and 'augmentation' (increase) collocating with 'nombre
des femmes dans les assemblés' (number of women in the National
Assembly), presented sarcastically and derogatorily, (evident on the
recordings and in my field notes):

114

Au moment présent me semble engagé sur tous les fronts, **pour conquérir** l'égalité des sexes **le droit d'exercer toutes les activités, l'abolition des sévices de tous genres, l'augmentation du nombre** des femmes dans les assemblés (ln 5-7)

At present, **it seems to me that women are engaged in all aspects** *to* **achieve equality of sexes,** *the* **right to practice all activities,** *the* **abolition** *of violence [by men] of all sorts, and* **the increase** *of women in the House of Assembly*

If we take Dahl's (2006) definition of culture as mutually constructed, learned and shared, we may insinuate that 'the culture' referred to by Honourable Etame is that of gender inequality, violence against women, division of labour and women not participation in decision-making – the parliament. He also criticises Cameroonian women for allegedly copying what happens elsewhere 'il n'est pas toujours nécessaire de copier la mode' (it is not always necessary to copy fashion). The quest for the equality of sexes, which is not traditional, is *negatively* juxtaposed with the quest to participate in all (deviant) activities, which include women dressing the way they want and drinking in public, a consequent loss of culture. As such, 'gender equality', a modern discourse, is constructed as an abuse of the culture and a weapon of cultural destruction. Juxtaposing 'gender equality' and these women's represented social practices can be seen as a discursive and rhetorical strategy - the speaker laments later in the text that 'we' have lost our customs and identity (ln 28-29). This loss may be interpreted as a consequence of (at least or closely related to) the fact that women no longer preserve the culture, rather, their current behaviour *conflicts* with the customary demands of social practices. I wish to emphasise here that he excludes men in this project of cultural preservation, implying an unquestioning acceptance of men's liberal (non-traditional) practices.

Other texts within the wider dataset similarly draw on the need to preserve and maintain 'our culture' and suggest that women especially are the preservers of this culture. The female Minister of Women's Affairs explicitly refers to women as preservers of social values (that is, including cultural values):

rôle de mère, très important, rôle d'épouse également, de gardienne des valeurs social positive.

Role of the mother, *very important, equally, role of the wife*, **guardians of positive social values**

This speaker is a woman and perhaps because she is also a politician, she moderates her language strategically so as not to lay the entire burden of preservation of culture only on women. Although she characterises the 'mother' as 'guardian of *positive* social values', she also lays the primary task of preserving the culture on the *family*, which necessarily includes men. She also subverts this discourse of women as 'preservers of *traditional* values' by adding a qualifier *positive* (implying some social values are not positive), and acknowledges the notion of a changing world by using the word 'modern' in promotion of *modern* social and cultural values:

La famille : base de [...] promotion des valeurs sociales et culturelles positives, modernes.

The family: basis... for the promotion of **modern** *social and cultural values*

Women as Modest
For a woman, display is dishonour (Swahili/Fulani proverb)

Modesty relates to humility, quietness, reticence, and not being concerned with self-pride. It is related to the social norms of the society in question and to (women) being (relatively) 'invisible' in public - in particular, not displaying evidence of their sexuality, as this may be perceived as 'flaunting' it. Publically visible women risk being seen as prostitutes; accordingly, the male MP in Appendix 1 indicates in that they bring their woes on themselves:

Je demande au MINCOF, est ce qu'il peut faire quelque chose pour amener la femme camerounaise à s'exhiber moins et à retrouver sa dignité dans les tenues qui la rend belle et respectable plutôt que sexy et désirable, car de cette tendance à vouloir être attirante a tous prix. La femme [...] s'expose aux vices qui sont: le harcèlement sexuel, la prostitution, le pros-élitisme, la pédophilie, (ln 18-23)

I ask the Minister of Women's Affairs what she can do to bring the Cameroonian woman to exhibit herself less and **regain her dignity** *in clothes that* **render her beautiful** *and* **respectable instead of sexy** *and* **desirable**, ... *Women [...] expose themselves to vices of sexual harassment, prostitution, pro-elitism [sic] and paedophilia*

Women's modesty is a focus of this text and related issues raised include public behaviour and dress style. Modesty is an issue because its absence is associated here with loss of culture and identity (though, ironically, traditionally women wore almost nothing). Being 'sexy and desirable' is presented in the text as immodest. This is achieved through the lexical juxtaposition and contrastive use of the words 'sexy' as opposed to 'beautiful', and 'desirable' as opposed to 'respectable'.

Walking 'naked' in public does not literally mean walking 'nude' but, simply, exposing more flesh than social norms require. Women within the Cameroonian society normatively do not expose their legs above the knees, their arms beyond the elbows or their stomach in public. It is possible that the women in question wore clothes that simply exposed their legs above the knee. Such exaggeration, typical of parliamentary debates and part of the rhetoric (see van Dijk 1997, Chilton 2004), is used as a discursive strategy to legitimate the construction of a model traditional Cameroonian woman.

Male homosociality is notably evident in Cameroon in (public) bars, and women's 'intrusion' into these spaces and consumption of alcohol is constructed as lack of modesty, in part because it is commonly considered that women who are prostitutes go to bars (ln 22-24) and 'good women stay at home'. Men in contrast are not constructed as immodest when they drink in bars or run after prostitutes and have free access to public space and uncritical social practices. The speaker refuses to acknowledge a changing world and prefers to stick with his entrenched notions of what a 'model Cameroonian woman' should be.

Conclusion

In presenting an image of a model Cameroonian woman, in which women are constructed as mothers, carers, cooks and preservers of culture and tradition but not men, the speaker of the main text, Honourable Etame, is clearly constructing women as very different from men. He draws on the discourses of 'Gender Differences' and 'Gender differentiated roles as beneficial' (Sunderland 2004), where society is demarcated between men and women with women having specific roles and duties and being expected to behave in particular ways.

In this chapter, I have identified some 'traditional conservative' discourses drawn on by MPs and ministers in the parliament to construct a model image of Cameroonian women, who also identify and criticise deviance from this image. I have examined the dominant discourses of domesticity, modesty and preservers of culture and how they help to create the image of a good Cameroonian woman. While society is changing both culturally and economically, several MPs and ministers can thus be seen to continue to draw on dominant 'traditional' discourses, which legitimate patriarchal control and dominance and sustain male hegemony.

Notes

1. Expressions such as 'A woman's place is in the kitchen' are prevalent even in institutional settings.

2. See Tegomoh (1999) on the case of Mary Bali, a successful Bamenda, Cameroon based business woman who builds a house, buys a car and marries a younger man and suffers the scorn of the society. Her accomplishments as a woman are seen as transgressions because, at that time, she accomplished what previously was masculine. Although things are evolving, such prejudices still exist in the country.

3. In the past in Cameroon, a woman who has few children was accused of eating her unborn babies through witchcraft. Today, that is explained (often incorrectly) through other things such as abortion.

4. Note that what Sunderland (2004) refers to as 'a discourse', Wodak (2001) perceives as a (sub)-topic. Wodak does not explicitly present a difference between 'sub-topics', 'topics' and 'discourse topics'.

5. The Cameroonian constitution was revised in 1996 recognising equal rights, but the 1982 Civil Code has not been revised, and still has clauses which limit women from carrying out certain activities if their husbands choose to limit them.

6. See footnote Error! Bookmark not defined. on the 1981 law on women's right to work (still effective today, although rarely enforced).

7. A 1972 law on prostitution required that all single women in towns who could not be seen as performing any particular job had to go back to their villages, and that women could not go to leisure spots without male companions. This law has not been revised.

8. See Reisigl and Wodak (2001).

Chapter Five

Legitimating 'A Model Traditional Cameroonian Woman'

Introduction

In this chapter, I analyse how MPs discursively legitimate discourses surrounding the notion of 'a model traditional Cameroonian woman'. I identify and analyse strategies used in the *construction* (referential) and *legitimation* (preservative/justification) of 'a model traditional Cameroonian woman'.

These discursive strategies relate to different textual dimensions. As Wodak (2001: 73) writes: as far as the discursive strategies are concerned, that is to say, systematic ways of using language, we locate them at different levels of linguistic organisation and complexity and are concerned in this chapter with

♦ How MPs label and construct men and women within the society through parliamentary discourse (referential strategies) (e.g. van Leeuwen 1996; Wodak 2001; Reisigl and Wodak 2001, van Dijk 2006).

♦ The arguments they use to legitimate their views (e.g. van Leeuwen and Wodak 1999, Wodak and Meyer 2009.

♦ Lexico-semantic and syntactic structuring of arguments (Reisigl and Wodak 2001).

♦ Rhetorical style (through the use of metaphors, proverbs, analogy).

♦ juxtaposition' (sometimes 'divide and rule').

An analysis of *referential strategies* presents the different strategies used to refer to social actors and how they contribute to their construction. Drawing on the negative or positive construction of these social actors, legitimation strategies are employed to legitimate the discourses drawn on in relation to these social actors. These are achieved in part through discursive strategies such as *arguments* which include 'It's the culture', gender differentiation, Moral appeal, Religion, and Geographical difference. Legitimation strategies can also be achieved through Mythopoesis, rhetorical strategies, and Juxtaposition and polarisation. I explain these in each relevant section.

Referential Strategies

Constructive discursive strategies serve to 'build' 'in-groups' and 'out-groups', creating a *positive self-representation* or a *negative other-representation*. This is mainly achieved through reference. In analysing reference, I draw (mainly) on van Leeuwen's (1996, 2009 forthcoming) *representation of social actors* model. Through referential strategies, social actors are seen to be behind every social action and are either included/named or excluded through suppression (complete lack of reference, even implicit of social actors) and backgrounding (where social actors maybe mentioned elsewhere in a text in relation to a different activity or implicit reference to social actors – van Leeuwen 1996: 39). In this section, I examine strategies used by the speaker to refer to social actors (Cameroonian women) as in-groups and corresponding out-groups to negatively or positively present them as model or bad (un)traditional women. It also looks at the suppression, backgrounding and foregrounding of social actions of Cameroonian men and women.`

As observed in the literature (see van Leeuwen 1996, Reisigl and Wodak 2001), referential strategies are linguistic means used to name and refer to social actors positively or negatively. I show more specifically how women are negatively presented in their actions for which they are criticised for being responsible for the loss of culture, and to legitimate the traditional image of a model Cameroonian woman. These strategies discoursally achieve the suppression, backgrounding, or foregrounding of social actors. These include:

- Genericisation/generalisation
- Ethnification/regionalisation
- Collectivisation
- Stigmatisation
- Victimisation
- Agentialisation/Activation

Ethnification/regionalisation, and collectivisation are all related to genericisation and generalisation (see below). Agentialisation/ activation, related strategies are also examined. This is not an exhaustive list but only the most important ones have been identified here. These strategies all relate to social action and here I examine which social actors are activated and referred to as agents (of the social actions), when and how. Are women for example activated and referred to as agents with regard to positive or negative actions? I examine these below.

Genericisation/Generalisation

Although different, these two strategies are related to each other. I distinguish between generalisation where members of a group are treated as homogenous, e.g. women in this case, and genericisation where a member of a group stands for all (see Wodak' 2001 singularising synecdoche). Genericisation and generalisation relate to social actors not being identified or referred to as individuals but 'completely undifferentiated'. It can be achieved through the use of

> collective singulars or 'particularising synecdoche' [which] is typical of stereotypes and prejudiced discourse, in which statements about persons are made in a levelling, generalising, essentialising and eternalising manner, in which groups of social actors are presupposed to be homogenous and are selectively ascribed a specific, allegedly shared, either negative or positive feature, trait, mentality (Reisigl and Wodak 2001: 63)

The strategy thus is used to achieve a wider effect by putting everyone from a social group into the same basket. In our sample text, Genericisation is achieved in a simple way through two different methods:

- Singular noun with a definite article - 'singularising synecdoche' e.g. **'la** femme (camerounaise)', *the (Cameroonian) woman* (ll 8, 19, 22 and 28).
- Plural noun with a definite article - 'pluralising synecdoche' **'Les** femmes (ll 11, 13) (realised in English as 'women')

(Cameroonian) women in these lines are however also *negatively* presented in this essentialising, generalising manner, as if they commit the same acts e.g. 'se déshabiller en public' (undress in public), (ln 9), or 's'expose aux vices' (expose themselves to vices) (ln 22). Also, they are negatively presented in sharing the same demands, which through a sarcastic tone are made to sound questionable, for example:

Au moment présent me semble **engagé sur tous les fronts**, pour **conquérir** l'égalité des sexes, **le droit d'exercer toutes** les activités, l'abolition des sévices de tous genres, **l'augmentation du nombre des femmes dans les assemblés etc.** (ln 5-7)

it seems to me that [women] are engaged in all fronts [aspects], to achieve the equality of all sexes, the right to practice all activities, the abolitions of all forms of violence [against women], the increase in the number of women in the National Assembly, etc.

It cannot be assumed that all Cameroonian women want 'equality of sexes' or all want the number of women to be increased in the parliament or to do all things men do. However, the MP in the text referred to them in a generalising (and thus inaccurate) manner.

When the male MP in the text calls on the Minister of Women's Affairs to do something about *the Cameroonian woman* (ln 29), he is in fact generalising from the 'deviant' practices of women from one locality – 'Sangmelima women' - to all Cameroonian women. In this 'synecdochic' reference, women of Sangmelima stand for all Cameroonian women. To justify the requirement for a general behavioural change/maintenance to preserve the image of a 'model traditional Cameroonian woman', the MP also generalises from these few women to the entire society through the use of 'singularising synecdoche' (Reisigl and Wodak 2001: 56) where the singular stands for the whole. In

[…] le premier et seul combat gagné jusqu'à lors par **la femme** camerounaise (ln 8)

*The first and only battle **won by the Cameroonian woman…***

'the Cameroonian woman' is used *generically* to represent all Cameroonian women. In his 394 word text, the speaker in fact uses the phrase *la femme [camerounaise]* 10 times. Such reference to social actors creates a 'sameness and homogeneity' (Reisigl and Wodak 2001), foregrounding the allegedly negative actions of women in *general* as destroyers of customs. *Generalisation* and *genericisation* are thus, strategies used to achieve a wider effect.

Ethnification/Regionalisation

Closely related, and indeed, a strategy which can be used to generalise, is ethnification/regionalisation (Reisigl and Wodak 2001: 50). In the text, 'deviant' behaviour is identified with women of a particular ethnic group, or region. Ethnification and regionalisation are categories which allow us to see how women are placed according to region[1]- here, (North, West) and ethnic[2] group (Bamoum, Sangmelima). This strategy polarises (and generalises) – here, it polarises and generalises women by positively representing some specific groups and negatively representing others. Although the MP's general argument is that Cameroonian women have changed, he however excludes women from certain ethnic groups and regions from his claims, who, he observes, adhere to the norms and customs of the people by behaving in 'acceptable' ways, and wearing traditionally expected clothes:

> J'ai vu la délégation des femmes de l'ouest qui sont passés avec les pagnes de leur région, les femmes du Nord sont passées avec leurs pagnes, les femmes Bamoums sont passées avec leurs pagnes, et dès que le défilé est fini, ces femmes sont rentrées dans leurs maisons, sauf les femmes de Sangmélima.

> *I saw the delegation of women from the* **west** *who passed wearing the wrappers [sarong] of their region, women from the* **north** *passed with wrappers,* **Bamoum** *women passed with their wrapper, and as soon as the march past finished, these women went back to their homes, except women from* **Sangmelima**

This of course enables him to *negatively* contrast women from Sangmelima with other women.

Table 5. 1   Regional and Ethnic Representation

Positive Representation	*Negative representation*
Women from the West	Women from Sangmelima
Women from the North	
Bamoun Women	

To return to the previous discourse strategies of genericisation / generalisation, ethnification / regionalisation are also used to *generalise* practices of women from one region/ethnic group to all Cameroonian women. Although women from the West of Cameroon and women from the North of Cameroon make up only about 40% of the total female population of the country, the MP still goes ahead to generalise the 'deviant' social practices of women of Sangmelima (even when they constitute less than 5% of Cameroonian women), and *over-generalises* from them to all Cameroonian women through (as indicated above) the use of singularising or pluralising or particularising synecdoche. The MP may be said to be using verbal coercion to protect masculine interests and to maintain male dominion (the status quo) within the society.

Stigmatisation

Stigmatisation is discussed in relation to negative ascription of social actors and social actions. I make a distinction between (the process of) stigmatisation and 'stigma words'. Reisigl and Wodak (2001: 55) for example discuss the use of 'stigma words' e.g. 'nigger' or 'Jew' in the discourse of racism. In this section, I examine how this male MP stigmatises social actors, referring to them not necessarily with 'stigma word(s)', but stigmatised ones. For example, the word 'sexy' is not a 'stigma word' in the Cameroonian society, but here has been stigmat*ised* by the speaker. Stigmatisation, as used in this section therefore, relates to negative ascription, branding, and name calling. It is achieved in part by juxtaposing positive

126

attributes of 'good women' with negative attributes of 'bad women' and negatively presenting others (bad women). Cameroonian women are negatively presented through stigmatisation by listing all their 'unacceptable' characteristics and practices while implicitly branding them as destroyers of culture. If we take for example,

Je demande au MINCOF, est ce qu'elle peut [sic] faire quelque chose pour amener la femme camerounaise à s'exhiber moins et à retrouver sa dignité dans les tenues qui la rend belle et respectable plutôt que sexy et désirable...

I ask MINCOF [the Minister of Women's Affairs] can she **do** *something to* **bring** *the Cameroonian woman to* **exhibit** *herself less and* **regain** *her* **dignity** *in clothes that* **render** *her* **beautiful** *and* **respectable instead of sexy** *and* **desirable**... ln 19-21,

When we examine the choice of verbs, we notice a string of material verbs: '*do* something to *bring* the Cameroonian woman to *exhibit* less' and '*regain* her dignity'; and wear clothes that '*render* her beautiful'. Together, these verbs connote something that has gone bad and greatly need repair —*regain* in particular connoting a return to the status quo. The juxtaposition of good attributes of women to bad ones therefore stigmatises those. There is also the use of the contrastive adverb 'plutôt que' – *instead of,* to stigmatise the 'sexy' and 'desirable' 'bad women' who 'exhibit' themselves. Thus such exhibitionist practices are stigmatised.

If we look at the catalogue of 'malpractices' below, we can identify how Cameroonian women are constructed in this speech. I look at the propositional content of some of the practices below.

    i.   Women *walk* naked in public (ln:8)
    ii.   Women '*stay*' in public (ln:9)
    iii. Women *drink* in bars (ln:9)
    iv. Women *abandon* children (ln:15)
    v.   Women *expose* themselves to vices e.g. prostitution (ln:22)

In i – v the MP explicitly uses these active material verbs to represent the negative practices. i – iii are stigmatised based on (Cameroonian) cultural expectations of women as regards dress code and social practices. The verbs in iv. (abandon) and v. (expose .. to vice) in themselves carry negative connotation within the context of usage. Some characteristics of women are also stigmatised as examined in the propositions below:

  vi. Women *are* sexy and desirable (ln 20)
  vii. Women *are* the cause of the loss of culture (ln 28)
  viii. Women *have* lost their dignity ln 19)
  ix. Women *have* forgotten religious principles/morals (ln 27)

vi - ix refers to negative characteristics that should not be encouraged and that the minister 'should do something about'.

Lastly, women's demands are stigmatised such as:

  x.   Women *seek* equal rights (ln 5)
  xi. Women *want* to be attractive at all cost (ln 20)
  xii. Women *want* to practice all activities [that men practice] (ln 5)
  xiii. Women *want* to increase female representation within the parliament (ln 6)

Lastly, x – xiii represent the things women are still seeking to do (even when what they are already doing is bad). These propositions reflect diverse but conservative expectations of women: political, social, religious and domestic. Konde (2005:37) observes that for men to 'maintain themselves in power and deny access of same to women, the patriarchs of Cameroon devised a culture of restrictions that were imposed on the majority of women'. It is the flouting of these restrictions that result in the stigmatisation of practices, characteristics and demands. Although Konde wrote this in the context of Cameroonian politics in the 1970s and 80s, I think strongly that elements of this ideology still run through the Cameroonian society. In The Cameroonian People's Democratic Movement (CPDM) party constitution (the ruling party and the party of the speaker of the text), one of the objectives of the Women's Wing (Article 47 a. and b., Appendix 6) specifies that the role of women within the party and in the women's movement is to mobilise Cameroonian women in the achievement of the political objectives of the party and to conceive and put in place programmes of a social, cultural and political nature. However, Article 48 of the same constitution spells out that the women's wing is *subject to the main party*. As observed by Konde, then, the women's wing of the CPDM can be seen supporting male MPs in their political ambitions. A demand for an increase in the number of women in the parliament (cf. ln 7) may be seen as challenging the status quo, that is, a male dominated parliament, by undermining male hegemony. It is therefore understandable that (some) MPs frown at women's *independent political* ambitions and *pro-independence* activities, for fear of losing their patriarchal grip on power - hence the negative 'other-presentation' of women in the text and arguments to legitimate the image of *a traditional woman*, one supposedly more controllable and dependent.

In analysing stigmatisation, I found it difficult to represent it as either a constructive strategy or a justificatory one (see van Leeuwen and Wodak 1999, Reisigl and Wodak 2001). Stigmatisation, I suggest, thus serves a dual function: constructing social actors negatively and justifying a change in social actions.

Agentialisation

This is a referential strategy used to negatively present others and legitimate the need for behavioural change - 'nous avons perdu nos coutumes' (we have lost our customs), ln 29. Social actors allegedly responsible for this loss of customs are given agency. Agency is realised through grammatical roles such as [grammatical] subject position, for example, 'the man beat the student, where *man* is an *agent* of the action 'beat' and *student* of the *patient* of the action. Van Leeuwen (1996: 33) observes that sociological agents are not necessarily grammatical agents and sociological patients not necessarily grammatical patients. Agency thus is analysed in the context of social *actors* and social *actions*. In this section, I examine how social actors are constructed as *agents* of those social actions being disapproved. I also examine how other actors in the text are presented as 'patients' of social actions.

Referring to *agency*, Halliday (2004: 164/165 [1985]) states that:
> every process has associated with it one participant that is the key figure in that process, that is, the one through which that process is actualised.... The medium could be self-engendering in which case there is no separate agent, or it is represented as engendered from outside, in which case there is another participant functioning as agent.

Agentialisation thus is achieved through the use of agentive *verbs*. These verbs could be 'self-engendering' as in *the glass broke,* where the action is not caused by an external factor, or *engendering* with another participant functioning as agent. Here there is a material process, as in *he beat the child* (Halliday 2004 [1985, 1999]). In this analysis, I examine agency where the action is engendering with an external participant. Here, there is an 'initiator' to the action, and material process verbs (Halliday 2004 [1985, 1999]) are used.

In the text, *agentialisation* is achieved by presenting 'women' as subjects of active verbs, e.g. '*they* abandon children', where the objects are the patients and sufferers of the actions of these women. Van Dijk (2006:373) describes this as 'local syntax' where the speaker uses active or passive verbs for specific ends. Women here are presented as agents or actors in clauses where they are initiators or perpetrators of allegedly negative practices (Table 5: 2). The speaker manipulates agency to discursively construct men as powerless as regards controlling the effect of women's 'negative practices' (thus unintentionally empowering women!). I look at some examples in the text where social actors are realised as agents or patients of social actions. In Table 5: 2 below, I present the different processes and the main agents and patients of each. We observe that the main actor is a woman. Grammatically, the Cameroonian woman/ women (*la femme camerounaise/ les femmes*) occupy the main subject positions in grammatical roles and are agents of the various actions.

Table 5. 2   Agency in Speech by Male MP, Honourable Etame

Action/Process	Agent	Line No	Patient
Merci monsieur le président de m'avoir donné la parole. *Thank you Mr President for giving me the floor.*	President	3	---
[Il] me semble engager sur tous les fronts pour conquérir l'égalité des sexes *It seems to me that [women] are engaged in all fronts to conquer [achieve] the equality of sexes*	(Implied)Women	5-6	Men (Implied)
Le premier et seul combat gagner jusqu'à lors est le droit de se déshabiller et de marcher nu en public *The first and only battle won so far [by women] is the right to undress and walk naked in public*	Women (Implied)	8-9	Society (implied)
Le droit de **boire** en public *The right to drink in public*	Women (implied)	9	---
Elles ont abandonnées des enfants. *They abandoned children…*	Women	16	les enfants (children)
Est-ce qu'elle peut faire quelque chose pour amener la femme pour s'exhiber moins et à retrouver sa dignité… *Can she do something to bring women to exhibit themselves less and regain their dignity*	Minister of Women's Affairs (do, bring, women exhibit, regain)	19	women
La femme […] **s'expose** aux vices *Women expose themselves to vices*	Women	22	Women (self/engendering)
Est-ce qu'elle peut faire quelque chose *Can she do something?*	Minister of Women's affairs	30	---

In the example below, **they** is grammatically foregrounded and occupies an agentive role, being the sole actor in the clause. Also, the emotive material verb 'abandon' is a transitive verb constructing women as agents with 'enfants' *(children)* as the patients:

Elles ont abandonnées des enfants (ln 15)
They abandoned children in bars

On the other hand, the example below shows the agents are at the same time the patients of their actions. This is achieved through the use of a reflexive pronoun **se** (herself):

La femme fonctionnaire, salarier, étudiante, élève, commerçante, etc., **s'expose** aux vices (ln:20)
The female civil servant, wage earner, student, merchant etc, **exposes herself** *to vices...*

The reflexive pronoun **se** in *s'expose* 'exposes herself' gives women double agency in that clause. Both 'la femme' and 'elle' are of course not only subjects of the sentences above, but also constitute the subject of the discussion. Use of the reflexive also constructs them as 'patients' at the same time as they are the sufferers of their own social actions (self-engendering), that is, it makes women *responsible* for these negative consequences (much as rape victims are sometimes blamed). The actual sociological agents, (that is the rapists for example) of these vices that women are exposed to are suppressed.

Foregrounded is reference to women as agents of *negative* practices (including an implied loss of culture). For example, in ln 9:

Le premier et seul combat gagné par la femme est le droit de se déshabiller et de marcher nu en public, le droit de boire en public

The first and only battle won by the woman is the right to undress and walk naked in the streets and drink in public

Although women in the above sentence are not grammatical agents of the sentence, of the verbs 'drink' and 'walk naked', they are however *sociological agents* as it is their actions that 'cause' such loss of culture.

Activation, a realisation of agentialisation, occurs when social actors are represented as 'active, dynamic forces in an activity' (van Leeuwen 1996:43). In negatively presenting the 'other' in the activation process, e.g. women in the active process of *abandoning* children in bars', patients are constructed *positively* as victims. They are deactivated and thus have no agency in the process of 'destruction' of the culture. The all-inclusive 'our' 'nous avons perdu notre culture' (we have lost **our** culture) calls for sympathy while excluding men as agents of negative actions. Two main groups of actors are presented as patients: *(the children)* and 'nous' *(we)*. This is because women are 'othered'- not really part of the 'us'. *Because* women are no longer there to care for the children, they (children) are abandoned in bars. There is 'common sense' knowledge here that if women are not there for the children, then there is therefore nobody for them. Men (who could logically have looked after the children at this time) are 'radically' *excluded* (van Leeuwen 1996: 38). The entire society is thus constructed as 'patients', emphasising the female care role. The use of the all-inclusive 'nous' and 'notre' are presumably intended to appeal to the entire society, making the problem a general one caused by the 'agents', women. However, women are excluded in this construction since they are the only actors nominated in the social action.

Legitimation Strategies
Legitimation in part relates to how different arguments are used to justify a particular position or point of view aiming at *conserving, reproducing* or *changing* identities (and practices), in this case, traditional and cultural identities. Van Leeuwen and Wodak (1999: 93) observe that strategies of justification (legitimation) attempt to 'maintain, support and reproduce identities'. Legitimacy transcends legality, and legitimation of certain practices or ideologies may not even be based on law (Reisigl and Wodak 2001:205). Legitimation is achieved typically, but not exclusively through argument. Argumentation strategies used by MPs include: 'It's the culture', Gender differentiation, Moral Appeal, Geographic differentiation and Religion. Other legitimation strategies include Mythopoesis (van Leeuwen and Wodak 1999:110), Rhetorical strategies and Juxtaposition.

Argumentation

Argumentation is concerned with rationally or logically convincing or persuading the reader or hearer to accept one's perspective (see Reisigl and Wodak 2001:70). The relationship between *legitimation* and *argumentation* is so close knit that it is difficult to separate the two concepts. However, legitimation is largely but not exclusively achieved through argumentation.

As Reisigl and Wodak (2001: 74-75) observe, within argumentation theory, legitimation of discourses can be achieved by means of topoi. Topoi, they note, are

> parts of argumentation that belong to the obligatory, either explicit or inferable, premises. They are content-related warrants or 'conclusion rules' that connect the argument or arguments with the conclusion or claim. They justify the transition from arguments to conclusion.

Central to the notion of topoi is thus the 'conclusive' aspect of arguments. Arguments are thus presented to legitimate the explicit or implied (desired) conclusion, and are 'conclusive' in themselves. Eemeren, Grootendorst and Kruiger (1987:65) also observe that arguments can be referred to as *topos*, where a topos is 'the *place* (their emphasis) from which the attacker can get his [sic] arguments'. Of course arguments are made with the assumption that the individuals concerned or groups share the same values, for the arguments to succeed. As Eemeren et al observe, 'the audience must agree with the point of departure which the speaker chooses for his argument and it must accept the argumentation schemata employed by him [sic]' (1987:65). Litosseliti (2002: 131) similarly sees arguments as 'a connected series of statements intended to establish a position (whether speech or writing), sometimes taking the form of an interchange in discussion or debate, and usually presenting itself as a sequence or chain of reasoning'. In discourse analysis, she sees arguments as a 'context situated 'battle' between discourses'.

Table 5. 3 Argumentation Strategies

Argument	Topoi (summary of the MP's Arguments)	Example
'It's the culture': (Reisigl and Wodak 2001)	Because it is *our* identity and culture, and we need to preserve it	Nous avons perdu notre identité, nous avons perdu nos coutumes *We have lost our customs and identity*
Gender differentiation (Myself)	Women are different from men and so should not want to do things men do	Il apparaît de toute évidence que le premier et seul combat gagné jusqu'à lors par la femme camerounaise est le droit de boire en public *Women have won the battle to drink in public [as men]*
Moral Argument (Litosseliti 2002)	It is not morally right for women to expose their bodies in public or expose themselves to prostitution	amener la femme camerounaise à s'exhiber moins et à retrouver sa dignité dans les tenues qui la rend belle *...bring the Cameroonian woman to exhibit herself less and regain her dignity in the dresses that make her beautiful.*
Religion (Reisigl and Wodak 2001)	Christians should not behave in certain ways especially women	Nous sommes chrétien, la femme a accouche Jésus. *We are Christians, a woman gave birth to Jesus*
Geographical differentiation (Myself)	We are Cameroonian women and so should not copy what European women do	Car un adage de chez nous dit ceci : 'qu'il n'est pas toujours nécessaire de copier la mode *A saying from our [culture] says this: it is not always necessary to copy fashion [from Europe]*

In order to negatively present [contemporary] Cameroonian women, reproduce and legitimate the 'model traditional Cameroonian woman, the MP condemns their social practices based on a number of arguments: culture and tradition, gender differentiation, moral appeal, religion and geographical differentiation. In the next sections, I examine these strategies. In the table above, I summarised how the MP's arguments construct Cameroonian women in terms of their political, social and moral behaviour including associated topoi.

'It's the Culture'

After having constructed 'traditional model Cameroonian women' as 'preservers of culture' (see chapter 4), Male MPs legitimate these constructions by drawing on the discourse of 'It's the culture' as an argument to legitimate the maintenance of traditional values. I define culture as a way of life for a given society. Culture may also be defined as beliefs (shared), customs, practices, and social behaviour of a particular nation or people. It creates meaningful contexts in which activity takes place (Roseberry, 1989). Culture as defined by Verhelst (1990) embodies

> every aspect of life: know-how, technical knowledge, customs of food and dress, religion, mentality, values, language, symbols, socio-political and economic behaviour, indigenous methods of taking decisions and exercising power, methods of production and economic relations (Verhelst, 1990).

It is both socially constituted (it is a product of present and past activity) and socially constitutive. Verhelst claims culture permeates and influences every aspect of life (see also Parsons and Shills 1990), it is not static but a process in a constant state of flux and adaptation to new contexts, demands, and needs. Parsons and Shills also note that 'traditional' cultural knowledge developed within a particular spatial and temporal 'context' or 'environment' as a dynamic process continues to change as people cope with new challenges and adapt to changing conditions. In a nation such as Cameroon faced with change and globalisation, conflicting ideologies and beliefs therefore emerge. Drawing on the discourse of culture as a legitimation strategy suggests 'culture' is 'good' and so can't or shouldn't be changed (although this is not possible), and thus we should maintain 'our identity' in the face of post colonial 'erosion' of 'our customs'.

These conflicting ideologies concern freedom and equality between the sexes, morality and freedom of action, equal access and equal participation in the public sphere, and women's emancipation. They have an impact on what the speaker terms 'customs' (conceptually related to culture)[3]. The speakers refer to 'nos coutumes' (our customs), that is, our way of doing things, 'our tradition', thus implicitly legitimating the rejection of change, because change leads to a 'loss' (of male dominance?) – 'Nous avons perdu notre identité, nous avons perdu nos coutumes' (We have lost our identity, we have lost our customs).

Although practices such as women drinking in bars are more common now in Cameroon, this in itself does not *justify* the fact that, culturally, for many, women *should* (be able to) drink in bars. The speaker is likely to be aware of public opinion on such matters, especially the opinions of the older generation, which can be illustrated by the quote from a newspaper article where an old woman frowns at the behaviour of her granddaughter and comments 'If this is what emancipation means, then women rather not be emancipated'. The speaker, I suggest, exploits this popular belief. He knows that the older generation of Cameroonians corroborate his ideas on the preservation of culture (even if it means discriminating against women). That is why he can justify his construction of a model/traditional Cameroonian woman through the topos of culture.

In her interesting response to the text quoted in chapter 4 (Honourable Etame's speech), the Minister of Women's Affairs backs up the position of women as preservers of culture:

> **La famille** ...cadre d'éducation à la base des enfants, **de promotion des valeurs** sociales... **des femmes de telle région sont rentrées chez elle, et tels autres ne sont pas rentrées chez elle, ce sont les valeurs culturelles positives** que doit...doit perpétuer par la famille. **Il s'agit donc de la promotion des valeurs sociales et culturelles positives**, modernes, pour développer le goût de l'effort, le goût du travail bien fait, le goût du respect de l'autre, de l'excellence sur tous les plans (FA1:94-101)

The family…setup of basic education for children, for the promotion of social values… **Women of such and such a region went home, and such and such women did not go home, these [i.e. the former] are positive cultural values** *that should be perpetuated in the family. These are therefore the promotion of modern, positive social and cultural values to develop the taste of effort, the taste of a job well done, a taste of respect of others and excellence at all levels.*

In the above extract, the female minister, also uses the topos of culture to legitimate the construction of 'a model Cameroonian woman'. She reaffirms the fact that women who went home (immediately after the celebrations) practice 'positive cultural values'. But her reference to culture *additionally* take note of the notion of modernity, making room for change. The use of the phrase *'modern, positive social and cultural values'* legitimates cultural change as long as (we can infer) this change is away from a repressive culture. Further, the loss or gain of positive values, and adherence to culture, are not ascribed only to women but to the *family*, an inclusive discoursal strategy where men are *included* in the preservation of culture. As such, modern 'positive [cultural] values' encourage respect for *all* others.

Thus, although the male MP uses culture to justify the need for Cameroonian women to remain as traditional as he and part of the society expect. Elsewhere, this topos is justified more in terms of *positiveness* of the traditional culture rather than conservative and possibly repressive cultural values. The focus is on the preservation and promotion of culture in terms of promoting it. References to the promotion of culture can be found in many different texts produced both by ministers and MPs during parliamentary sessions. Questions by two MPs focused on promotion and preservation of culture and an *Answer* to a question from a Minister also focuses on that. Elsewhere, an MP asks the Minister of Communication what the place of (Cameroonian) culture is in the national media. He questions why the national media does not preserve culture by promoting it through radio and TV programmes. He also blames the media for promoting the consumption of foreign culture through films, music and other radio and TV programmes at the expense of the Cameroonian culture.

Nous avons 300 tribus avec un patrimoine culturel diversifie et riche dont seul votre Ministre devrait conduire ces activités en faveur de la promotion de la culture nationale. Je ne suis pas encore satisfait, mais mon inquiétude concerne principalement les danses et les musiques traditionnelles ainsi que les chorales. Les danses traditionnelles et les musiques religieuses présentées sur les antennes de la télévision nationale sont peu diversifiées alors qu'il en existe une grande variété dans nos villages. Les équipes de reportage de la CRTV semblent manquer de bonne volonté de dynamique et même de moyens pour des rendre dans ces zones rurales (MQ6 : 653-661).

*We have **300 tribes with a rich and diversified cultural heritage**. Only your ministry can manage these activities in favour of **the promotion of the national culture**. I am not yet satisfied but my principal worry concerns traditional dance and music as well as choral music. There is little diversification of traditional and choral music shown on television when there exist a wide variety in our villages. CRTV [Cameroon Radio and Television Cooperation] seems to lack the good will and even the means to reach these rural zones*

Although not indicated directly in the above text, it is implied that there is under-exploitation and lack of promotion and consequently no preservation of the Cameroonian culture. We thus observe the topos of the preservation of culture in the above text. In the same vein, Honourable Adamu Ndam Njoya questions the Minister of Culture about why 'our rich cultural heritage is not being exploited in terms of 'moral values'. He argues that Cameroonian culture can help to cultivate positive 'moral and native values'. Such values he claims may help to reduce corruption.

Culture may be seen as a 'grand narrative' (Baxter 2003) in the legitimation of discourses on the construction of a model traditional Cameroonian woman. This is because several strategies to legitimate the discourses about 'model traditional Cameroonian women' draw on this discourse/argument of 'It's the culture'. However, I would argue that however 'positively' appeals to preserve traditional culture are made, appeals to 'culture' will always be problematic in the achievement of women's equality in cameroon. The maintenance or reconstruction of the 'model traditional Cameroonian women' is I suggest, legitimating gender discrimination and male dominance.

Gender Differentiation

The topos of 'Gender differentiation' relates to discourses that construct women as desirably different from men in terms of practices which have implications for the way they are represented within discourse (see Sunderland 2004, Baxter 2003). As Sunderland observes, gender differentiation tends to be seen as normal and unproblematic and often not associated with disadvantage. However, I use the phrase here to include discourse which articulates or takes for granted in particular, a gender division of labour/roles. The topos of 'gender differentiated roles are beneficial' is key in the representation of a 'traditional/model Cameroonian woman'. As observed by Konde (2005), this discrimination or division of roles and duties along gender lines has been necessary in order for men to maintain the power relations between men and women. Gender division of labour is therefore essential for the sustenance of male supremacy. A change in the status quo is accordingly threatening to gender and power relations. It is evident from the text that women changing and taking up practices that were exclusively male is a key issue for the speaker and apparently for the community. Gender roles traditionally ascribed to women were centred around the home and in serving fathers, husbands and children. That women are apparently abandoning these duties/roles and taking up new ones such as being active in politics, and even asking for equality, are differences from before, as highlighted in the excerpt below:

> Au moment présent me semble engagé sur tous les fronts, pour **conquérir** l'égalité des sexes, le droit d'exercer toutes les activités, l'abolition des sévices de tous genres, l'augmentation du nombre des femmes dans les assemblés etc. (MQ1: 4-9)

> *At the present, it seems to me that [women] are engaged at all fronts to conquer [the battle] of equality of sexes, the right to practice all activities, the abolition of violence of all sorts, the increase of the number of women in the National Assembly etc.*

The speaker explicitly notes the fact that there is a difference between the social situations of the two sexes. It is not clear whether or not he advocates the maintenance of this situation. However, he gives a negative and divisive presentation of the efforts of women to bridge this gap, claiming that women are *engaged in a battle to conquer.* We should note the use of the word conquérir (to conquer) as opposed to *gagner* - 'to win', signifying a worthless battle. 'Conquerir' also connotes a lot of effort to defeat an enemy (although not named in the text).

The MP uses 'gender differentiation' as a legitimating strategy, selectively ascribing certain roles and functions to a particular sex and criminalising / stigmatising the activities of the other. In *Cameroon Tribune,* this selective strategy is echoed by a female journalist in the excerpt below:

> 'From time immemorial, women have been considered the weaker sex. Biological, physical and even social reasons are used to justify the assertion. However, this whole perception might soon be put to question following the **"manly" attitude of some women... Drinking in bars is no longer the reserve of men.** Our daughters, sisters, aunties and mothers drink and heavily too. Some smoke ... just like some men do... **"If this is what emancipation means, then women rather not be emancipated", one old mother said (with tears in her eyes)** (*Cameroon Tribune* July 13th 2006)

Although the author of the article does not seem to question emancipation, here, she however uncritically reflects the ideas of 'an old mother'[5] (definitely not of the generation of those seeking emancipation) who, like the MP, does not approve of gender equality. 'Emancipation' is a selective term and carries here a negative connotation when equated with women's social practices especially related to drunkenness. Such a selective strategy is similar to that used by the MP in presenting women's practices. 'Gender differentiation' arguably serves men's interests and legitimates their freedom and dominance. Masculine practices are not judged in the text above but when women want some freedoms, it becomes an issue, and problematic. What is *selected* as of interest for public consumption by a social actor may be to satisfy the different interests of the different generations functional within this society (see van Leeuwen 1996 on *exclusion* and *inclusion*). This older woman (who is 'apparently in tears at the situation') confirms discourses of gender as difference, and of men as free (to drink and get drunk) and women relegated to the private sphere. Men's own social practices – drinking and dressing in public are suppressed in the text and no mention is made of them. This exclusion is strategic in criminalising women, even when, as indicated, men also have deviant social practices.

Moral Appeal

The notion of morality ties in with societal and cultural values. It is concerned with what is regarded as wrong or right (see Litosseliti 2002). This is always complex and the notion of morality is always subjective. In a society caught between tradition and modernity, it is particularly difficult to define what is morally right or wrong, even within one setting or community of practice, in part because what is considered proper or decent in one generation could be considered to be morally wrong by another (or vice versa). There is always change, each generation usually seeing the next as more deviant than the previous. Since the late 20th century, for example, Cameroonians have had the propensity to copy foreign practices (especially from watching TV). Different individuals and generations often look to different 'authorities' e.g. 'the culture', the church, for moral guidance, and globalisation plays a role here. There are also differences between rural and urban areas – villages and cities.

Litosseliti (2002) observes that moral claims can be expressed, sustained or challenged from certain moral *positions*. Different groups articulate different positions and the meaning of morality is continually being challenged and contested.[6] In the text under study, the speaker sees *traditional* morality as being challenged (by women) through some social practices he sees as unacceptable.

As van Leeuwen and Wodak (1999: 108) observe, moral argument can be achieved discursively through a 'straightforward description of what is going on (here the MP telling the story of women's social practices) rather than an explicit formulated legitimatory argument'. The mechanisms of moralising may also include the 'discourse of values' (van Leeuwen and Wodak (1999: 108) relating to culture, for example). Below, I examine some lexical traces of social practices which the MP sees as inappropriate, appealing for change in the moral behaviour of these members of the society.

These traces include negative evaluative phrases such as: 'se déshabiller en public[7]' (to undress in public), 'marcher nu' (walk naked); 'boire en public' (to drink in public), others include: 'rentrées dans les bars' (went into bars), plutôt que sexy' (rather than being sexy), '[et] désirable', and 'être attirante' (being attractive). The above traces are all morally evaluative arguments, appealing for public maintenance of the status quo.

An apparent lapse in morality may actually have a *symbolic* function here with minor changes implying greater change in gender and power relations within the community in general. If this is the case, the only way then for traditionalists to sustain or maintain their grip on women is to condemn the new practices and try to legitimate the old ones through moral arguments, rather than argue for gender equality and freedom.

Requesting for women to regain their dignity in the text suggests a loss of moral values:

> …Amener la femme camerounaise à s'exhiber moins et à retrouver sa dignité dans les tenues qui la rend belle et respectable plutôt que sexy et désirable, car de cette tendance à vouloir être attirante a tous prix. (MQ1: 19-22)

> **…bring the Cameroonian woman to exhibit herself less** *and* **regain her dignity** *in clothes that render her beautiful and respectable instead of sexy and desirable, for there is the tendency to want to be attractive at all costs.*

The arguments are made with the presupposition that the audience share the same moral values (e.g. women should not 'exhibit themselves'). The target audience are generally members of the speaker's generation and gender and are likely to agree with his argument since they share the same moral and traditional values. The speech is therefore an appeal to reinstate moral values, a strategy to construct a perfect image of a model/traditional Cameroonian woman.

We should note the juxtaposition of *beautiful and respectable* against *sexy and desirable*. One cannot apparently be beautiful and sexy at the same time nor simultaneously respectable and desirable. These qualities thus polarised. A closer look at these words suggests connotations of conservatism and responsibility of the first pair and a sense of freedom and independence of the second, the second also being a threat to existing power relations between men and women. Being sexy and being desirable gives a measure of *power* to women, that is, control over their sexuality. Although these words are uttered in a political context (where men have more power), they are indicative of how much power and control men may feel they are losing in the new social sphere. Moral arguments thus justify these claims in the construction and representation of the 'model traditional Cameroonian woman', an idea they have been used to. Van Dijk (2006:359) observes that by invoking a traditional ideology, 'our good things' and 'their bad things' are emphasised. Moral appeal reproduces the inequality between men and women and therefore can be seen as conservative and repressive, as issues like women's freedom (say, to have a drink in a public place) are considered immoral. The articulation of discourses of morality is indicative of the conservative nature of a male-dominated society, when men still want complete control over women and their activities. 'Appeal to morality' I suggest, is based on ideological differences especially due to global changes affecting traditional practices within the Cameroonian society in relation to contemporary ones.

The Minister of Women's Affairs similarly dwells on the preservation of moral values, this time explicitly, with lexical traces as shown below:

...Le président de la République... lutte contre... la pauvreté morale.

The President of the Republic **fights against moral poverty**

and

...de sensibilisation et de **promotion des valeurs morales** et sociales positive ainsi que celle de protection de la femme contre les déviances sociales. Ces actions se matérialisent par l'éducation morale et physique aussi bien que les jeunes filles des systèmes scolaires que des femmes

144

...the sensitisation **and the promotion of positive moral** *and social values as well as the protection of women against social deviances. These actions are* **materialised through moral and physical education** *as well as young girls and women in school systems.*

The Minister's direct reference to moral issues is a response to the complex ones raised by MPs. She reclaims the notion of morality positively by arguing for the 'promotion of *positive* moral values', through moral education of young girls and women. Education in knowing what is good and what is bad can help Cameroonian men and women to be selective for example in what they copy from the internet.

Le renforcement des capacités des femmes en matière de l'utilisation rationnelle optimale et positive des NTIC, en les mettant justement en garde contre les effets néfaste des NTIC

The reinforcement of women's capacities in the rational, optimal and positive use of ICTs, by protecting them against the negative effects of ICTs.

Religion

'Religionisation' is an argument identified by Reisigl and Wodak (2001: 50), and used in their analysis of racial discrimination. This refers to the use of 'religionyms' (terms of reference) such as 'Christ', 'Jews', 'Muslims'. In Reisigl and Wodak's account, religionyms are used in the discourse-historical approach to exclude/include and justify racial discrimination, and to name and represent social actors either as in-group members or out-group members. Below, I examine a religious argument more in relation to social actions, where it is used to justify particular moral (non-)actions and the representation of an ideal Cameroonian woman. Christianity itself is a colonial/post-colonial discourse (thus not indigenous – traditional) but used here conservatively to legitimate a construction of a model traditional Cameroonian woman.

Cameroon is a pluralistic country, and the MP chooses to use not only a Christian icon but a key Roman Catholic one to support his argument. He assumes his audience understands the symbol and 'personality' of the Virgin Mary, and that they accept this as *positive* (which many may not).

145

On a toujours dit de la femme : 'ce que femme le veut, Dieu le veut'. On a toujours dit que 'la femme est la mère du monde', la femme accouche l'homme, la femme accouche la femme. Nous sommes chrétien, la femme a accouche Jésus. Nous avons perdu notre identité, nous avons perdu nos coutumes

What a woman wants, God wants. It has always been said, the woman is the mother of the world. A woman gives birth to a man; a woman gives birth to a woman. We are Christians. A woman gave birth to Jesus Christ. We have lost our identity, we have lost our customs

In the text above, we see close reference to religious terms – 'God', 'Jesus', 'mother of Jesus', 'Christian'. Non-Christians within the parliament are thus effectively excluded. He therefore proceeds to use 'Her' as an ideal image of a Cameroonian woman, although, paradoxically, this is contradictory. He is using a Judeo-Christian icon to portray a *model, traditional* Cameroonian woman within the context of culture and tradition, but this image or icon is not indigenous to Cameroon and is far from representing a perfect image of a *model traditional* Cameroonian woman. The MP therefore, uses a religious and a (post)colonial discourse (see Huntington 1993) to legitimate tradition. His legitimation of the construction and representation of a model Cameroonian woman could thus be said to be a reconstruction of a 'model (non)-African Catholic woman'. Just as Reisigl and Wodak's (2001) identification of the topos of religion to *discriminate*, I argue that religion is used in this context to project masculine hegemony and feminine modesty. The mother of Jesus Christ, a woman, is seen as a symbol of femininity and morality by Catholics, and the MP does not hesitate to draw on this comparison to legitimate his claim that Cameroonian women should look up to her as a moral model. His next phrase after this reference: 'nos avons perdu notre identité, nous avons perdu nos coutumes' (We have lost our identity, we have lost our customs) may imply he is looking up to this figure as a model.

Geographical Difference

What I call the topos of 'geographical difference' has not been used within the discourse-historical approach although related arguments such as *ethnification* and *nationalisation* have been (Reisigl and Wodak 2001: 50). Legitimation through geographical difference here refers to national and world geography. This topos is employed when the speaker juxtaposes or rather polarises the North against the South, presenting one region as 'good' and the other as 'bad'. Using the strategy of geographical difference to legitimate positive social practices, the speaker polarises the north of Cameroon with the south and also the Northern Hemisphere with the Southern Hemisphere. While the North of Cameroon represents maintenance and preservation of cultural values, the northern hemisphere (western world) represents loss of these values.

I begin with the polarisation of 'Nord' (North) Cameroon (Figure 5.1) with the South, where the north is constructed as symbolising purity, tradition, moral uprightness, and of course 'good' women. Women of the 'south', that is, women of Sangmelima, are represented as non-conformist. They do not conform to traditional norms and practices. By juxtaposing the geographical north[8] of Cameroon with the geographical south, the speaker argues that women from the north conform to traditional norms and practices whereas women of Sangmelima (south) do not. This is indicated through nomination of national geographical regions with reference to good and 'bad' practices.

> J'ai vu la délégation des femmes de **l'ouest** qui sont passés avec **les pagnes** de leurs régions, les femmes du **nord** sont passées avec leurs pagnes, les femmes **Bamoums** sont passées avec **leurs pagnes**, et dès que le défilé est fini, ces femmes sont rentrées dans leurs maisons, sauf les femmes de **Sangmélima** (laughter...) qui sont rentrées dans les bars.

> *I saw a delegation of women from the west who passed with their wrappers [sarongs] of their regions, women from the north passed with their sarongs, Bamoum women passed with their sarongs, and as soon as the march past finished, these women went back to their homes, except the women of Sangmelima [...] who went into bars.*

The speaker thus nominates the different regions of the country in terms of positive and negative presentation with regard to social practices.

Figure 5. 1   Regions of Cameroon Showing Sangmelima

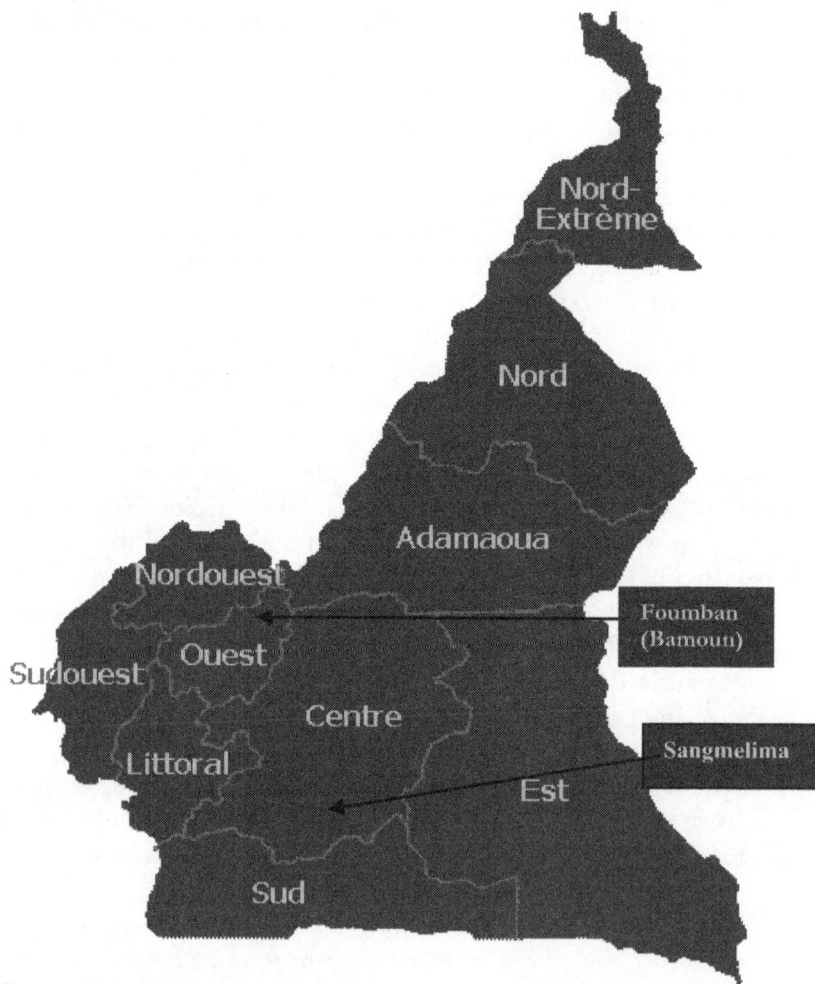

Figure 5. 2   Geographical Representation of Cameroonian Women

▪ North→ Good, where North	➡ 3 Northern Regions→ Essentially Muslims
▪ West→Good, where West	➡ North West and West Regions→ Bamilike and Grassfielders, both Christians and Muslims
▪ West→ Good, where West	➡ West Region→ Bamoums- Essentially Muslims
▪ [South]→Bad, where South	➡ Centre, South and Littoral Regions→ Sangmelima, Essentially atheist and Christians

In the speaker's argument on *National* geography, that is, the geography of Cameroon, the 'north' is used to symbolise moral uprightness and preservation of traditional values. In the above representation, religion is relevant although not made salient by the speaker. The north consists mostly of Muslims, whose culture is to cover up, whereas the south is mostly Christians, who are more liberal with their dressing. Also women of Bamoum are Muslims, perhaps why they belong to the 'good' group.

On the other hand, the northern *hemisphere* (Europe and America) does *not* signify moral uprightness and maintenance of traditional values but rather corruption of these values. Cameroonian women are criticised for copying 'negative' practices (from elsewhere). When the speaker says, 'Car un adage de chez nous dit ceci: "qu'il n'est pas toujours nécessaire de copier la mode"' (Yet one of our proverbs says: it is not always necessary to copy fashion), speaking from a parliamentary setting, the phrase 'chez nous' may be read to signify *Cameroon*. He does not say from where or from whom this fashion is being copied. However, as a Cameroonian, and an African, I read it to mean 'the West' (Europe and America) because I know that women copying western style is, frequently, problematic to

149

Cameroonian men (see footnote 50 and 'it's the culture' discourse). Although the text includes no explicit references to other geographical locations, its implicit reference to what happens elsewhere is key. By making such utterances as 'il n'est pas toujours nécessaire de copier la mode' (it is not necessary to copy fashion), the speaker is referring to western dress styles, which he implies do not suit Cameroonian women, though for cultural and ideological reasons.

This interpretation is supported when the Minister of Women's Affairs, in response, interdiscursively draws on the topic of 'geographical difference' to criticise the MP's view, arguing that the world is a global village. As such, she challenges the argument based on geographical difference in the construction of 'good' and 'bad' women'. The MP's assessment is thus subjective and selective: with my knowledge of the culture and the people, I read this as advocating certain modes of dressing and not others. The emphasis here is not on decency in terms of body coverage but rather geographical origin of the fashion. Yet, this construction of western fashion as negative is thoroughly partial and gendered because *men* generally wear clothes designed in Europe and elsewhere, and styled like those clothes won by men in Europe, again, we see women as being positioned as the 'guardians' of culture.

The implicit construction of the northern hemisphere against the southern hemisphere within the data can be represented as follows:

Figure 5. 3   (World) Geographical Discursive Construction of Social Practices

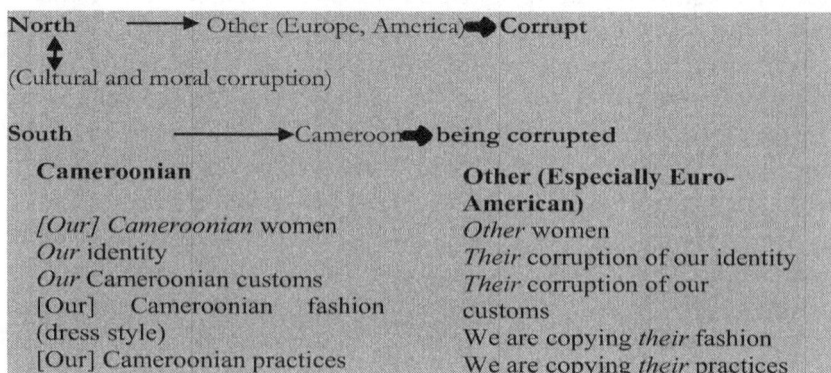

North ——→ Other (Europe, America)➡Corrupt

↕

(Cultural and moral corruption)

South ————→Cameroon➡being corrupted

Cameroonian	Other (Especially Euro-American)
[Our] Cameroonian women	*Other* women
Our identity	*Their* corruption of our identity
Our Cameroonian customs	*Their* corruption of our customs
[Our] Cameroonian fashion (dress style)	We are copying *their* fashion
[Our] Cameroonian practices	We are copying *their* practices

The use of the collective pronoun 'our' serves to represent 'us' and 'others,' *our* ways and *their* ways. The *'our'* pronominal serves the function of assimilation and inclusion (Cameroonians and our culture) (see van Leeuwen 1996: 49) and exclusion of others and their culture. Highlighting only women's changed social practices thus may be associated with the discourse of women as 'preservers of culture', and consequently, with 'maintaining' traditional culture, a very conservative discourse. Notable also is the emphasis on the kind of dress women from these 'model' regions wear: 'elles ont passé avec leurs **pagnes'** (they passed with their wrappers [a sarong-like garment]). This particular dress style is particular and traditional to Africa South of the Sahara. Anything different is seen as imported from the western world, and thus not traditional.

Using the strategy of geographical difference to legitimate his claim for 'the preservation of our culture through the maintenance of traditional values by women', the ideological 'west' is representative of deviance. In his terms, it is inconceivable for Cameroonian women (to want) to emulate women of the 'west' in terms of behaviour. Using nationalist and ethnic ideologies, the speaker constructs 'our' *culture, identity* and *values* as under attack from the 'west' through its influence on change in various social practices which affect especially children, men and some women and which are perpetuated by some (deviant) women.

Mythopoesis

Van Leeuwen and Wodak (1999:110) describe *mythopoesis* as legitimation through the *telling of stories*. Two types of tales can be told: moral tales and cautionary tales. In moral tales the hero follows socially legitimate practices while in cautionary tales, 'the hero(es) engages in socially deviant behaviour that results in an unhappy ending' (Van Leeuwen and Wodak 1999:110). In the study, we see evidence of a cautionary tale. The speaker presents his characters - women of Sangmelima - as potential heroes in the story of the March 8 events. These heroes however are presented as practising socially deviant behaviours which results in the *abandonment* of children (and, more widely, possible loss of culture).

151

Mythopoesis as a legitimation strategy is achieved here linguistically through the art of narrative. The speaker uses the first person in his narrative and gives an 'eyewitness account' of what he saw and claims is negative:

> **nous avons** vu des exemples dans la fête du 08 mars hmmm où les femmes quand elles ont défilé. *J'en ai* vu à Sangmélima ou les femmes on défilé, les femmes avaient leur pagne du 08 mars. **J'ai vu** la délégation des femmes de l'ouest qui sont passés avec les pagnes de leurs régions, les femmes du Nord sont passées avec leurs pagnes, les femmes Bamoums sont passées avec leurs pagnes, et dès que le défilé est fini, **ces femmes sont rentrées** dans leurs maisons, sauf les femmes de Sangmélima (laughter…) qui sont rentrées dans les bars. **Elles ont abandonnées des enfants dans les bars** de ' la radio équatoriale' (MQ9-16)

> *We saw examples during the March 08 festival, hmm where women were marching. I saw it in Sangmelima where women marched; women had their March 8 wrappers [sarongs]. I saw a delegation of women from the west who passed with the wrappers [sarong] of their region, women of the north passed with the wrappers of their region, Bamoum women passed with the wrappers, and as soon as the march past finished, these women went back to their houses except the women of Sangmelima [...] who went into bars. They abandoned children in the Radio Equatorial Guinea bar*

In this extract, we see elements of story telling: there is a narrator, narrating from his perspective – using a first person point of view. The story has protagonists, there is a plot, and there is a conclusion. The speaker is narrating the events of March 8th 2004 to members of parliament, is telling them a story with women as protagonists. These protagonists are presented negatively and their actions have negative consequences, which he presents. He sums up these consequences in a regretful tone, the consequences being:

a) abandoning children l.16
b) women being sexually harassed and raped l.22
c) paedophilia l.22
d) loss of identity l.29
e) loss of customs l.29

This story is thus a *cautionary tale* resulting in an unhappy ending. In narrating such stories, the speaker presumably aims to present a vivid picture of the negative social practices of women. He negatively presents 'the other' by cataloguing the negative consequences in order to justify his point that we are losing our culture and women are at the centre of is destruction. This strategy also serves to justify the need to maintain and sustain 'our' 'traditional' practices which constitute 'our identity and customs.' The moral of the story' is thus that (model) women should therefore desist from such un-cultural practices.

Rhetorical Style

Rhetorical style is a strategy which relates to the skill of using language effectively and persuasively, enhancing the seriousness of the matter (van Dijk 2006: 378). In this text, it is achieved with the use of hyperbole, emotions, metaphors, proverbs, analogy, and word play. This particular discursive style has been little referred to in discourse analysis. In fact, only bare reference has been made to it (see Wagner and Wodak 2006). However, I observe the use of this strategy for different effects in the representation and construction of a 'model traditional Cameroonian woman'. Lee and Lin (2006) do however identify a similar rhetorical strategy they call *epideictic rhetoric* in their analysis of newspaper editorial discourse and self-censorship. *Epideictic rhetoric* focuses on 'meting out praise, blame or censure for contemporary actions and issues' (Lee and Lin 2006). In meting out blame, the MP exaggerates using *hyperbole*. I examine this below.

The MP in the text uses the strategy of exaggeration is employed through *hyperbole* to present practices he does not agree with and also to negatively present others and positively construct the image of a model Cameroonian woman. For example, when he says 'the first and only battle won by Cameroonian women is the right to undress and walk naked in the streets', we know that these women did not literally walk naked. They were simply dressed in a relaxed style which he finds 'offensive' or 'untraditional'. Also, he states that women 'abandoned children in bars'. He can't possibly have known what childcare arrangements the women made but it seems obvious that this has been exaggerated to suggest the extent of the problem and seek for sympathy to justify his claim that women's social practices are not benefiting the community. The efforts of women are also mocked and their 'successes' stigmatised through the use of negative hyperbole. After enumerating the different battles women are apparently involved in, it is stated that the only battle won so far is the right to 'walk naked in the streets and drink in public', 'le Premier et seul combat gagné par les femmes est le droit de marcher nu en public et de boire en public'. This is evidently not true as the MP knows, and as shown by the Minister of Women's Affairs in her response to this text. This use of hyperbole could be seen as indicative of the MP's fears. Through such exaggeration, he uses what van Dijk (2006: 379) describes as 'emotional appeal' in both manipulating and legitimating his appeal for 'model traditional Cameroonian women'.

Use of *emotions* is another rhetorical style used by the MP in the text. When he appeals to members of parliament and the public of the negative consequences of poor dressing and drinking habits and in particular the neglect of children, the MP is using emotional appeal to legitimate and justify the need for Cameroonian women to be *traditional* because not looking after children properly is a terrible thing.

The use of *metaphor* is also employed by the MP, Honourable Etame, especially war metaphor, to illustrate the determination of women to 'conquer' inequality:

> Au moment présent me semble **engagé** sur tous les fronts, pour **conquérir l'égalité** des sexes le droit **d'exercer** toutes les activités, **l'abolition** des **sévices** de tous genres, l'augmentation du nombre des femmes dans les assemblés etc. Il apparaît de toute évidence que le premier et seul **combat gagné** jusqu'à lors par la femme camerounaise est le **droit** de se déshabiller et de marcher nu en public, le droit de boire en public

> *At present it seems to me that the [women] are **engaged** at all **fronts** to **conquer** the equality of sexes, the **right** to practice all activities, the **abolition** of all forms of violence, the increase of the number of women in the parliament etc. It seems in all evidence that the one and only **battle won** by the Cameroonian woman so far is the **right** to undress and to walk naked on the streets, the right to drink in public.*

154

The MP presents women as waging a war against an unnamed enemy. He himself does not point to anything like 'men' or 'patriarchal structures' or repressive traditions, a notable *absence* (see van Leeuwen 1996 on 'exclusion') though all these maybe *implied*. He uses war metaphors such as 'engager', 'conquerir', 'exercise' (as in practicing activities women have been previously excluded from), 'combat, and 'gagner'. This image is also captured by lexical traces such as 'abolition' collocating 'violence', 'conquer', 'battle', social inequality and lack of freedom to practice all activities and political misrepresentation (increase in the number of women in parliament) all also collocate. However, the *tone* of the text as suggested by my field notes is that of an *MP in Power* who sees women's fight for equality as not worthwhile, a basis for his claim. His use of this war metaphor may be read as creating the impression of a big effort for a small thing, which is not even worthwhile. Although he presents women as fighting a war, he may also be construed as fighting back by arguing for a change in practices (perhaps since this 'success' is threatening male hegemony).

Using *Proverbs* is another form of rhetorical style and is very effective in the Cameroonian and African society. Chinua Achebe observes that, 'proverbs are the palm oil with which words are eaten' (Achebe 1958). Proverbs, though they serve as analogies, are sometimes believed to be 'true' by the community using them; they are mostly spoken in formal and quasi-formal settings, generally to caution, instruct and advise. Although both men and women use proverbs within the Cameroonian community, observation suggests men use them more to indicate a mark of wisdom and status within the society. Proverbs are a preferred part of rhetorical style amongst older people. While they serve as words of caution and advice, they sometimes aim to summarise what is to be said in a few words. Using this strategy, the MP quotes:

> Car un **adage** de chez nous dit ceci : 'qu'il n'est pas toujours nécessaire de copier la mode mais de porter ce qui te va'. On a toujours dit de la femme : 'ce que femme le veut, Dieu le veut'. On a toujours dit que 'la femme est la mère du monde'.

> *An adage in our [culture] says: 'it is not always necessary to copy fashion but to wear what suits you'. It is always said of a woman that 'what a woman wants, God wants'. It is always said that 'a woman is the mother of the world'.*

155

These three proverbs expressed in the excerpt above are all used analogously to legitimate his representation of a 'model traditional Cameroonian woman'. Through these proverbs, women are positioned as superior in some limited sense ('mothers of the world') (see also the topos of religion), implying that women demean themselves by carrying out certain (non-maternal) practices. The use of proverbs as a rhetorical strategy (bearing what is socially accepted as truth) implies that women are important within certain constrained spheres *and* should not abuse this position with deviant social practices.

Selective lexicon and *Local syntax* are other discursive rhetorical strategies proposed by van Dijk (2006). A *selective lexicon* relates to selective choice of words to negatively present others and positively present self, and includes some social actors and actions and suppresses or backgrounds others through absences – 'missing' social actors and actions (see van Leeuwen 1996: 38). In the data, selective lexicon is evident through the use of words with a strong negative connotation. The association of words such as *war, conquer, battle,* and *win,* with negative practices such as walking *naked,* drinking in *public* and *abandoning children in bars; and* women who 'expose themselves' collocating with *'prostitution', 'sexual harassment',* all selectively present negative effects of women's pursuits. Similarly, *children, our customs,* and *our identity* are presumably also selectively used to draw sympathy and legitimate. Honourable Etame's choice of words then is not *random* or even balanced but highly selective to suit his purpose. He did not include the role of men, for example in child care, nor did he seek to find out the reasons why women are fighting battles in the first place.

Non-presentation of counter - arguments is a further rhetorical strategy used here by the MP. Not presenting any counter-arguments allows social actors to emphasise only their own arguments and viewpoints while effectively suppressing others. This relates broadly to Van Leeuwen's (1996) notion of *suppression,* but of counter-arguments rather than social actions and social actors achieved through absences within the text. Counter-arguments which could have been brought into the text (perhaps than to be challenged) such as these have been strategically suppressed:

♦ If men drink in bars, why should women not also do the same?

- ◆ Why is it only women who should take care of children and not men?
- ◆ Why is the preservation of tradition and customs only the task of women?

The Honourable Etame could have brought in all these, with the purpose of 'destroying' them, but did not. Worth mentioning is also is complete related lack of reference to (that is, absence of) *man, men* or *fathers* in the text, nor is there any reference to the duties or the role of men within the society. Also note the suppression of expressions such as

- ◆ Sangmelima women went into bars to drink **with** *m*en
- ◆ **Men were not at home** to take care of children

(which would have 'justified' the 'abandonment' claim). Men are thus suppressed through non-presentation of the above arguments, and their role in the social actions concerned – childcare and drinking in bars suppressed.

As observed by Chilton (2004) and van Dijk (1997), the rhetorical style is an aspect of parliamentary discourse and MPs are engaged in a 'battle' of arguments and counter arguments. As Walsh (2001) also observes, the very nature of parliament discourse itself, and also the physical presentation (e.g. of the UK parliament) connotes confrontation. It is therefore unsurprising that, Honourable Etame confronts the Minister of Women's Affairs using such a rhetorical strategy.

Juxtaposition and Polarisation

This is another strategy to achieve positive self-presentation and negative other-presentation. Juxtaposition occurs in the text when the MP puts lexical items, phrases and even paragraphs in contrastive but adjacent positions to achieve certain effects. He does this by polarising 'good' practices with 'bad' one and 'good' social actors with 'bad' one. Juxtaposition and polarisation work *together* when positive self-representation (through positive attributes) is juxtaposed with negative other-representation (through negative attributes) to polarise 'good, model traditional Cameroonian women' with 'bad, deviant' ones. In particular:

- Lexical juxtaposition: belle/sexy (beautiful/sexy); respectable/désirable (respectable/desirable); North / [South] Sangmelima
- Juxtaposition of *Noun Phrases* – Les femmes du Nord / les femmes de Sangmelima ;
- Juxtaposition of *Verbal phrases :* 'Ces femmes **sont rentrées dans leurs maison'** / les femmes de Sangmelima …**sont rentrées dans les bars**
- Juxtaposition of paragraphs: written text contains two main paragraphs: one presenting the bad practices of women and the other the image of a model woman. This is reflected in the spoken version by change of tone and change of style. The first paragraph draws on the narrative style (telling a story), and the second paragraph on cautionary tone (advising women).

Within this analysis, juxtaposition serves to *polarise* negative and positive (traditional) social and moral values. Practices such as 'going home after events' and 'staying in bars to have a drink' are polarised, and women from different regions of the country are similarly juxtaposed and polarised with each other, representing women from certain regions as better than women from other regions as (indicated above). It places side by side 'good' and 'bad' social practices such that the difference between them can be highlighted to serve the purpose of the speaker. Putting side by side extreme practices implying 'if it is not good, then it is bad', with no middle range positions, serves to legitimate specific social actions and delegitimate others, in this case, a 'model traditional Cameroonian woman' and a modern deviant one (the familiar angel/whore discourse, gendered, but only for women). This strategy makes constant use of opposites within the legitimation process.

In Table 5.3, I summarise the different discursive strategies discussed above, effective in the construction and legitimation of the discourses about 'a model traditional Cameroonian woman'.

Table 5.4 Summary of Discursive Strategies for the Legitimation of 'A Model Traditional Cameroonian Woman'

Author	Strategy	Linguistic Means	Examples from Data	Translation
Reisigl & Wodak 2001, Wodak 2004, van Leeuwen (1996) (Partly myself)	**Referential**	Deictics	Nous, Nos, Elles, Ces femmes	We, us, they, these women
		Collectives	Les femmes, des enfants, les étudiants	Women, children, students
	Genericisation/ Essentialisation	Generic nouns: plural or singular with a definite article (singularising synecdoche)	Les femmes camerounaises, nous sommes chrétiens	The Cameroonian woman
	Ethnification/ Regionalisation	ethnonyms	Les femmes Bamoun, femme du Nord, femme de Sangmelima	Bamoum women, women from the North, women from Sangmelima
	Stigmatisation (Myself)	Negative other presentation	Les femmes [sont] sexy et désirables	women [are] sexy and desirable
	Agentialisation/ Activation	Subjects of active verbs Active verbs	Les femmes…sont rentrées dans les bars. Elles ont abandonnées S'exhiber, S'exposent, Amener	Women went back into bars, they abandoned children Exhibit, expose themselves, bring

Table 5. 4   Summary of Discursive Strategies for the Legitimation of 'A Model Traditional Cameroonian Woman' (Contd)

	Legitimation Argumentation			
Reisigl & Wodak 2001, Wodak 2004	Gender as difference (Myself)			
	Moral Appeal			
	'It's the culture' (Myself)		Nous avons perdus nos coutumes	We have lost our customs
	Appeal to religion Myself		Nous sommes chrétiens	We are Christians
	Geographic differentiation (Myself)		Femme du Nord, femme de Sangmelima [femme du Sud]	
Van Dijk 2001, 2006	**Rhetorical**	Hyperbole	Le droit [...] de marcher nu en public	The right to walk naked on the streets
		Metaphors	Conquérir, combat gagné	To conquer, battle won
		Proverbs (Myself)	Ce que femmes veut, Dieu le veut	What a woman wants, God Wants
		Word Play		

Table 5. 4 Summary of Discursive Strategies for the Legitimation of 'A Model Traditional Cameroonian Woman' (Contd)

	No counter arguments		
	Lexicon	Negative lexicon	Prostitutes, drink in public, walking naked,
	Local Meanings	Many/few details	Few details about men's activities
	Local syntax	Passive/active sentences	They abandoned children…
Other legitimation Strategies	**Juxtaposition/ Polarisation**	**Myself**	Femmes de Sangmelima vs. other women

Some of the strategies have been previously identified in literature and are noted within the first column of the table. I present the source of the strategy (from literature or identified within this study), linguistic means, and example from the data. Ones newly identified are not marked by any reference and are indicated in Column 1 and 2. Bold fonts are the 'macro-strategies' (see van Leeuwen and Wodak (1999) while regular font (same column (2)) are the 'sub-strategies' of these macro-strategies. Also empty spaces on table are a result of strategies whose examples cannot be represented within the table. However, these have all been discussed in the analysis.

Conclusion

In this chapter, I have identified and analysed some discursive strategies used to construct and legitimate discourses of a perfect model of an ideal Cameroonian woman identified in Chapter 4. In this way, I show not only what male and female MPs talk about, and the *quantity* of their talk (see Chapter 3), but also some telling discourses *about* women (and thus available to speakers), and how various representations of women are achieved.

The Referential strategies identified and analysed include Genericisation/Generalisation, Ethnification/Regionalisation, Stigmatisation, and Agentialisation while legitimation strategies included arguments such as *'It's the Culture, Gender Differentiation, Moral Appeal, Religion,* and *Geographical Difference.* Other legitimation strategies examined within the chapter included Mythopoesis, Rhetorical Style, and Juxtaposition and Polarisation. Some of the strategies identified have been used in literature, for example, ethnification and regionalisation (see Reisigl and Wodak 2001) and others have been newly identified such as 'Geographical difference, Gender differentiation and Juxtaposition within the analysis. Discursive strategies identified within the discourse historical approach have been found valuable in analysing the legitimation of a 'model traditional Cameroonian woman'. However, within the analysis of this text, there was a need to identify new strategies to explain some legitimation processes.

In the next chapter, I set out to identify *counter* discourses to the traditional ones analysed in this Chapter. While the previous speaker constructs women as normatively domestic, and guardians of culture and in many ways and subordinate (to men), I show how women can resist and challenge such constructions by drawing on available new 'progressive' discourses of change, gender equality and women's empowerment. In Chapter 6, then, I identify some of these 'progressive' discourses, again using one key text, analyse how women and men are constructed through these discourses, and how the Minister of Women's Affairs legitimates them through different discourse strategies.

Notes

1. Cameroon is divided politically into regions and these regions are named geographically, e.g. North, West, and South (see map on Fig 5.1).

2. Cameroon has more than 250 ethnic groups (see 1.2.1), amongst which are the Bamoums mentioned in the text.

3. In the dataset, I observe that culture is used in a sociological sense to generally refer to customs and traditions of the Cameroonian people.

4. Use of this excerpt corresponds to the DH-CDA approach which advocates cross-text intertextuality, with documents outside the data incorporated into the analysis (see Wodak 2001).

5. Note choice of words: 'mother' and not 'woman'. Mother here connotes compulsory heterosexuality. Note also the use of the word conquérir (not gagner), signifying a worthless battle.

6. See also Baxter (2003) on non-fixity of meaning generally.

7. In Cameroon, there is a prime ministerial text banning women from wearing trousers to certain government offices including the Prime Ministry and the Ministry of Finance. Note also the traditional costume in the late 19th and early 20th century where women covered only their genital areas. This is still practiced during some traditional ceremonies today and it is therefore problematic to see such modern dressing as immoral.

8. Politically the northern and western Regions are: the Far North, North, Adamawa, West and North West Regions. The Centre, South, and Littoral are considered southern Regions. The Far North, North and the Adamawa Regions constitute the Grand North of Cameroon.

Chapter Six

Modern 'Progressive' Gendered Discourses in the Cameroonian Parliament

Introduction

In this chapter, I identify and analyse *modern* 'progressive' gendered discourses in the Cameroonian parliament and how they are 'legitimated'. Analysing discourse as 'modern' or 'traditional', and as 'conservative' or 'progressive' is setting up a binary as discourses can only be described as conservative or progressive from a particular standpoint. From a CDA perspective, this is almost inevitable as the analyst has to take a political stance – one which often supports the oppressed. I see modern, 'progressive' discourses as new discourses that challenge 'patriarchal' values, opening up the possibility of and advocating *improvement* in conditions of the disadvantaged group, here, women. 'Progressive' gender discourses in doing so aim at countering (negative) discrimination against women, for example, in employment and education. 'Progressive' discourses articulated seek to challenge normative masculine thinking in Cameroon

In this chapter, I examine these progressive gendered discourses, discursive strategies (legitimation strategies) and the arguments presented to constructed and justify gendered practices. I also examine how social actors intensify or mitigate their utterances as regards power relations.

Legitimating 'progressive' discourses within this chapter will be viewed from a 'modern feminist' perspective, although 'the feminist' ideology here does not draw fully on western feminism, but an African one (see Atanga et al. 2010 forthcoming), which accepts certain aspects of African/cameroonian culture. I examine interdiscursivity to show how speakers draw on discourses of others to either counter them, or to legitimate their own discourses. I also analyse interdiscursivity to show the pervasiveness of a discourse within the parliament.

The Data

The data for this chapter is mainly drawn from the speech of the Minister of Women's Affairs, Madame Catherine Bakang Mbock (see Appendix 2). This was produced in a Question-and-Answer Session June 2004 in response to the speech by the Honourable Etame François (see Appendix 1). I have selected this text as the primary text for analysis in this chapter for two reasons: first, because it is a response to the primary text used in Chapters 4 and 5 (Appendix 1), which questions women's 'battles' for gender equality and increase of women in the National Assembly, and women's social practices as a whole, and is thus properly contextualised. Secondly, I choose the text for its contrastive, positive, modern 'progressive' gendered nature. However, although I use the text as the key text for analysis in this chapter (following the discourse-historical tradition ; see Wodak, 2001), I also intertextually draw on discoursally related texts and material from the Cameroonian parliament during the period within which this text was recorded. I also draw on other texts outside the data.

In the following sections, in accordance with the discourse-historical approach, I present the historical and sociological contexts of the modern 'progressive' discourses identified and gender relations in Cameroon and link these to the public/political sphere and in particular the parliament of Cameroon. I interdiscursively show some current tensions between modern concepts, behavioural patterns and traditional practices. After identifying and naming a key macro-discourse of 'Positive Action for Women', I then proceed with the identification and naming of the discourses (sub-topics) about 'Positive Action for women', traces of which are, I will show, evident in these parliamentary debates. I also show how these discourses are intertextually related, and also aspects of wider interdiscursivity. The Question and Answer genre within parliamentary discourse means that the Minister, Madame Catherine Bakang, (re)articulates discourses drawn on by 'questioner' (Appendix 1) and re-contextualises them as she interdiscursively draws on them. She also, I argue, *appropriates* some of them (Sunderland 2004: 30) in what can be seen as a progressive way.

Modern 'Progressive' Discourses: Context

I identify some available 'progressive' gendered discourses, starting with two macro-discourses which can also be seen as 'overarching' discourses. These are 'Positive Action for women' and 'Gender partnership'.

'Positive action' may mean 'positive discrimination' or 'affirmative action' with regard to the promotion of women in the society. However, currently in Cameroon, there is some positive action for women, but no positive discrimination, as there isn't any legislated quota system (for women). Positive action is meant to promote and encourage women and create equal opportunities (for women and men) in community policies and activities. Positive action is designed and indeed, I suggest, needed to counter overt, non-subtle discrimination against women based on traditional patriarchal practices within a given society – at least, in the short term.

Constant reference by the Minister (author of the text) to women's *promotion* and *elimination of all forms of discrimination* against them in the Cameroonian parliament triggered my identification of this macro-discourse, these being traces of it. Also, other traces include the lexical items *modern* and *positive*. Like other discourses, Positive Action can be identified through such linguistic traces, like consistent use of certain lexical items, collocations, and presuppositions. With regards to presuppositions (see Fairclough 2003; Norrick 2001), I identify what Sunderland (2004: 29) calls 'informed insights' and 'shared assumptions'. All these traces provide 'warrants' (Swann 2002) for my identification of these discourses.

The macro-discourse of 'Positive Action for Women', has, I suggest, been interdiscursively drawn in a large part from the Beijing Declaration (1995) and the UN Millennium Declaration (2000) which are both concerned with Positive Action in their focus on women (and which themselves indirectly draw on modern discourses of women's empowerment prevalent since the late 1960s). The Millennium Development Goals (MDGs) (see below) have increased the public understanding of the need for positive action for women. The MDGs[1] are to:

1. eradicate extreme poverty and hunger
2. achieve universal primary education
3. promote gender equality and empower women

4. reduce child mortality
5. improve maternal health
6. combat HIV/AIDS, malaria and other diseases
7. ensure environmental sustainability and
8. develop a global partnership for development (quoted from www.un.org/millenniumgoals)

All these goals have either direct or indirect implications for women and for gender relations, and I examine the specific implications of these goals below.

Ways of 'seeing the world' or 'thinking about it' change over time and *new* discourses – including more 'progressive' ones - emerge accordingly. Lexical cues for Positive Action for Women and Gender Partnership from my close paraphrase of the MDGs above include 'promote', 'empower', 'improve', 'poverty', 'partnerships', 'development', 'girls' and 'women' evident in the goals above collocate syntagmatically are also abundant in my own data. In particular, they include

♦ *promotion* ...de la *femme camerounaise APP 2: ln 22, 27, 41, 57, 102, 103,*

♦ *promotion du genre, le partenariat homme/femme, APP 2: 27*

♦ *l'amélioration* de la vie de la *femme camerounaise. APP 2: 22*

♦ *la femme connaît ... une évolution ascendante qu'il convient certes ... APP 2 : 25*

♦ *d'améliorer ... dont les signes positifs s'observent à travers les actes quotidiens FA: 24*

♦ *partenariat homme/femme, APP 2: 17, 27, 43*

♦ les *partenaires au développement* afin *d'engager des femmes APP 2: 53*

♦ La lutte contre les *IST/VIH/SIDA APP 2: 115*

I recognised the Macro-discourse of Positive Action from various linguistic traces – forms of 'marks on [the] page' (Talbot 1995: 24) through to 'repetition' (Fairclough 2003: 124). The above lexical and syntactic traces (noun phrases, verb phrases and adjectival phrases) therefore cued what looked like a macro-discourse of 'Positive Action for Women' and associated topics and discourses.

Context: Political Developments Surrounding Gender in Cameroon

Following the requirement of the discourse historical approach, the wider socio-historical context of the discourse needs to be analysed. The link between gender and political relations and gendered discourses need to be analysed. Discourse and gender relations need to be studied against the background of the Cameroonian society, as well as the governmental (parliamentary) viewpoint. I indicated the impact of the creation of a women's ministry in Cameroon and events which helped shape gender issues in Cameroon, particularly the United Nations' Fourth World Conference on Women in Beijing in 1995 and the 8 Millennium Development Goals (MDGs) in 2000 (see above). Here, I examine how the 8 goals are specifically related to women's issues in Cameroon.

1. To eradicate extreme poverty and hunger: Mostly women are poor due to lack of education, land rights and lack of employment opportunities.
2. To achieve universal primary education: Achieving (only) primary education does not improve the lot of women greatly. Good jobs are mostly available to graduates and postgraduates[2].
3. To promote gender equality an empower women: This third goal focuses directly on 'gender', 'equality', 'empowerment' (see below).
4. To reduce child mortality: is directly linked to gender (childcare and parenthood are associated with womanhood, see chapter 4).
5. To improve maternal health is again directly linked to women's issues (many women die from childbirth, and childcare is generally the direct responsibility of women[3]), Child mortality and maternal mortality are most times related to poverty.
6. To combat HIV/AIDS, Malaria and other diseases: Again related to the 4th and 5th goals are the 6[th.] The effect of HIV/AIDS and malaria are felt mostly by women and sex with an HIV positive partner also results in risks of pregnancy, high maternal deaths and also child mortality

7. Goal number 7 on environmental sustainability may seem not to affect women, but mostly women carry out subsistence farming (in Sub-Sahara Africa) and are most affected by environmental degradation. Thus the preservation of the environment has the greatest impact on the lives of women as they greatly depend on land for subsistence.
8. The development of a global partnership is a macro goal which relates to international cooperation; it impacts on the day-to-day lives of women through various projects.

The third goal is the most important as it concerns most Cameroonian women and tends to encompass all the other goals. The full MDGs were not as such the focus of any parliamentary debates in my data. However, government ministers and MPs intertextually draw on the discourses associated with them as will be shown in this chapter.

Cameroon has signed a number of conventions about discrimination against women including the 1951 convention stipulating equal remuneration of wages for both men and women doing similar jobs ratified in 1970; the 1953 convention on the political rights of women; and the CEDAW (Convention for the Elimination of all forms of Discrimination against Women) in 1979. The government even created a Ministry of Women's Affairs in 1984, and much more recently, the Cameroon Poverty Reduction Strategic Paper (2003) recognised gender equity in the country. These however have only minimally reduced discrimination against women and male dominance within the society. Forms of discrimination include political, economic, legal, social and cultural discriminations (CEDAW Cameroon Report 2000[4]), although most discrimination within the system is more de facto than de jure. Although there are some available legal responses to discrimination, the lack of a legal definition of discrimination and its very general characterization in the Criminal Code means acts of discrimination cannot always be identified, let alone dealt with (see Ngo Som 2000).

Politically, few women are appointed to positions of responsibility and there are none in some positions like governors of regions[5]. While there are no laws that discriminate against women in political life, women continue to be under-represented in decision-making circles (as illustrated in Chapter 3). Between 1960 and 1999, the percentage of women in the parliament rose from 0.8 to 14.5. However, since 1992, the percentage of women in the multi-party assembly actually dropped sharply from 26 (14.5 per cent) to 10 (5.5 per cent) in 1997 (see **Table 6. 1**), 11% in 2004/2005, the period of data collection. This decline is due to small numbers of women being nominated, people not voting for women, the failure of some political parties to include women in electoral lists (Ngo Som 2000), and more so the de facto system in place, which is also suggested by own findings (see Chapter 3) of women's relative and disproportionate silence.

Table 6. 1   Percentage of Women in the National
              Assembly since 1960

Year	Number of members	Number of women	Percentage of women	Remarks
1960-1965	137	1	.8	Assembly of federated states
	50	2	4	Federal Assembly
1966-1970	141	2	1.4	Assembly of
1970-1973	137	5	3.6	federated states
	50	2	4	Federal Assembly
1973-1978	120	7	5.8	Single chamber:
1978-1983	120	12	10	one party system
1983-1988	120	17	14.2	
1988-1992	180	26	14.5	
1992-1997	180	23	12.8	Single Chamber: Multiparty system
1997-2002	180	10	5.5	Double Chamber (Functional
2002-2007	180	20	11.11	Single): Multiparty system
2007 -	180	15	08.3	

Source: *Cameroon Tribune* **No. 6644 of 21 July 1998. [2002-present, myself].**

This failure to appoint women to positions of responsibility also arguably has a part to play in maintaining and perpetuating stereotypes about women in decision-making positions, that is, that women are not good at decision-making: generally emotional, not rational, and accordingly better suited as wives and mothers, their place being at home.

Post-Beijing Gender Issues in Cameroon:

In this section, I look at gender issues after 'Beijing' in 1995, issues of gender equality, the representation and construction of Cameroonian women, and the work of non-governmental organisations in the fight for gender equality.

During the 1995 United Nations' Fourth World Conference on Women, 189 member states unanimously agreed to the Beijing Declaration and Platform for Action, committing themselves to ensuring women's equal access to, and full participation in, power structures and decision-making. Cameroon was one of these 189 countries. More than 10 years down the line, however, there is little achievement in Cameroon. The Cameroonian government and the National Assembly in particular appear not to have taken their commitment seriously as little is done to achieve them: gender mainstreaming,[6] which is practiced in other countries, is not evident. Some Scandinavian countries such as Sweden and Norway (see van de Ros 1994, 2005), some EU countries (see Wodak 2003) and some African countries (Ghana, South Africa and Rwanda for example) in their mainstreaming policies insist on gender quotas in their parliaments. Table 6.1 indicates that there is no mainstreaming in the Cameroonian parliament and the quantitative analysis of female representation in political parties and volume of talk in Chapter 3 of this book confirms this. Some members of parliament rather make a joke of all these goals, especially those relating to gender equality. Members of the public and even members of parliament still discriminate in discourse against women, for example, in the name of 'culture' (see MP's claim that 'we have lost our customs' App 1, ln: 28). Male hegemony is thus evident despite the ratification of international protocols and conventions and even national strategic papers. And as I have shown, attempts by members of the public to practice or institute gender mainstreaming are often

172

seen as deviant and against the culture (see Chapters 4 and 5)[7]. There are still material, non-subtle issues such as:

- education (fewer women in higher education in the southern regions of Cameroon and low girl-child enrolment in the North of Cameroon)
- female circumcision has not been legislated against
- domestic violence against women (legitimated through bride price and culture)
- forced marriages (child brides still prevalent)

Women's voices in Cameroon are marginal and they still have to fight to overcome gender discrimination both in the formal and informal sectors. In the private sector especially, there is discrimination in employment as employers complain about absence of women during maternity leave. Some women, especially those working in the private sector do not have the benefits for fear of losing their jobs. Women who are promoted to positions of responsibility have a double 'burden' as added to their jobs, they still carry full responsibility of the house work. However, there are some voices which contest and resist these gender discriminatory practices legitimated through a patriarchal culture, and fight for positive action for women, hence this chapter.

Against this background, I present and analyse the macro-discourse of what I call 'Positive Action for women' based on assumptions of the desirability of women's promotion generally and gender equality. I examine how men and women are constructed against the background of change and global processes. I also look at the tensions in the Cameroonian parliament between these 'progressive' discourses of women's promotion, gender equality and the empowerment of women, and more traditional discourses.

'Positive Action for Women'

'Positive action' could be viewed as aiming at countering discrimination against minorities and in this case women. It may or may not include positive *discrimination* (e.g. when making a job appointment or increasing the number of women in the parliament). 'Positive Action for Women' can be identified as a modern, 'progressive' overarching macro-discourse advocated through discourses such as 'Women's Promotion', 'Women's Protection', 'Women as Agents of Development' (see Awasom 2005), and 'Elimination of all forms of Discrimination'. I consider 'Gender partnership' as a macro-discourse, as on its own, there are many other discourses. An analysis of discourses relating to Positive Action for Women shows how women construct themselves and are constructed linguistically by others.

The overarching macro-discourse of 'positive action for women' is evident in different parliamentary sessions largely through women explicitly pointing out issues requiring positive action for women. The Minister of Women's Affairs draws extensively on this macro-discourse. Other female parliamentarians take up the issue of positive action in different parliamentary sessions. I provisionally identify and name the discourses in this chapter following Sunderland (2004). Discourse identification and discourse naming are done in part through a range of linguistic traces. The figure shows that these discourses all overlap and interdiscursively draw on each other. Some of the discourses tend to articulate others, for example, 'Women's promotion' articulates 'Women as decision-makers' in its traces. However, each discourse, though overlapping with the other is so strongly articulated that each is analysed differently. The same discourse is evident in different texts and genres within the wider dataset - hence the need for an analysis of intertextuality and interdiscursivity.

'Women's Promotion'

'Women's Promotion' tends to encompass other discourses and could be seen to be (almost) synonymous to 'positive action'. 'Women's promotion' relates not only to the promotion of women to higher positions of responsibility, but the general and total promotion of women in all aspects of their lives, that is, in the different areas inter alia education, economics, and politics leading to their general empowerment in the society. The main lexical cue to this discourse is the word 'promotion' in association with *women*. The Minister of Women's Affairs refers to 'la promotion de la femme (camerounaise)' (promotion of Cameroonian women), 'la politique de promotion de la femme' (the politics of the promotion of women) through state instruments such as the constitution, and the promotion of women in areas such as education, and an increase in the number of women in the parliament (see APP 2: ln. 22, 41, 52, 53, 65, 115). 'Promotion' directly collocates with 'women' - for example, App 2, ln.22: 'la promotion ...la femme camerounaise', ln.115: 'de promotion de la femme'. Promotion *also* collocates with *'genre'* (gender) equates with elevating women to equal status with men (thus a promotion), for example, ln.27: 'la promotion du genre' (the promotion of gender). The lexical term 'promotion' is also found in the text to collocate with 'positive moral and social values', e.g. ln.109 'promotion des valeurs morales et sociales positive'. As well as 'promotion' functioning as a lexical cue for this discourse, the Minister also articulates the phrase 'renforcement des capacités – *the reinforcement of (women's) capacities* (1.29). She also draws on women's promotional discourses and discourses of 'gender sharing' intertextually from the international scene as I show below.

This large excerpt from the speech of the Minister of Women's (Appendix 2) shows her articulation of the promotion of women discourse:

> ... l'implication directe et personnelle du chef de l'état, son excellence Paul Biya dans la **promotion** et **l'amélioration** de la vie de la femme camerounaise. A ce titre, faut-il le rappeler, la femme connaît sous le renouveau une **évolution ascendante** qu'il convient certes de parfaire et **d'améliorer** mais dont les **signes positifs** s'observent à travers les actes quotidiens de la vie publique (APP 2 :22-27)

> ... *the direct and personal implication of the Head of State, President Paul Biya in* **the promotion and amelioration of the life of women in Cameroon.** *It should be noted that in this light, during the regime of this president, women have known* **a progressive evolution** *which brings about* **positive signs** *that can be observed through daily actions in* **public life** *(my emphasis)*

Here, we see contextualised lexical traces of the discourse of 'Promotion of Women': not only 'promotion', but also, the associated 'progressive' 'evolution' and 'public life'. This discourse is a key 'supporting' discourse for 'Positive Action for women', as one strategy for and indicator of positive action must be promotion. As noted, this discourse is not only produced within the Cameroon parliament but nationally and internationally; it can thus be seen as intertextually drawn from other promotional discourses within the society and the wider world. 'Promotion of women' is a contemporary discourse and is, we can claim, intertextually drawn in part, from MDG 3: 'to promote gender equality and empower women'. Women are discursively constructed within the text in Appendix 2 as needing promotion in many domains such as education in general, health (education and prevention of diseases), political involvement, the fight against poverty, gender partnership and development of women's capacities. We see therefore that the discourse of women's promotion is intertextually linked with other discourses e.g. surrounding health and poverty.

This discourse can be considered 'progressive' as promotion is a positive action, intended to improve women's lives. However, women are also, by definition, necessarily discursively constructed as *disadvantaged*. There is therefore a tension in considering this as a *'progressive'* discourse. The very act of 'promoting women' may suggest that women are incapable of promoting themselves, and therefore need others (by implication decision makers who are mostly men) to promote them.

The Minister is thus walking on a tightrope as this discourse *still* constructs men as the more powerful, active agents. This is of course why 'quotas' are sometimes resisted by the very groups they are designed to empower.

'Women Need Protection'

I identify a 'Women's protection discourse' as one which focuses on the protection of women from injustices both physically in society (for example, sexual violence) and by the law (e.g. discrimination). This new discourse has not yet been provisionally identified and named in the literature to my knowledge. Direct lexical traces of this discourse are found in APP 2: ln 105-106:

> ... de promotion des valeurs morales et sociales positive ainsi que celle de **protection de la femme contre les déviances sociales**

> *... the education, sensitisation, and promotion of moral values, positive*
> *social values and also* **the protection of the woman against**
> **social deviance** [ills]

Also, implicit traces of this discourse are identified in other text
from the parliament where women are seen as victims of societal
ills and require the law to protect their rights. These ills range from
rape, to unwanted pregnancies and the contraction of sexually
transmissible infections including HIV/AIDS (APP 2: 115). The
perpetrators of such ills are often identified as men. In the example
below, a female MP in a Discussion session (Appendix 3) presents a
situation where women in prison are victims of rape and resulting
pregnancy:

> Mon souci se situ au niveau de la jeune fille et des femmes
> qui sont emprisonner. Vous avez dit que si une femme est
> enceinte, on ne pourrait pas l'enfermer. Mais quand une femme
> se trouve enceinte en prison, parce que les femmes prennent
> les grossesses en prison, elle donc, elles subissent des viols en
> prison par des prisonniers et même les gardes. Il serait grand
> temps excellence de faire en sorte que les femmes aient leurs
> prisons et les hommes leurs prisons. Moi j'ai déjà eu à préparer
> des naissances pour des femmes en prison. (App3: 10-18)

> *My worry is at the level of the young female prisoner. You said that*
> *when a woman is pregnant, she cannot be locked up.* **But when a**
> **woman finds herself pregnant within the prison**, *because*
> *women get pregnant in prison, she then,* **she has been subjected**
> **to rape** *in prison by prisoners and even prison guards. It is high time*
> *for Your Excellency to do something for women to have their own prisons*
> *and men to have their own prisons. I have had to prepare for childbirth*
> *for women in prison.*

She presents women as (sociological, if not linguistic) 'patients'
(van Leeuwen 1996) e.g. 'a woman finds herself pregnant' (APP 3:
12), 'women get pregnant' (APP 3: 13) who need protection from
negative social actions. She suppresses the agent (pregnant by
whom?) but focuses on women's victim status – an object of negative
actions. A further lexical cue of this discourse is the phrase '*been*

subjected to rape' but here, agents are specified. It should be noted how use of the definite article - **la** jeune fille et des femmes qui sont prisonniers' (APP 3: 11), *(the)* in (the young girl and women who are prisoners) essentialising women in prison. They are grammatically presented as patients as they are passive actors and beneficiaries of negative actions.

Although the female MP and the Minister of Women's Affairs articulate this discourse of 'women's protection', they do so from different perspectives. The female Minister articulates the discourse with regard to the general protection of women from negative social practices while the female parliamentarian represents women as victims of physical violence who need to be protected from predators (men) by the law, by the system using its 'instruments' such as the constitution and the penal code. As patients these negative actions, they need positive action.

Female prisoners are also presented as 'objects' of abuse since they are in mixed sex prisons, victims either of male prisoners or the prison guards themselves. Their subject positions as victims are presented from a particular perspective to achieve certain ends: that is, the introduction of laws that protect female prisoners and provide separate prisons (consequently better facilities) for men and women. It is argued here that women are victims since they need the protection of the department of law and order who are in charge of fighting social deviance.

'Elimination of all Forms of Discrimination Against Women'
Intertextually drawn from a UN organ, it is based on the Convention on the Elimination of all forms of Discrimination against Women (CEDAW). 'Elimination of discrimination against women' is closely intertextually linked to the 'Equal opportunity discourse', arguably the other side of the same coin, which, although not discussed in this book, I also consider modern, 'progressive' discourse in support of 'Positive Action for women'. This discourse is made relevant in the data by the speakers themselves. In Chapters 4 and 5, this discourse was constructed negatively by Honourable Etame, accusing women of requesting for the elimination of all forms of discrimination, but in this chapter, it is viewed as a potentially 'progressive' discourse as it is articulated by the Minister

of Women's Affairs in relation to the overt discrimination against women in Cameroon and even in the parliament. Reference to a 'discourse' (in this sense) can be positive or negative, depending on who is articulating the discourse and to what ends (as I show below).

Lexical cues of this discourse can be found in the Appendix 1, the question of Honourable Etame to the Minister of Women's Affairs on women seeking the elimination of all forms of discrimination against them:

> Au moment présent me semble engagé sur tous les fronts, **pour conquérir l'égalité des sexes le droit d'exercer toutes les activités, l'abolition des sévices de tous genres, l'augmentation du nombre** des femmes dans les assemblés (App 1 : 5-7)

> *At present,* **it seems to me that women are engaged in all aspects** *to* **achieve equality of sexes,** *the* **right to practice all activities, the abolition of violence [by men] of all sorts, and the increase of wom***en in the House of Assembly*

And the Minister of Women's Affairs responds with lexical traces such as 'discrimination' (l.50) and its opposite 'égalité' (equality) found in APP 2: 51 (see below), and highlighting the mission of her ministry. Of course, the Ministry of Women's Affairs was created to promote and fight for gender equality and the elimination of all forms of discrimination against women:

> *The politics of the promotion of the woman has been a recurrent and constant preoccupation of the President of the Republic. This was once more manifested when* **the head of state created an autonomous ministry of women's affairs and entrusted it with the mission to elaborate and put in place measures and policies that protect the rights of the Cameroonian woman in the society, the abolition of all forms of discrimination against the woman, and an increase in equality in the political, economic, social and cultural domains.** *To put that in practice, my ministry in collaboration with other developmental departments have enabled women, as the MP Etame Francois pointed out strongly,* **to break through and gain equality in gender [issues], the right to participate in all**

179

activities, the abolition of all forms of violence, and an increase, and this we all witnessed yesterday, in the number of women in the National Assembly *etc.* (see APP 2: 46-56 for version in French)

In the excerpt above, the Minister restates the mission statement of her ministry. The last 4 lines are *implicitly* about the elimination of all forms of discrimination against women. The Ministry of Women's Affairs has as a mission to get women to achieve equal opportunities in every field. Her ministry, she notes, has as its mission 'd'élaboration et de mise en œuvre des … à la disparition de toute discrimination à l'égard de la femme'(APP 2: 51), that is, to put in place measures to *protect* the rights of Cameroonian women and *the abolition of all forms of discrimination* against them The 'Elimination of all forms of discrimination against women' discourse is central to the speech of the Minister of Women's Affairs and constitutes a dominant discourse within her ministry. Here, she is attempting to make it less marginal in the parliament as a whole. However, it does not go without resistance – this was a response to a male MP, Honourable Etame, who *criticised* the elimination of discrimination against women, claiming that women have abused this principle. (Recall that he equated this so-called 'elimination of *all* forms of discrimination' with a weapon by women to destroy 'our customs' and to licence deviant practices such as women 'walking naked in the streets' and drinking in public places).

Other traces are found in one June 2005 Question-and-Answer session where two male MPs question gender discrimination in sports including against female footballers and female athletes:

Dite nous quelle est la politique concrètement qui va relever notre football … Pourquoi on relève notre championnat national pour qu'on a un championnat junior, pour qu'on pense au football féminin, qu'elle est d'une manière générale la politique sportive de votre ministère

Tell us what concrete policy that will save our football … why don't we change our national championships so that we can have junior championships, think of feminine football, what is the general sports policy in your ministry?

Also,

> Il nous a même revenu que notre médaillé d'or, médaillé or aux jeux olympique d'Athènes n'avait même pas eu le soutien de son pays le Cameroun.

> *It has come to our knowledge that our [female] gold medallist, the Olympic gold medallist in Athens did not even have the support of her native country Cameroon.*

Another MP questions the masculine focus of the media on football and the budget allowance for male football compared to other forms of sport (including women's football). He thus contests the discrimination in the financing and media coverage of this particular female sport and other sporting events. Although the MP recognises the negligence of the state in its discrimination against this (female) athlete, interestingly, he does not dwell on it nor does he give the gender perspective any prominence. However, I see it as a step in acknowledging the achievement of women in Cameroonian society and the 'other side of the coin' of promotion and positive action for women in not discriminating against them in sporting activities.

Gender Partnership

'Gender partnership' is a macro-discourse and relates to male-female *genuine* partnership in all social activities, professional and domestic, and is a counter-discourse to the practice of gendered division of roles (see 'Gender differentiation'). Lexical traces of the 'Gender Partnership' discourse are mostly found in the main text under analysis here where the female Minister in her response to Honourable Etame, who strongly observes that there is the need for men and women to work in close partnerships, what she calls 'male/female' partnership. Lexical traces of this discourse can be found in APP 2: lines 29, 48/49 and 147. In the excerpt below, she notes:

> Le véritable combat de l'heure ...reste bien ... la promotion du genre, le partenariat homme/femme, la contribution nécessaire de chaque genre à l'édification de la société (APP 2 : 25-28)

181

The real fight of the moment remains the promotion of gender, male/female partnership, the necessary contribution of each gender to the edification of the society.

She juxtaposes the phrases 'promotion of gender', 'male/female partnership' and 'contribution of each gender' to relate to men and women working together for the benefit of the society. She intertextually draws this discourse from developmental discourses that are articulated within the community calling on men and women to work together towards developing the society. This discourse can be seen as a modern, 'progressive' discourse because it elevates the status of women to *equal* partners with men (in development) in the promotion of the society:

> le maintien de la tranquillité, de la paix et cohésion social ainsi que celui de l'ordre publique, est une exigence fondamentale **qui interpelle les hommes, les femmes,** les pouvoirs publiques, **les partenaires aux développements** pour une **approche systémique et un partenariat actif, durable,** pour le bonheur de nos populations. (APP 2: 123-127)

> *the maintenance of tranquillity, peace and social harmony as well as public order is a fundamental exigency,* **which calls on men, women,** *public authorities, and partners in development for a systematic* **approach and an active and sustainable partnership, for the well being of the people.**

This discourse in the wider Cameroonian society is becoming dominant especially in international non-governmental organisations and other development funding bodies. Its lexical traces are abundant through constant reference to women and men working together in partnership in the development of the society. This discourse is also intertextually drawn from the international scene especially from the Inter-Parliamentary Union[8], which has a 'gender partnership' group with a mission to ensure that there is constant and explicit partnership between men and women. Its mission is to serve interests and visions of both men and women equally in activities and decisions. 'Gender partnership' competes with a discourse of 'Gender differentiation' which suggests that if women gain, men may lose, and therefore a resistance to gender sharing or gender partnership. Being equal partners entails women and men being partners in the decision-making process, as I show in the next section.

'Women as Decision-Makers'

I view the discourse of 'Women as decision-makers' concerned with women's 'active' and 'equal' participation in the decision-making process especially in the parliament. Traces came from primarily from a 'protest' by an MP that women are seeking *equal* representation in the Parliament (see App 1) and the Minister's response in App 2 arguing for equal opportunities, elimination of discrimination against women and participation of women in decision-making, that is, an increase in the number of women in the parliament. Although women are generally not constructed in popular discourse as decision makers in the Cameroonian community, their very presence in the parliament nevertheless indicates they are de jure part of the decision-making process.

Linguistic traces of this discourse have been identified in APP 2, the Speech of the Minister of Women's Affairs and also in the question asked by Honourable Etame (App 1). In APP 2: 4-8,

Permettez-moi …de présenter mes chaleureuses félicitations du haut de cette tribune, à l'honorable Eyenga Blandine [clapping] pour **sa brillante élection de la loi du 08 Septembre portant à 20 le nombre de député femme à l'assemblé nationale**

Permit me …to present, from this high tribune, my warm congratulations to Honourable Eyenga Blandine (clapping) and for the brilliant voting of the law of 08th September, **bringing the number of female parliamentarians to 20 in the National Assembly.**

And APP 2: 52-56,

mon département ministériel s'y emploie, **en collaboration avec les partenaires au développement à fin d'engager des femmes** comme l'honorable Etame François forte opportunément relever, à conquérir l'égalité des sexes, le droit d'exercer toutes les activités, l'abolition des sévices de tous genres, **l'augmentation, et cela nous l'avons vécu encore hier, du nombre de femme dans l'assemblé**

183

my ministerial department has taken upon itself, **with the collaboration of *partners in development to engage women,*** *as honourable Etame has* strongly *indicated, to* achieve *the equality of sexes, the right to participate in all activities, the abolitions of violence of all sorts,* **and the increase, and that we witnessed yesterday, the increase of female parliamentarians in the national assembly**

The Minister points out to the presence of women in the parliament and an increase as well, while she advocates for women to be engaged in decision making. At the same time, she intertextually draws on Honourable Etame's claims in the previous text, and challenges his initial 'put-down' claims that the only battle won by women so far is the right to walk naked and drink in public. Showing women as being elected into parliament and an increase in the numbers in this assembly is counter-discourse.

In another text – in a Discussion session, June 2005 - (APP 3), a female MP presents herself and other female MPs as leaders and who are proactive in taking decisions that affect women. On the topic of separate prisons for women and men, she notes:

Amenez nous un texte, je serai le premier à défendre cette [sic] texte. Qu'il y est des prisons d'hommes et des prisons des femmes. **Je vous assure que les femmes qui sont ici rejoindront à moi pour défendre ce texte pour qu'on augmente le budget pour que vous puissiez faire des prisons des femmes.** (APP 3:24-28)

Bring us the text; I will be the first to defend this text for there to be male prisons and female prisons. I assure you that the women who are here will join me to defend this text so that the budget can be augmented so that you can construct prisons for women.

A 'sisterhood discourse' (united we are more powerful!) may also be identified here – that is, women coming together irrespective of party leaning to fight for a common goal. In calling on the Minister (of penitentiary administration) to present a text so they can take a decision on it for the benefit of women in the country, this female MP discursively constructs female MPs as agents who can bring about change by taking decisions that affect women.

Decision-making processes by women are indications of women who are well-educated and are leaders. Constructing women as decision makers is thus progressive and positive. We can argue that this discourse is loosely related to 'Gender partnership' discourse examined above between men and women in decision making, with women now *also* having access to decision-making.

'Women as Agents of Development'

'Women as agents of development' is a dominant discourse in the developing world whose origin can be traced back to intergovernmental agencies working on development; (e.g. Plan International, UNICEF)[9] and focus on women in the development process. Previously in Cameroon, women tended to be excluded by development agencies (see Fonchingong 2005), but this exclusion was recognised (by development agencies themselves) as a mistake and the current discourses construct women as (main) agents of development. Research suggests that women are in fact better agents of development than men, e.g. a female NGO director in Senegal observes that 'if you want to develop Africa, you must develop the leadership of African women' (Manuh 1998),[10] because women are often closely associated with *farming*, children's education, and family finances, AND educating women is seen as educating the family, a good way to reduce ill-health in children. Such current literature links development to good governance and good governance as achievable only when there is gender parity.

A discourse of Cameroonian women as agents of development has been previously identified by Awasom (2005). There are indeed more Cameroonian women engaged with NGO work geared towards development, especially in sustainable environmental management and agricultural development. Development projects in the areas of community health and social relations in the community also tend to be staffed by women. It is therefore unsurprising that members of parliament therefore call on government to promote women in their country's development process. Women are discursively referred to by the Minister as 'actors in development' (APP 2: 30-31), 'partners in development' (APP 2: 53), and 'agents of development' (APP 2: 109-110).

le renforcement des capacités des femmes pour jouer
sainement et en responsable leur rôle ... les actrices de
développement (APP 2: 28-31)

*the reinforcement of women's capacities to reasonably and responsibly
play their role... [as] actors of development*

Also noteworthy is the explicit reference to women as 'agents' of
development' in APP 2: 108 - 'rôle de mère... et d'agent de
développement' (the role of mother ... and agent of development).
This is a reason for the promotion of women in this domain. This
discourse also constructs women as active agents of development
being one of their primary roles (see APP 2: 30-31, and 109). 'Women
as agents of development' is thus an empowerment discourse and
serves as discoursally promoting positive action for women.

'Globalisation'

Globalisation is generally viewed in economic terms, often
relating to business expansion at international levels. In this book, I
choose to see it as 'internationalisation', not only from an economic
perspective but also with a socio-cultural and political dimension. I
see globalisation in this section to relate to the mix of foreign cultures
and practices with local ones, and contrary to 'localisation' which I
see as the conservation and preservation of local cultures and
practices.

In APP 2, the Minister of Women's Affairs makes reference to
globalisation and to the world as a global village. This reference is
in relation to the different social and cultural practices that are being
acquired by men and women in the society. She observes that:

La restitution du problème de l'accoutrement des femmes dans
le contexte de la mondialisation. L'honorable député relève
pour sa part que 'le premier et seul combat gagner jusqu'à
lors par la femme camerounaise est le droit de se déshabiller
ou de marcher nu en publique, le droit de boire en publique'.
Je réfère Kay Marc Gloire, un écrivain célèbre qui disait que
'le monde est un village planétaire'. Le Cameroun ne saurait
déroger à cette exigence par ce qu'il vit et évolue avec la
mondialisation dont les contours malheureusement ne sont
pas toujours bien maîtriser par tous (APP 2: 61-67)

To redress the problem of women's dress [it should be put] in a context of globalisation The Honourable Deputy, on his part claims that 'the first and only battle won so far by women is the right to undress and walk naked in public'. I will refer to Kay Marc Gloire, a celebrated writer who said 'the world is a global village'. Cameroon will not be left out in this exigency because it lives and evolves with the process of globalisation whose outcomes cannot always unfortunately be controlled by all.

The Minister situates women's social practices within the context of globalisation and defends these practices by drawing on a 'globalisation discourse'. Although she does acknowledge the drawbacks of the globalisation process, she however does not blame women for 'deviant' social practices but brings in other social actors:

N'oublions pas que les jeunes filles, ou les garçons enviaient justement les comportements déviants aussi bien des hommes que des femmes. ... Dès lors, il ne s'agit pas en somme, d'un problème de femmes ou hommes mais s'un problème de société (APP 2: 73-77)

Let us not forget that young girls, or boys equally envy these deviant behaviour, as well as men and women ... Hence, it is in all, not only a problem of men or women, but a societal problem

Thus men and not only women as indicated by Honourable Etame, also acquire these 'deviant' practices through the globalisation process.

The discourse of globalisation is strongly articulated in this speech considering the post-coloniality of the context of production, and the hybridity of cultures (see Chapter 4 on clash of cultures). Globalisation thus is seen as a societal phenomenon that has to be dealt with, and which, although having positive contributions to the society, also is a problem to both men and women.

Drawing on the 'globalisation discourse' the minister thus explains both positive and negative social practices without blaming women as responsible for loss of culture. This discourse of globalisation entails that the age of 'localisation' is over and we have to deal with globalisation, while preserving 'local/traditional' 'positive social values', - pragmatic indication that some of these traditional values are *not* positive (to women especially).

In this chapter, I have provisionally identified several discourses that articulate positive action for women. These discourses construct women in a positive way and see them as functioning in a changing society where they are active (positive) social actors. Having shown how these discourses construct women positively and, I argue, 'progressively' in these social actions, I now examine how these positive actions are legitimated. I examine different discursive strategies used to construct women and justify these positive actions.

Notes

1. These are the actual wording of the MDGs and for more information on the goals, see http://www.un.org/millenniumgoals

2. Few women attain especially higher education in Cameroon with less than 10% as university senior academic staff http://www.acu.ac.uk/womens/single5.pdf

3. Nsamenang (2000)

4. www.un.org/womenwatch/daw/cedaw/23sess.htm

5. http://www.un.org/womenwatch/daw/cedaw/cedaw23/cameroon.pdf

6. Mainstreaming a gender perspective is the process of assessing the implications for women and men of any planned action, including legislation, policies or programmes, in any area and at all levels. It is a strategy for making the concerns and experiences of women as well as of men an integral part of the design, implementation, monitoring and evaluation of policies and programmes in all political, economic and societal spheres, so that women and men benefit equally, and inequality is not perpetuated. The ultimate goal of mainstreaming is to achieve gender equality. Mainstreaming includes gender-specific activities and Positive Action, whenever women or men are in a particularly disadvantageous position. Gender-specific interventions can target women exclusively, men and women together, or only men, to enable them to participate in and benefit equally from development efforts. These are necessary temporary measures designed to combat the direct and indirect consequences of past discrimination. http://www.ilo.org/public/english/bureau/gender/newsite2002/about/defin.htm

7. This may be because mainstreaming, gender equality and women's empowerment are all contemporary discourses and challenge the status quo, seeking to transform gender relations in Cameroon.

8. http://www.ipu.org/wmn-e/gender.htm

9. See http://www.plan-international.org/wherewework/westafrica/cameroon/http://www.unicef.org/infobycountry/cameroon_27281.html

10. http://www.un.org/ecosocdev/geninfo/afrec/bpaper/maineng.htm

Chapter Seven

Discursive Strategies in Legitimating 'Positive Action for Women'

Discursive strategies as 'plans of action with various degrees of elaborateness, the realization of which can range from automatic to conscious and which are located on different levels of our mental organization' (Van Leeuwen and Wodak 1999: 92). These strategies can range from intentional ones by the speakers to (*importantly*) legitimate their claims or unintentional ones which may come up subconsciously, with societal legitimation in the background.

In Chapter 5, I analysed the discursive strategies used to legitimate 'traditional' gendered discourses. The strategies were mainly constructive (referential) and justificatory strategies which served to build in-groups and out-groups, and sustain and maintain (through legitimation) the status quo. These were very valuable in analysing the legitimation of the discourse of a 'model traditional Cameroonian woman'.

In Chapter 6, I identified and analysed what I call 'progressive' gendered discourse on 'Positive action for women'. The discourse of 'Positive action for women' entails 'negative' actions towards women being in place, that need to be challenged and countered. Positive action seeks to challenge repressive traditional practices that discriminate against women. To legitimate discourses, social actors draw on constructive strategies not only to construct in-groups and out-groups, but to positively or negatively (re)present self and others within discourses. Speakers also draw on legitimating macro-discursive strategies such as *Transformatory strategies* which 'attempt to transform a relatively well-established situation into another, of which the speaker ... may already have formed an image' and aim to change the social constructions of women (van Leeuwen and Wodak 1999: 93, Reisigl and Wodak 2001: 43) and *Destructive strategies* (Reisigl and Wodak 2001: 43) which serve to 'demolish a status quo' (van Leeuwen and Wodak 1999: 93). In this chapter, I analyse how they serve to 'demolish' traditional *arguably oppressive* construction of a 'model Cameroonian woman' (see chapter 5) and 'destroy' negative practices while 'transforming' (potentially negative) social practices to positive actions for women.

Salient is the fact that the Minister of Women's Affairs does not (generally) draw on a binary representation of gender relations, but rather a mutually constructive identity and partnership, thereby discoursally demystifying male hegemony and empowering women. The binary presentation or polarisation of men and women (as well as binary notions of tradition and modernity, public versus private), are deconstructed in her discourse. I see this as an attempt to justify and transform the dominant discourses of gender division of roles and male hegemony, to a discourse of 'Gender partnership' and 'Gender equality, main discourses of Positive action for women'. Although there is an attempt by some Ministers and MPs to deconstruct binaries to legitimate positive actions, they sometimes 'strategically' draw on the notions of gender difference to legitimate positive action for women. These macro-transformatory and destructive strategies are realised through different arguments.

As well as referential (constructive) and argumentative (transformatory and destructive) strategies, other discursive strategies are relevant, in particular *mitigation* strategy (Reisigl and Wodak 2001: 83). Mitigation is effective as it is a language of prudence and deliberation, used to 'force through' ideas that are in fact subversive. These strategies are presented in Table 7. 3 and analysed in the sections that follow.

Referential Strategies

In this section, I identify and analyse some referential strategies used in the main data (the Minister's speech and other data) to achieve positive presentation of women (and negative presentation of 'other'). These referential strategies are used to refer to or name social actors. Actors are thus either included in the discourse or (notably and/or strategically) excluded. Drawing on referential strategies, speakers construct women through 'positive self presentation.

The different referential strategies identified and analysed in this section are elision, as an exclusionary strategy, specification, agentialisation, passivation, victimisation, and essentialisation/genericisation. As observed by Reisigl and Wodak (2001: 47), exclusionary strategies could be employed to conceal persons responsible for discrimination and also sometimes to conceal those being discriminated against. In contrast, in the data available, although social actors are backgrounded, they are not named to strategically include all social actors (both named and backgrounded) in the social action being solicited.

Positive reference to social actors is also achieved in the text through **specification** of these actors in the process of articulating discourses of Positive Action for women. This is achieved through 'individuation' (see van Leeuwen 1996) or specific use of proper nouns – names of persons positively involved in the Positive Action. The Minister of Women's Affairs for example names Paul Biya - the President of the Republic [of Cameroon] - for his promotion of Positive Action:

> l'implication directe et personnelle du chef de l'état, son excellence **Paul Biya** dans la promotion et l'amélioration de la vie de la femme camerounaise. (APP 2:22-24)

> *There is the direct and personal involvement of the Head of State, His Excellency Paul Biya in the promotion and the improvement of the life of the Cameroonian woman*

The strategy of specification therefore is used here to name social actors directly involved in positive social actions for women that directly benefit women. In contrast, in the excerpt below, the speaker also nominates and specifies the social actor *responsible* for a particular positive action for women (but has not (yet) carried out). Specification can therefore be seen here as strategic.

> monsieur le ministre, le ministre délégué chargé euh…, **le ministre délégué chargé auprès de la ministre de justice chargé du politique pénitencier** [sic] a quand penserai vous séparer les femmes et les hommes (APP 3 :20-23)

> *Mr Minister, Mr Minister Delegate in charge euh …,* **The Minister Delegate of Justice in Charge of Penitential Policy,** *when do you think you will separate male and female prisons?*

The strategy **Elision**, identified as a referential strategy is an extension of van Leeuwen's (1996) notion of exclusion of social actors through *suppression*. Elision refers to the (*intentional*) omission of social actors and is discursively achieved through ellipsis, agentless clauses, passives and use of infinitives. Here, the Minister of Women's Affairs' strategy appears to be *not* to name social actors in the process of Positive Action for women. She presents a whole series of social actions without naming their associated actors. These are indicated in the excerpt below through the use of blanks _:

> Le véritable combat de l'heure, qui constitue une préoccupation majeur pour le Président de la République reste bien **la lutte contre la pauvreté**—; je voudrais dire la pauvreté morale, et **la promotion du genre** —, le partenariat homme/femme, la **considération mutuelle** —**,** la contribution nécessaire de chaque genre à l'édification de la société, **le renforcement des capacités des femmes**—(APP 2: 25-29)

> *The real fight of the moment, which constitutes a major preoccupation of the President of the Republic, remains the fight against poverty —; I mean moral poverty, and the promotion of gender, male/female partnership, mutual consideration —, the necessary contribution of each gender to the edification of the society, the reinforcement of women's capacities —…*

The omission signs above after the bold texts indicate *elision*: cases of agentless clauses, that is,

Ln 26:   *the fight against poverty* **[by whom]?**
Ln 27   *the promotion of gender [relations]* **[by whom]?**
Ln 27   *mutual consideration* **[by whom]?**
Ln 28-29   *reinforcement of women's capacities* **[by whom]?**

Such omissions are arguably strategic in the sense that in not naming specific persons in the process of Positive Action, all persons are included in this process. As regards that, syntactic constructions of these agentless clauses, they are nominal clauses without verbs. All the verbs in these clauses have been 'nominalised', for example, instead of a verbal clause like the 'minister should reinforce women's capacities', where a social actor is named, we have a nominal clause 'the reinforcement of women's capacities' with the actor suppressed. The strategy of *elision* is arguably used progressively here so as not to background or suppress any social

194

actors and exclude their voice, as may be the case in the discourse of racial discrimination (see Reisigl and Wodak 2001, van Dijk and Wodak 2000, van Dijk 2005). It is used to include *all* social actors – women, men, NGOs, parliamentarians, organisations in the accomplishment of the social action.

Previously in Chapter 5, *agency* was used as a strategy by a male MP, Honourable Etame, to present women as agents of negative actions which included 'our loss of culture'. In this chapter, I examine how social actors are constructed as agents of negative or *positive* social actions, depending on what the speaker wishes to highlight. *Agentialisation* (see van Leeuwen 1996: 33/49) is achieved grammatically through the presentation of social actors (agents) as (sociological) subjects of active clauses; agents are not however always grammatical subjects of sentences.

In the main text, in discussing what can be done to promote women in the Cameroonian society, the Minister of Women's Affairs names a number of agents whom she considers vital for the implementation of positive action for women. The Minister, in the excerpt below names agents of positive actions

Les **associations** et **ONG, courroies de transmission entre les pouvoirs publiques et des populations** mènent à leur niveau des actions d'éducation et de sensibilisation des femmes. Au total, le maintien de la tranquillité, de la paix et cohésion social ainsi que celui de l'ordre publique, est une exigence fondamentale qui interpelle les **hommes**, les **femmes**, les **pouvoirs publiques**, les **partenaires aux développements** pour une approche systémique et un partenariat actif, durable, pour le bonheur de nos populations (APP 2 : 121 - 126)

*Associations and **non-governmental organisations, agents** of transmission between the public authorities and the* **population** *at their own level are carrying out actions in the education and the sensitisation of women. All in all, the maintenance of tranquillity, peace and social solidarity as well as public order is a fundamental exigency, which calls for* **men, women, public authorities,** *and* **partners in development** *for a systematic approach and an active and sustainable partnership, for the well being of the people.*

195

Without the involvement of key actors as agents of change, the goal to achieve the promotion of Cameroonian women may not be successful. The minister therefore lists these actors/agents in her presentation, calling on government and non-governmental bodies, as well as institutional and non-institutional bodies in the achievement of these goals. In APP 3 (Appendix 3), in a discussion session, a female MP, Honourable Mebanda for example presents prisoners and prison guards *negatively* as agents of rape. Contrary to the Minister who names agents of positive actions, the female MP, Honourable Mebanda names agents of negative actions. In the example below, the agents of negative actions are positioned in a by-clause, but function as agents of the action of the verb *to rape* even though they do not occupy the sentential subject position.

Elle donc, elles subissent des viols en prison par des prisonniers et même les gardes (APP 3 : 14)

They undergo rape in prison by prisoners and the guards themselves

Here, male prisoners and prison guards are presented as agents of negative action, a threat to women, and have been thus negatively constructed to achieve a specific goal - the separation of male and female prisons. By explicitly presenting the male prisoners and prison guards as threats to female prisoners, Honourable Mebanda presumably hopes to better achieve her goal of appealing to the government that it is imperative to take immediate action, given the shocking nature of her claim.

While agentialisation is a referential strategy used to either positively or negatively present social actors in relation to Positive Action for women, the strategy of *victimisation* constructs women as victims of physical abuse (by men) or structural negligence by the system or the laws of the country. In focusing on the need for Positive Action for women in her speech, women are also presented as victims of negative actions and are constructed as victims of negligence. If they were not neglected, there would be no need for positive action. Thus in the phrases:

la volonté politique en matière de promotion de la femme
the political will to promote women'

'la politique de promotion de la femme *(APP 2: 45 - 47)*
The politics of the promotion of the woman'

The nouns *'women'/'woman'* are the objects of the transitive verb 'promote' and of the nominalised 'promotion': Cameroonian women are objects of 'promotion' because they are victims of some form of discrimination (here, neglect).

Constantly representing Cameroonian women as *patients* of actions of others (well-intentioned and otherwise) is a discursive strategy to achieve sympathy towards the idea of women as victims of some social and political discrimination. In APP 3 for example, Honourable Mebanda, a female parliamentarian uses the discursive strategy of *victimisation* (women as victims) to legitimate her call for Positive Action for women. She presents the case of women as victims of rape in prison by male prisoners and prison guards. She also presents women as victims of a system that puts men and women in the same prisons. She describes the case vividly, presenting women as defenceless victims who really can do nothing about their plight:

> quand une jeune fille de 18 ans va en prison, **c'est sur qu'elle sortira de la malade de SIDA, ou sa vie est condamné et en faite**, un homme ne peut pas attraper la grossesse en prison, c'est la femme qui subit cela. Donc vraiment, trouvez un aménagement pour la femme et surtout pour la jeune fille, (APP 3 :32 – 35)

> *when a young girl of 18 goes to prison, it is certain that* **she will come out with AIDS, where her life is destroyed** *and in effect, a man does not get pregnant in prison, it is the woman who undergoes that. So, really, find better conditions for the woman and especially the young girl, I thank you*

Thus there is the need for the law to intervene on their behalf. They are subjected to rape, pregnancy and become infected with HIV/AIDS (see excerpt further down), what worse things can happen to a woman in prison. This speaker uses this strategy effectively in achieving her goal: women have been presented in the text as victims of abuse in prison hence the need for positive action. By presenting them as victims, negative agency (see above) has been ascribed to *other* social actors.

The last referential strategy I examine is *essentialisation* (see Holmes 2006, Stone 2004, and Holmes and Meyerhoff 2003). Women are often essentialised and referred to as a common entity with the same characteristics and problems, as fixed with the same issues preoccupying them. This strategy is achieved linguistically through the use of definite articles and a singular noun (e.g. *the* Cameroonian women, the woman, the young girl, see excerpt above).

Essentialising women with the use of the singular definite article and the singular noun suggests that it is typical for women who go to prison to be raped, get pregnant and contract HIV/AIDS. Reisigl and Wodak (2001) call this sort of essentialisation 'singularisation of synecdoche'. Such essentialisation in the reference to women as victims in the data may be claimed to be a positive and *strategic essentialisation* in the sense of Holmes (2006), and used *politically* (Spivak 1996) to achieve greater good for all the women of Cameroon and despite the fact that it ignores diversity, women are essentialised with the use of the definite article and the singular noun.

> This has been manifested once again when the Head of State created an autonomous ministry with a mission to elaborate and put in place relative and respective measures for **the rights of the Cameroonian woman** in the society, **the end of all forms of discrimination against the woman** and the improvement of the guarantee for equality in the political, economical, social and cultural domains. (APP 2:47 - 52)

While certain measures are being welcomed, the implication is that most, if not all Cameroonian women are suffering from discrimination. The use of *strategic essentialisation* as a discursive strategy, though problematic, may strengthen the effect of the discourse of Positive Action for women; Cameroonian women characteristically undergo discrimination, it is even more pressing for there to be measures to eliminate this (for example, for the separation of prisons for men and women).

Mitigation/Intensification Strategies
Mitigation is shown by Reisigl and Wodak (2001) to be a strategy where speakers use the language of prudence and deliberation to 'force through' ideas that are subversive or 'to ease the anticipated

unwelcome effect' of an argument (Martinovski 2006, Fraser 1980). What I find interesting in mitigation in the text is that although all the speakers mitigate their language, they do so for different ends. Wodak (2001) observes that mitigation could serve as an expression of prudence and deliberation (and could be achieved through the use of modalities). I identify mitigation through modality, but also verbs of permission and gratitude, weak adjectives/nouns, and diminutive adjectives. An analysis of mitigation reveals that these female speakers mitigate when they challenge dominant (patriarchal) social practices within the society and counter negative prejudices against women (which they all are doing here) - in conformity with the norms of the wider society where women are not expected to challenge men. For example:

> **Permettez moi**, honorable députés à l'assemblé nationale de formuler des réserves quand à l'affirmation selon laquelle, le premier et seul combat gagné jusqu'à lors par la femme camerounaise est le droit de se déshabiller ou de marcher nu en public, le droit de boire en public (APP 2 : 15-18).

> **Permit me** *Honourable Deputies of the National Assembly* **to present reservations with regard to the claim that** *the first and only battle won by the Cameroonian woman so far is the right to undress herself and drink in public*

Here the Minister of Women's Affairs is countering Honourable Etame's claim on women's social practices but she mitigates her language with a verb of permission 'Permit'.

She also uses a weak noun 'reservations', which is a very weak objection to the honourable's claims. This may be explained from the genre of parliamentary discourse or for an ironic effect. It may also be seen as a strategy to counter negative claims, yet employing politeness strategies (something to be considered for future research).

The Minister also mitigates because she disagrees with the claims made by the Honourable MP. She thus challenges social linguistic practices (e.g. challenging men in public) with a face saving strategy (of the MP's face), but does not fail to then challenge male perceptions of women's social practices –

Il s'agit incontestablement ici d'une appréciation excessive qui occulte des multiples combats mener et gagner tant par les femmes elles mêmes (APP 2 : 19-20).

This **incontestably** *constitutes* **an excessive assessment** *which* **conceals the many battles fought and won** *by the women themselves…*

After mitigating in lines 14-18 above, she thus challenges in the next lines (19-20). The impact of this challenge on the audience may however have been reduced by her mitigated expression 'Permettez-moi, honorable députés à l'assemblé national de formuler des réserves' – 'permit me honourable MPs of the National Assembly to present reservations'.

Table 7. 1 Mitigation Strategies

Female MP/Minister	Linguistic mitigation strategy	Example
Minister of Women's Affairs	Modal verb + verb of saying	• je voudrais **dire** la pauvreté morale (I would like to say moral poverty…)
Hon Ndo		• je voudrais **ajouter** ma modeste voix (I would like to add my modest voice) • May I therefore **appeal** on the entire chamber…? (original English)
Hon Njini		• j'ai eu **l'impression** en lissant les texts (I have this **impression** from these texts that…) • je voulais aussi **souligner** que (I would like to **underline**…)
Hon Mebanda		• j'aimerais par exemple **reprendre** l'article 583 (I would like for example to **repeat** article 583…)

Table 7. 1   Mitigation Strategies (Contd)

Hon Mebanda	Use of reductive quantitatives, Negations	▪ 'je me rend compte **qu'il n'y a pas beaucoup** d'aménagement pour les femmes' ('I have noticed that there *are not many* facilities for women')
Minister of Women's Affairs	Verbs of permission And gratitude	▪ **Permettez**-moi … pour présenter mes chaleureuses félicitations **(Permit** me to [...] present my congratulations) ▪ Permettez-moi, honorable députés … de formuler des réserve **(Permit** me to formulate my reservations)
Honourable Njini Honourable Ndo	Weak Adjectives/ nouns	▪ j'avais tout juste une petite préoccupation, (I had just a **little** worry) ▪ je voudrais ajouter ma **modeste** voix (I wanted to add my modest voice to the voice)
Hon Njini	Verb of feeling/ thinking	▪ I think my colleagues … are with me
Hon Mebanda	Orientation to addressee and modality	▪ A quand **penserai vous** … (When do you think you would separate prisons between men and women)
Minister of Women's Affairs	Initial orientation	▪ je souscris justement à ce question, (I acknowledge this question…)
Hon Njini	Speaker oriented	▪ j'ai eu l'impression en lissant les texts (**I** have the impression from reading the texts that...)
Hon Mebanda		▪ On the contrary, I have a worry…
Hon Ndo		▪ **Je** voudrais ajouter ma modeste voix (**I** would like to add my modest voice)

201

Table 7. 1   Mitigation Strategies (Contd)

Hon Njini	Use of diminutives	• j'avais tout juste une **petite** préoccupation (I have just a little preoccupation) • ma **petite** préoccupation tout à l'heur c'était (my little worry of a moment ago was…) • Moi, j'aurai souhaité **un peu** que (me, I would like a little [sic] to wish that…)

In APP 3, the female MP Honourable Mebanda similarly starts her speech with mitigated language to challenge an article in the proposed Penal Code put forward by a male Minister of Justice.

Je félicite le gouvernement …par contre **j'ai un souci** (APP 3 : 8/10)

I congratulate the government… however, I **have a worry**

Previously (in APP 3: 4), that is, a few lines earlier, she had called this worry 'little' – 'j'ai **un petit souci'.** Her use of the diminutive adjective 'little' and her reference to the problem as a 'worry' discoursally downgrades magnitude of the problem –which is rape, pregnancy and possible infection with HIV.

After mitigating her introduction of this 'worry', and being booed at for even daring to accuse men of rape (as my field notes indicate), she intensifies her language.

IL **SERAIT GRAND TEMPS** EXCELLENCE DE FAIRE EN SORTE QUE LES FEMMES AIENT LEURS PRISONS ET LES HOMMES LEURS PRISONS (APP 2: 15-16)

IT IS **HIGH TIME** *YOUR EXCELLENCY THAT WOMEN HAVE THEIR PRISONS AND MEN HAVE THEIR PRISONS.*

There are two markers of intensified language here: the use of high pitch (as indicated by capital letters) and the use of markers of intensification 'it is high time'. Other markers of intensified language include the use of imperative verbs: 'Amenez nous un texte' – 'bring us a text (APP 3:14), and 'trouvez un aménagement pour la femme' – Look for [alternative] accommodation for female prisoners and girls (APP 3: 34-35). Honourable Mebanda challenges the minister to do his job to improve the status of women in prison (positive action), the men in the national assembly (who boo and heckle her), and the status quo: where men engage in libertine sexual practices. A woman using intensified language violates the linguistic norms of the unacknowledged community of practice that exists outside the parliament (see Eckert and McConnell-Ginet, 2007). Conforming to parliamentary norms of frank talk (see also Chilton 2004) worked negatively for this speaker (Honourable Mebanda) in terms of the heckling. She is challenged for talking too much by the Speaker of the House, though through discourse, she empowers herself as a woman fighting for Positive Action for other women.

Argumentation Strategies

Arguments are used to legitimate certain discourses and here I examine transformatory strategies to legitimate discourses of 'Positive Action for women'. As Wodak (2003: 672) observes, men have dominated the professional field and the public context for so long that women now have to 'justify' their presence in these domains: 'They often have to compete with conservative stereotypes, whereas men are spared this kind of legitimation pressure'. There is thus a need for women to argue for Positive Action and for the analyst to examine the different arguments used in the legitimation of discourses for Positive Action for women.

Below, I identify the legitimation strategies for positive action for women, and the arguments used within each strategy. I examine the different topoi (concluding warrants, see Reisigl and Wodak 2001), and I identify other (my own) strategies such as the use of particular discourses and appeal to global tendencies for the legitimation of the discourse of 'Positive Action for women'. In Table 7. 2, I present these strategies.

These arguments are different from those in Chapter 6 because different strategies are used to legitimate the discourses of positive action for women. While the arguments in Chapter 6 are mostly justificatory and preservative (of a model traditional Cameroonian woman), those in this chapter focus on transformation of the status quo.

Table 7. 2   Argumentation Strategies to Legitimate 'Positive Action for Women'

Legitimation Strategy	Topoi	Argument in my own words
Authorisation (Van Leeuwen and Wodak 1999)	Appeal to authority either to persons or institutions or legal or authoritative documents	If the President of the Republic says so, who are you to dispute?
Moral Appeal (Litosseliti 2002); Moral Evaluation (Van Leeuwen and Wodak 1999)	Moral values	Why would women and men share the same prisons?
	Human rights	Doesn't every Cameroonian deserve to have human rights respected as the constitution stipulates?
	Health	Why would we not protect our women from STIs and HIV?
Discourses of Women as Victims (myself)	Victimisation	Why would women be victimised in their own country?
Appeal to global tendencies (myself)	Globalisation	Why would Cameroon be left behind in an age of globalisation?

Legitimation through Authorisation

Authorisation means using authority to legitimate *societal* actions (van Leeuwen and Wodak (1999: 104). Authority can be individual or institutional, that is, where the individual has been vested with institutional authority. It could be impersonal, such as the Law, international conventions or established documents such as the Bible or the Koran. Legitimation is expressed through authorisation either by 'a saying verb with the relevant authority as subject ... or a circumstance of attribution' (van Leeuwen and Wodak 1999: 104), for example, 'I would like to **repeat** article 583' (APP 3: 6).

Discourses on 'Positive Action for women', mostly legitimated by female MPs and the Ministers of Women's Affairs, are articulated in part through such authorisation. They make reference to authority – someone in whom institutionalised authority is vested like the 'President of the Republic' (APP 2: 28), 'Head of State' (APP 2: 22) and 'Paul Biya' (APP 2: 23). The Minister of Women's Affairs refers to the involvement of the President of the Republic by positioning him as an active agent in the process of women's development, noting that Positive action for women is a main preoccupation of the Head of State and citing:

> **l'implication direct et personnel du chef de l'état, son excellence Paul Biya** dans la promotion et l'amélioration de la vie de la femme camerounaise (APP 2: 21-24)

> *the **direct and personal implication of the Head of State Paul Biya** in the promotion and amelioration of the lives of the Cameroonian woman*

By implicating the Head of State as a direct agent in bringing about positive action for women, the Minister of Women's Affairs is using his authority to legitimate her own discourses on Positive action for women.

Another form of such legitimation through the use of authority is when the Minister quotes an author to justify the fact that the world has become a global village and women are learning from experiences across the world:

> Je réfère Kay Marc Gloire, un écrivain célèbre qui disait que 'le monde est un village planétaire'. Le Cameroun ne saurait

205

déroger à cette exigence par ce qu'il vit et évolue avec la mondialisation dont les contours malheureusement ne sont pas toujours bien maîtriser par tous *(APP 2: 65-67)*.

I refer to Kay Marc Gloire, a renowned writer who said, 'the world is a global village'. Cameroon will not be left behind from these exigencies because it lives and evolves with globalisation whose effects cannot unfortunately be mastered by all

Other forms of *authorisation* to legitimate discourses of Positive Action for women are in the form of legal texts. I identify the use of the constitution of Cameroon and articles from the penal code as authoritative documents in the Authorisation strategy of legitimation:

pour revenir a cette question qui concerne une femme citoyenne camerounaise, qui a des droits, et des devoirs reconnu à tout être humain sont une question de paix, de croyance et de religion prévu dans **le préambule de la constitution de Janvier 1996,** et à **d'autres instruments nationaux** (APP 2:42-45)

to return to the question which concerns the rights of Cameroonian female citizens, who have rights and duties recognised by every human, we come to a question of peace, belief, and of religion **as is stated in the preamble of the constitution of January 1996** *and* **other national documents**

The use of 'as is stated' with reference to the constitution legitimates Positive Action for women ('the rights of female Cameroonian citizens').

Reference to International events and conventions such as the theme of the International Day of the African Child of 2004, which was "Family and Child" are also used as arguments for Positive Action. Such a strategy also legitimates 'Gender partnership' discourses by highlighting the place of the family, where men and women work together for the betterment of society. Interdiscursive drawing on a counter discourse of 'Family and Child' serves to undermine the 'Women as domestic' discourse.

La famille est donc appeler à se renforcer d'avantage pour que l'éducation et la formation reçu puisse permettre d'avoir un citoyen moderne ou une citoyenne moderne pour faire la fierté du Cameroun. Et c'est à ce fait que le thème de la 14ème édition de la journée de l'Enfant Africain a porté sur « Famille et Enfant » (APP 2 :90 - 93)

The family *is therefore called to become stronger, so that the education and training received may allow* **modern citizens to be the pride of Cameroon.** *And it is because of this that the theme of the 14th edition of the African child day focused on* **"Family and Child".**

Honourable Mebanda cites the Penal Code to justify the fact that male and female prisons should be separated.

Et j'aimerais par exemple reprendre l'article 583 où ... la page sécuritaire qui faisait du prisonnier un exclus de la société. ... par contre j'ai un souci. Mon souci se situ au niveau de la jeune fille et des femmes qui sont des prisonniers.

I would love for example to repeat article 583 where ...*the prisoner [is made] an outcast of the society ... on the contrary, I have a worry. My worry is situated at the level of young girls and women who are prisoners.* (APP 3:8-19).

By citing that article (583) she questions women's plight, which is not taken care of by the law, as are other issues. By citing the law, she can justify that it should encompass benefiting women in relation to the particular issues of rape and pregnancy (see discourse on women's protection). If the law is designed to serve women positively, as in having an article protecting them from prison assaults including rape (e.g. requiring separate prisons), this would be a good form of Positive Action.

Legitimation through Moral Argument

As Litosseliti (2002:129) observes, social actors make 'moral claims and express, sustain, or challenge certain moral positions'. Moral arguments appeal to values, claims about 'right' or 'wrong'. Speakers construct values and identities through discourse and their arguments are often shaped by their understanding of gender as well as morality (Litosseliti 2002). Discourses on Positive Action for women have also been legitimated using moral argument.

Let us take the case of raped prisoners cited above. In the argument against women sharing prisons with men, moral arguments are *implied:* for example, 'vous ne pouvez pas savoir ce que les femmes subissent dans les prisons' (you cannot imagine what women are subjected to in prison). These moral arguments are based on socio-cultural norms which construct, not only the illegality but also the *immorality* of rape. It is morally wrong for somebody to be raped, which is tantamount to violation of human rights:

> quand une jeune fille de 18 ans va en prison, **c'est sûr qu'elle sortira de la malade de SIDA, ou sa vie est condamné** (APP 3 : 32-33)

> *when a young girl of 18 goes to prison, it is certain that* **she will come out with AIDS, where her life is destroyed**

It is therefore not normally acceptable for women and men to be in the same prison. People who are supposed to protect others (prison guards) cannot be the same people neglecting their moral obligation by morally and physically assaulting these very persons (again, this is implied).

Other topoi drawn on within is moral argument is the topos of *human rights.* Women are entitled to human rights, and the education of women on their rights is advocated: 'l'éducation de la femme aux droits … de la femme' (APP 2: 131). Women's rights discourses are accordingly legitimated with topos of human rights, as articulated by the Minister in the example below:

> Ainsi, pour revenir a cette question qui concerne **une femme citoyenne camerounaise, qui a des droits**, et **des devoirs reconnu à tout être humain…le préambule de la constitution de Janvier 1996**…Celle-ci s'est manifesté une fois de plus quand le chef de l'état créait un ministère autonome et qui confiait les mission d'élaboration et de mise en œuvre des mesures respectives et relative **au respect des droit de la femme camerounaise dans la société,** à la disparition de toute discrimination à l'égard de la femme… le droit d'exercer toutes les activités (APP 2: 37-41, 47-55)

To come back to the question which concerns a **Cameroonian female citizen who has rights and duties recognised by everyone [...] and the constitution of 1996** *[...] and this has been manifested once more when the Head of State created an autonomous ministry with a mission to elaborate and put into place respective and relative measures* **with regards to the rights of the Cameroonian woman** *in the society, the disappearance of all forms of discrimination against the woman...* **and the right to practice all activities.**

The use of the argument, that is, that women 'have rights', women 'with a right to practice all activities' and the 'regard' of the rights of the Cameroonian women recognised by the constitution, are all expressed to legitimate the fact the there needs to be more positive action for women with regards to their rights as women, citizens, and human beings. Elsewhere a male MP, Honourable Tasi, also raises this and although he does not make reference to *women's* rights, I still find his words relevant to discourses on women's rights. He observes that 'human rights do not necessarily get protected only if a detriment has been suffered [sic], a special detriment...'. Another male MP, Honourable Ndinda Ndinda, also observes that '**cette projet de loi** va apporter le bonheur, la prospérité et la garanti de joie et de **liberté individuel** de tous les peuples camerounaises' (**this bill** will bring us wellbeing, prosperity and the assurance of happiness and **individual liberty** to all the people of Cameroon). Although their references to the benefits of new law are not necessarily referring to the benefits *women* will acquire, a good legal system can be assumed to benefit not only male members of the community but also its female citizens (assuming these laws are not discriminatory), and it can be assumed that all citizens would agree with this, at least in principle. To draw on 'human rights' for issues concerning women is thus to use an *accepted* moral argument.

Legitimation through Discourse of Women as Victims

I see the articulation of certain discourses as a discoursal strategy to achieve specific aims. Discourses that position women as victims of sexual violence and inequality are used here to legitimate and justify the need for Positive Action for women. Women are constructed as victims of violence and injustice in the community, but, here, such discourses *legitimate* the need for Positive Action for women in order to eliminate the injustice:

> On me dit, 'Honorable, il y a une femme qui est prête à accoucher et elle n'a pas où emballer son enfant'. Elle a donc attrapé la grossesse où ? Dans la prison !! Est-ce que cette femme qui a attrapé cette grossesse dans la prison peut être libérée ? (APP 3:17-20)

> *I am told, 'Honourable, there is a woman who is ready to give birth and she has nothing to cover her child with. Where has she got the pregnancy from? In the prison!!! Can this woman who has become pregnant in prison be liberated?*

In the excerpt, Honourable Mebanda highlights one of the issues and then points out that, there is a need for a 'text' to be put in place such that women will not be exposed to such inequality and abuse. She moves on to indicate that she will be the first to vote such a text into law. Speakers also legitimate positive action by articulating other related discourse that position women as victims, e.g. *'Women's Promotion'* and *'Women Need Protection'*.

Legitimation through Appeal to Global Tendencies

Globalisation is a contemporary concept and refers to the restructuring not only of societal but individual thoughts and values, including modern values associated with gender relations and implies modernisation of discourses to include *discourses of change* (Fairclough 2001:231). An appeal to global discourses such as 'Gender equality', 'Elimination of all forms of discrimination against women', 'Women's promotion and empowerment', 'Women as partners/ agents of development, and 'Gender partnership' are drawn upon by different parliamentary speakers, as I have shown. These discourses can all be seen as discourses of change to legitimate Positive Action for women.

Conclusion

'Positive Action for women' is a contemporary discourse in Cameroon. It is however seen by (some) Cameroonian men (and women) as a strategy to licence deviant and negative practices, as well as subvert the status quo. It is seen as a 'feminist' discourse where feminism may be fashionable (among some women) though popularly perceived by men as a misandrist (hatred of men) discourse. This means that Positive Action needs to be fought for through a range of discursive strategies in the parliament (as shown in Table 7. 3 including strategies of legitimation in the articulation of Positive Action discourses.

In this chapter, I have identified different discursive and legitimating strategies for Positive Action for women and analysed how these are legitimated within the parliament. Two macro-discursive strategies were identified and analysed in this chapter. First were *constructive* (*referential*) strategies which served to construct in-groups and out-groups, and positively present 'self', while negatively presenting 'other'. Referential strategies identified within the chapter include the representation of social actors as *agents* of positive or negative action (depending on the effect highlighted), and women as *victims*.

The second macro-discursive strategy I examined in this chapter is the 'transformatory strategy' which serves to legitimate change, that is, a transformation of the status quo. *Transformatory* strategies include *arguments* drawn on. Another major transformatory strategy drawn on by speakers is mitigation. As indicated within this chapter, the *mitigation* strategy serves a different purpose from that identified by Reisigl and Wodak (2001) in their analysis of discourses of discrimination. While in discriminatory discourses mostly powerful social actors mitigate their language when discriminating against (racial) minorities. I have shown that rather minority (relatively powerless) social actors (women) mitigate their language to 'force' their ideas through thick wall of patriarchy. Fighting against institutional and cultural barriers, women in parliament then try to legitimate the need for a positive action in a context where men tend to 'fear' this very action. From my analysis, these speakers in the parliament have effectively used discursive strategies in positively presenting Positive Action and arguing favourably for it.

Table 7.3   Discursive Legitimation Strategies for the Discourses of 'Positive Action for Women'

Discursive Strategies	Linguistic Means	Grammatical Realisation	Example in my Data (paraphrased in English)
Referential/ Nomination (and exclusionary strategies)	Elision/ exclusion	Ellipsis, agentless phrases Use of passives,	Strategic backgrounding of social actors. e.g. • 'le renforcement des capacités des femmes pour jouer sainement et en responsable leur rôle premier de mère' (the reinforcement of women's capacities [by whom] to effectively and responsibly play their primary roles as mothers) • 'Je voudrais effectivement rappeler la manifestation de la volonté politique en matière de la promotion' (I effectively wish to remind us of the political will in relation to the promotion of the woman).
	Specification	Individuation- use of proper nouns	'que l'implication direct et personnel du chef de l'état, son excellence Paul Biya dans la promotion et l'amélioration de la vie de la femme camerounaise' (the direct and personal involvement of the Head of State, **His Excellency Paul Biya** in the promotion and improvement of the life of the Cameroonian woman)
	Agentialisation	Actors as agents of positive actions for women	'ministre délégué chargé auprès de la ministre de justice chargé du politique pénitencier. a quand penserai vous séparer les femmes et les hommes' (**Minister** to separate prison between males and females')

Table 7.3 Discursive Legitimation Strategies for the Discourses of 'Positive Action for Women' (Contd)

		■ 'le chef de l'état créait un ministère autonome et qui confiait les missions d'élaboration et de mise en œuvre des mesures respectives et relative au respect des droit de la femme camerounaise dans la société'. **(the head of state created an** autonomous ministry of women's affairs and entrusted it with the mission to elaborate and put in place measures and policies that protect the rights of the Cameroonian woman
	Agents of negative actions	■ 'elles subissent des viols en prison par des prisonniers et même les gardes' (Male prisoners and prison guards rape female prisoners [Women claim victim status for positive values]
	Victimisation /Passivation	Women as objects/victims of the actions (realised as grammatical subjects of passive sentences)
		■ ' elles subissent des viols' (She was raped) ■ 'les femmes prennent les grossesses' (She was made pregnant) ■ 'les effets néfaste des NTIC' (the negative effects of ICTs) ■ (She is a victim of bad use of ICTs) ■ (A victim of poverty)
	Essentialisation : as if women have the same problems and attributes	Use of definite articles plus singular nouns to represent all
		■ 'la politique de la promotion de la femme' (The politics of the promotion of **the woman)**

Negative actions highlighted to achieve positive effects. Damaging discourses

Table 7.3 Discursive Legitimation Strategies for the Discourses of 'Positive Action for Women' (Contd)

Argumentation	Presented in **Error! Reference source not found. Error! Reference source not found.** as arguments for the *legitimation* of discourses for the Positive Action for women	
Intensification	Use of Imperatives	■ 'trouvez un aménagement pour la femme et surtout pour la jeune fille' Look for a means to improve to lives of women and especially the young girl. ■ 'amenez nous un texte' Bring a text for us
Mitigation/ intensification	See **Error! Reference source not found.**	

Chapter Eight

Summary, Recommendations and Conclusion

Introduction

The original motivation for this book was to examine gender and language in Cameroonian political systems. This was as a result of my observation as a Cameroonian that women are largely excluded from traditional political set-ups, of which the core ruling bodies are all male. This peripheral participation of women in traditional politics influenced me to carry out research in a modern political domain which does not (in principle) discriminate against women. An ideal context for such an investigation was the parliament. I therefore sought to look at the discourse and linguistic practices in this modern political system. In this final chapter, I attempt to bring together the various strands of the study. I summarise the findings and their significance, and contributions to gender studies and feminist linguistics, I also examine the limitations, and then propose some ways forward in terms of further research.

Summary of Findings

Based on the different research questions that were asked at the beginning of the study, I present a summary of the findings concerning gender differences in talk in the parliament, gendered discourses including the discursive construction of men and women and the legitimation of these discourses, and also aspects of gender and power in the parliament.

Gendered Differences in Talk the Cameroonian Parliament

My first (overarching) research question was 'What gendered differences are evident in the Cameroonian parliament?'. This was analysed in Chapter 3 of this book. Contrary to current 'western' research which largely rejects analysis of gender relations in quantitative terms, and perceives much sexism as 'subtle' (see e.g. Walsh 2001, Wodak 2003, Lazar 2005), I carried out a 'gender differences' analysis to show that sexism in the Cameroonian context may not be subtle but overt, at least in the quantity of talk (by men and women) in the parliament. This aspect of the study aimed to contribute to a broad picture of gender relations within the Cameroonian parliament. The gender differences analysis also served as a basis for the understanding of the articulation of 'traditional' (conservative) and rather marginalised 'progressive' gendered discourses, and their legitimation.

The results confirmed other findings that women are marginalised and men tend monopolise verbal space in public institutional talk (e.g. James & Drakich 1993; Walsh 2001; Christie 2003; Baxter 2002, 2003; Holmes and Meyerhoff 2003). In this study, men were more verbose in the parliament in that female MPs on average spoke for less that 5% of the total talking time though they represent 11% of the total number of parliamentarians (that is, 20 women out of 180 MPs). Women's speeches (in both Question-and-Answer and Discussion genres) were also far shorter than men's, with an average length of 3 minutes compared to men's average of about 6.5 minutes. These different indicators of women's silence (relative to men) can be interpreted as a form of historically gendered, indirect silenc*ing,* given the fact that, traditionally, women did not speak in public.

In addition to looking at such gender differences in talk, I also looked quantitatively in Chapter 3 at differences in how women and men were talked to, that is, how they were addressed in the parliament. An analysis of Titulation showed that although female MPs in Cameroon earned their parliamentary seats in the same systematic way as men (through votes and without any gender mainstreaming), they were not equally addressed as 'Honourable' within the parliament (see Table 3. 2 and Table 3. 3). From the data sampled, all female parliamentarians were always and systematically referred to as 'Madame' whereas their male counterparts were referred to using various political titles – for example, 'Honorable', 'Député', 'Monsieur le Deputé', sometimes their political titles emphasised e.g. 'Honorable Député Ndinda Ndinda', MDQ3: 208. The term 'Madame' (from French) is commonly used in Cameroon to connote married women, giving them respect and highlighting the fact that the woman addressed as such is the wife of somebody. Very traditionally, to avoid offending a married woman or her husband, its usage is then generalised to all women whose marital status is not known. Usage of Madame within a parliamentary setting is however unnecessary since MPs have an alternate title of respect - *Honourable*. Such differences in Titulation, I suggest, are aspects of the discursive *construction* of the identity of female politicians within the Cameroonian parliament. These gender differences in address, I also suggest, relate in particular to how within the Cameroonian parliament, men tend to be constructed as professional and women, still, as primarily domestic (see 'Women as domestic' discourse). The differences in address thus relate to the gendered discourses identified in the data constructing women generally as wives and mothers[1] rather than as professionals and politicians. Even in parliament, then, the social roles of women politicians are emphasised rather than their professional titles.

Gender Discourses and their Legitimation

The second key issue examined in this book was 'What gendered discourses are evident in the parliament and how are they legitimated?' This overarching issue was examined in the book in three different chapters looking at the 'traditional' gendered macro-discourse of a 'Traditional Model Cameroonian Woman' (chapter 4), the legitimation of this macro-discourse (Chapter 5) and a counter macro-discourse of 'Positive action for women' and its legitimation (Chapter 6 and 7).

Using a (Discourse-Historical) Critical Discourse Analytical approach, I thus first identified and analysed 'traditional' gendered discourses available within this community of practice (Chapter 4) and how they are legitimated within parliamentary debates (Chapter 5). 'Traditional' discourses identified in the study were generally based on a traditional gender division of roles and spaces and ideologically enforced male hegemony. Dominant 'traditional' discourses such 'Gender differentiation' constructed women primarily as domestic, with associated roles such as family carers, cooks and other primary duties associated with mothers and wives. 'Woman as mother and wife' discourse was particularly dominant, articulated by both male and female parliamentarians (although to different ends), constructing Cameroonian men and women as '(compulsorily) heterosexual' (Rich 1980). Discourses that construct women's primary roles as wives, mothers, cooks and family carers generally serve to negatively mark and de-legitimate their presence in the public sphere, especially in domains of power and authority.

217

These discourses were generally legitimated through the topoi of culture and tradition, with culture functioning as a 'grand narrative' (Baxter 2003). This gendering of the work place (Holmes 2006a, 2006c) where such public spaces relate to power and authority mean that the parliament is constructed as a largely masculine domain. The discourses were also indicative of how sex and gender norms and roles have 'historically been central to the structure of power relations' and to the organization of cultural categories in Cameroon (Mbembe 2001:7).

Patriarchal, hegemonic, traditional and sexist discourses that position Cameroonian women in conservative ways however can be resisted. In Chapter 6, available modern 'progressive' counter discourses which resist and challenge traditional social practices were identified and examined as were how they legitimate positive action for women.

The Minister of Women's Affairs (Appendix 2) for example draws on a macro-discourse of what I call 'Positive Action for Women.' Discourses such as wide promotion of women (e.g. participation in parliament) and 'Gender partnership' are articulated within this macro-discourse. An alternative voice to the traditional 'It's the culture' discourse is thus articulated and women are thereby constructed as active agents of development, decision-makers, and thus not primarily domestic; and especially members of parliament, (and, indirectly, men more widely) are challenged by this female minister from a 'political high ground' to be involved in the promotion of Cameroonian women.

'Positive Action for Women' is here legitimated through different discursive strategies (see Wodak 2001, Reisigl and Wodak 2001). Referential strategies construct women in more affirmative ways, giving them agency in positive action, while at the same time problematically representing them as 'victims', patients of negative actions (e.g. rape). Using 'globalisation' as a discursive strategy, change is presented as something which cannot be ignored by any society or community. Other arguments to legitimate 'Positive Action' included health, for example, the risks women face with regard to sexually transmissible infections including HIV/AIDS), and gender equality (thus countering the 'traditional' discourse of 'Gender differentiation').

Negotiating Power Relations

After identifying different gendered discourses in parliamentary debates, and the discursive strategies social actors employ to legitimate them, I moved on to examine how power is negotiated within the parliament with regard to how individuals are positioned powerfully or powerlessly within competing discourses. Through Chapters 4 - 7, I address the overarching question 'How are gender and power relations negotiated in the Cameroonian parliament?'. I examined how social actors are powerfully or powerlessly positioned within different available discourses and subject positions and how, as agents, they shift, sometimes strategically, between these positions of power. Such an analysis indicated that social actors might be constructed as power*ful*, for example, Honourable Etame François, can also be seen as power*less* in various ways. Within the same speech event, and within the 'patriarchal' society, the Honourable is empowered by discourses that construct women as traditional, but disempowered by competing discourses of change and women's emancipation. Similarly, Honourable Mebanda was arguably empowered by her discourse when she constructed herself as an MP who helps women in prison, but was then disempowered by the Speaker of the House of Assembly when he made reference to being separated from her husband because (as I interpret it) she talks too much. Such an analysis showed that Cameroonian men, although empowered by culture and tradition, are certainly not discoursally powerful all the time, and that women, although constructed and positioned as powerless by discourses that construct them as wives and mothers, are *socially* and *institutionally* empowered when they take up their professional subject positions (of MPs or Ministers). Further, my analysis shows them to also be discoursally powerful some of the time.

CDA enabled me to examine dominant macro power relations in the Cameroonian parliament, and to identify dominant gendered discourses and the discursive strategies used to construct social actors and legitimate arguments.

Contributions of the Study

This study has gone some way to filling the gap in the literature in the area of gender and language (specifically political discourse) in Cameroon and has highlighted the relationship between gender, language and power within public, and institutional settings more broadly.

Other contributions of this study are of three broad types: contributions to gender studies and feminist linguistics (gender differences, gendered discourses, and gender and power relations in institutional settings), contributions to gender and political linguistics, and contributions to theory.

Gender Differences in the Parliament

Current studies in gender and language have largely moved away from a quantitative, 'gender differences' paradigm claiming this is a binary approach which polarises subjects into two groups, often socially, if not biologically essentialising them, often seeing language use as a *reflection* of gender, rather than as *constructing* it. Current researchers also claim that many gender relations and issues of discrimination and power are today very 'subtle' (see Bergvall et al. 1996, Holmes and Meyerhoff 2003, Lazar 2005).

Studies of gender differences (West and Zimmerman 1977, 1987; Fishman 1978/1983) however served as pioneer work in analysing gender differences in language use within particular groups. And studies of gender differences are not entirely incompatible with social constructionist approaches (Cameron 2003: 187): for example, they identify what has been socially constructed, as well as point to *how*. Cameron adds that with gender differences, sometimes leading to generalisations, accomplished through quantitative analysis, are also 'not incompatible with contemporary feminist views of gender as social construct and social practice' (p. 197). Holmes (2006) points out that such quantitative studies can sometimes be relevant to present *strategic essentialism* for political reasons. In an African context where gender stereotypes are salient and discrimination often far from subtle, I thought it necessary to start by highlighting the quantitative distribution of talk by and about women and men in my research setting, the Cameroonian parliament. My main findings and contributions in the study of 'gender differences' are as follows:

♦ The study also showed that male Cameroonian politicians highlight the social status of women (but not men) in this setting at the expense of their professional/political status, through the use of their *social* titles (*Madame* rather than the available *Honourable*).

♦ In an era where women in Cameroon are predominantly marginalised in decision-making positions, but where women's rights and empowerment are highlighted internationally, it was not surprising that women's preoccupation in parliament was women's rights rather than other national issues, as reflected by their choice of topics (Table 3. 9) Men's topics in the parliament were more varied and included gendered topics, although most of the time their concerns were articulated through conservative discourses.

♦ Using a large quantity of recorded data (parliamentary talk), this study established a useful baseline data of gendered verbal participation in the Cameroonian parliament. This showed that the issue at stake is not only female *physical* representation in the public sphere or decision making bodies, that is, women's *presence*, but also their *functional* representation, that is, representation through active verbal participation and *positive contributions* in terms of amount and type of talk. The problematic quality and quantity of female participation in public discourse is relevant to gender mainstreaming in other organisations which are interested not only in the number of women in decision-making positions, but also the quality of women's talk within these organisations.

Gendered Discourses

One of the main concerns of this book has been to identify both 'traditional' and 'progressive' gendered discourses that are articulated within the Cameroonian parliament (meaning that these are available *outside* the parliament), how parliamentarians accordingly discursively construct their own and others' gendered identities through language, and the different strategies employed to legitimate the discourses. Findings in the study indicate that

221

♦ Although both men and women in parliament draw on 'traditional' discourses such as those surrounding motherhood, men tend to articulate and legitimate them conservatively, legitimating male dominance, while women tend to appropriate them and positively and strategically *utilise* their 'primary' roles as mothers and wives to *challenge* the dominant traditional interpretations of these discourses to bring out new (progressive) meanings.

♦ Cameroonian male politicians articulate and endorse discourses that highlight *gender as difference,* that is, discourses that in practice uphold male hegemony and dominance, and foster inequality. These differences are legitimated through the justification of the need for 'us' to preserve 'our culture', adhere to (Christian) religious practices, and mark geographical differences between Cameroonian women and women from elsewhere.

♦ Women parliamentarians however resist these discourses by drawing on 'progressive' counter discourses such as gender equality, women's empowerment, gender partnership and the elimination of all forms of discrimination against women to legitimate positive action for women. However, they also positively appropriate the discourse of *gender as difference* to celebrate femininity through their multiple roles of career women, mothers and wives. In their speeches, they negotiate the different subject positions of politicians and their gender identities as mothers and wives.

Gender and Power Relations

Although men are generally constructed within the Cameroonian society through powerful and dominant gendered discourses such as those we might call 'Men as public' and 'Men as heads of the family' (by implication born to lead; not discussed in this book), the analysis has shown that Cameroonian women are neither socially nor discoursally powerless all the time. Even when faced by a situation where they could be silenced by patriarchal hegemonic gender and institutional power relations, they tend to challenge, contest and resist these relations. This was evident in both the speeches of the female minister Madame Catherine Bakang Mbock and the female MP, Honourable Rose Mebanda. As such, Cameroonian women can be seen as powerful depending on the discourses that are being drawn on by them or others at specific moments. It was accordingly shown in the analysis that although male MPs are generally positioned by wider societal discourses (e.g. 'Gender differentiation' and 'It's the Culture'; and as powerful, both as members of parliament and as men, these MPs were rendered powerless at certain moments within a speech event by a counter discourse. For example, Honourable Etame was shown in the analysis to occupy a powerful subject position of *a man* and *an MP*, but, in his own speech, he is rendered socially and institutionally relatively powerless by the subject position of an MP in front of a more powerful position - the minister further, he also intertextually draws on discourses of women's emancipation, which position him as no longer in control of society as he once was. Trying to legitimate the maintenance of 'A traditional model Cameroonian woman' therefore shows the status quo is being threatened, and thus his (and other men's) power over women.

On gender and political linguistics, there have not been many studies in the area, with researchers such as Walsh 2001, Shaw 2000, and Christie 2003. In Cameroon in particular, there is a paucity of research in this area linking language to power and in political settings in particular. It is my hope that this study will contribute to the area of gender and political (parliamentary) discourse analysis, not only to the virgin area in Cameroon but Africa in general.

Theoretical Contributions of this Study

Although gendered discourses have hitherto been identified in Gender and Language literature (Rich 1980, Baxter 2003, Sunderland 2004), this study is unique in identifying gendered discourses characteristic of a developing country - Cameroon. Discourses of (Third World) *development* often represent women as better managers in the development process (see Fonchingong 2006, Fondo 2006, Fonjong 2001) but this study highlights the articulation of particular discourses of 'Gender partnership', 'Women as decision making', and 'Women as agents of development'. These discourses are dominant in the institutional texts surrounding third world development.

223

Particular to this study as well is the identification of an 'Its the culture' discourse as a dominant legitimation strategy to justify both the preservation of tradition and culture (by women, see the discourses of women as preservers of culture) and to maintain male dominance in a changing globalised society with new practices and discourses of gender, gender roles and gender relations. This legitimation strategy is common and characteristic of post-colonial communities (see Said 1985, Huntington 1983). This study has therefore been useful in identifying legitimated gendered discourses that are characteristic beyond Cameroon to developing world.

Although CDA researchers inter alia have identified different discursive strategies used in legitimating different discourses, I have identified certain additional strategies that I think are peculiar to this study and perhaps the contextual background. For example, in the legitimation of 'traditional' discourses that uphold male hegemony and reject positive change for women, male MPs use discursive strategies such as these below to legitimate the preservation and maintenance of the status quo:

- *Gender as difference (Gender Differentiation)* – women are different from men and should not try to copy male practices or otherwise seek to be equal.
- *Geography* – Cameroonian (African) women are unique and different from other women and so should not try to copy what happens elsewhere; this is in turn justified through a discourse which sees women as the main *guardians* of culture.
- *Juxtaposition* - good women vs. bad women, whores vs. Madonnas, women, as previously indicated from one region are better than women from others.
- *Culture* – The status quo *should* be maintained following the Cameroon government's plan to preserve the nation's culture and traditions.

Mitigation strategies (a contribution to CDA, hitherto identified in DH-CDA as strategies used largely by powerful groups to legitimate negative practices and soften negative utterances, (Reisigl and Wodak 2001: 85) are used in here by powerless groups (women) to legitimate positive practices. Mitigation is used in the context of gender discrimination by the 'weaker' group (women), not to 'minimise [negative] events' (2001: 110) as in racial discriminatory discourses, but to *highlight* and *underline* negative events against the marginalised group in a way that can also be read as (intended to be) ironic.

Self-Reflexivity and Limitations of the Study

In this study of gender differences, gendered discourses and relations of power within the Cameroonian parliament, I have assumed various 'subject positions' and have tried to remain reflexive. Davies underlines that the 'effects of self-reflexivity are to be found in *all* phases of the research process from initial selection of topic to final reporting of results' (Davies 2002: 4; my emphasis). I was reflexive (from a CDA perspective) by declaring my political stance as an African feminist[2], *'in solidarity with* Cameroonian women[3]' (see van Dijk 2001: 96; Reisigl and Wodak 2001: 33).

My identity as a female professional Cameroonian woman affected my choice of research area and, I suppose, my analysis has been partly influenced by this subject position. However, as Wetherell (2002: 16) points out, 'separation [of selves] is impossible'. I have in fact brought my various identities into this piece of research. First of all my cultural identity (born and raised in a Cameroonian village) cannot be ignored as well as my gender identity as a woman and a mother. Added to these identities is the fact that I am not only educated, but have worked in an institutional setting (the University). I am different from my research participants as among other things I am neither a politician nor a parliamentarian. However, we share a common subject position of working in public institutional settings.

While my multiple identities (Wodak 2003) have been a strength as I drew on my cultural knowledge and context related meanings of words and expressions, and the specific Cameroonian English and French, it has also been difficult to keep my voice out of the analysis as a Cameroonian who has lived and worked within this context. It is likely, if not inevitable, that while carrying out the qualitative analysis, my ethnic, historical, academic and professional background have influenced the interpretation of the data. While this is valuable (especially for a 'participant observer' and indeed FPDA sees the researcher's 'voice' as just one among many (Baxter

2003: 37), and the researcher as 'not a disembodied' critic but 'interested members of specific societies and social groups with specific points of view' (Reisigl and Wodak 2001: 35), I might have read meaning into expressions different from that intended by the speakers. Such limitations might have been minimised with the use of interviews of MPs to examine how they construct themselves as male and female politicians in terms of gender roles and power relations. However, due to time constraints, and the scope of this book, this was not possible. However, as indicated, my 'insider' position and cultural knowledge provided me with useful insights into cultural meanings, as in the case of the Minister of Women's Affairs appropriating 'traditional' gendered discourses of motherhood (see App: 29-30).

I might also have over-generalised in places: as Antaki et al (2003) points out, '[t]here is a danger of extrapolating from one's data to the world at large'. I have tried not to do this, but, in any case, as Cameron (2001: 138) notes, my conclusions may not apply to everyone but they do say something about someone and are indicative of the society I come from. Certainly, I have pointed to the *availability* of macro-discourses and discourses within current Cameroonian society.

In my data collection and analysis, I did not draw on the reflexive voices of the social actors as (as indicated); I did not carry out interviews or feedback the results of my analysis to the researched. This goes against one of the principles of FPDA, that is, polyphony (see Baxter 2003: 67), which requires the researcher to include all participants' voices in the research. Through interviews social actors might also have opened up and shed more light on their different subject positions in the parliament and how they (un)consciously negotiated relations of power within this institution, and indeed on my *own* interpretations. This was not practical for this research due to time limitations on my part and the busy schedule of the research subjects[4], as well as the geographical and institutional setting of the data[5].

Finally, one can never finish analysing a text. There is always more to say, as another researcher may actually come out with brand new material from the same texts. However, due to limitations of time and space, some aspects of analysis have been saved for future research.

Suggestions for Future Work

There are a number of future directions with which this research could continue in order to further explore and contribute to the study of gender, language and relations of power in institutional settings in Cameroon.

First, the study only focused on the question of power, gendered discourses and differences in the parliament. Other studies might also usefully examine masculine verbosity in public discourse within other public spheres such as courtrooms, board rooms and other public administrative positions to assess its prevalence and specific institutional manifestations within Cameroon. Studies in other institutional settings would also be able to identify if women's social roles are similarly highlighted at the expense of their professional roles, in particular, through titulation.

A broader study would extend to other African and other developing countries, to identify different strategies women use in public talk in negotiating gender and power relations in 'patriarchal' societies, and how they contest these and position themselves and other women as power*ful*.

Conclusion and Final Words

Growing up as a young girl, I often wondered why only men were members of the *Kwifor*, a ruling traditional men-only society in Cameroon. I later observed that only men could be leaders of the village, and only men were administrators of the sub-divisions, the provinces (and still are) and even the nation as a whole. However, as time went on, these stereotypes were being challenged when also I saw female heads of modern institutions, ministers, and female members of parliament. I came to ask myself how these women coped in these still 'masculine domains'.

As I went through life I realised these challenges were not only faced by these relatively powerful women but all 'modern' Cameroonian women, myself included. With my 'multiple' and 'complex' identities, I ask myself how I can best protect my rights as a citizen, arguing for equal opportunities, equal access to jobs and positions of power and responsibility, and getting my voice heard in public spheres, while maintaining my identity as an African woman who often still, supposed to be a 'preserver of culture and tradition' and all it entails? These are complex subject positions most Cameroonian women have to problematically negotiate on a daily basis.

In this study, I have come a long way in understanding in particular how women in decision-making positions in Cameroon discursively construct themselves and legitimate their positions in these male-dominated communities of practice. Further studies of gender and discourse within the public sphere will give greater insights into this complex situation, and, more importantly, will be able to monitor challenge and *change,* of which I hope this book has provided some illuminating examples.

Notes

1. A woman and a frying pan belong to the kitchen (Spanish proverb, Schipper 2003).

2. Being an African feminist means having the influence of western feminism, yet conscious of 'positive' African values.

3. Actually van Dijk talks of the 'oppressed' and Reisigl and Wodak of 'empathy with victims of discrimination'.

4. Parliament holds for 30 days, three times a year and, during sessions, MPs are involved in committees (which are in camera) or attending plenary sessions. It was therefore difficult to arrange interviews within these periods.

5. Travelling from the UK to collect data in a 30-day margin meant that it was difficult to schedule interviews as after the sessions, MPs generally go back to their constituencies. However, part of the difficulty was my own time constraints.

References

Abdela, L. (2000). 'A Strategy for Women's Empowerment in Cameroon'. Yaoundé. British Council Cameroon.

Abdela, L. (2000). 'From Palm Tree to Parliament: Training Women for Political Leadership in Public Life'. Gender and Development, 8(3), 16-23.

Achebe, C. (1958). *Things Fall Apart*. London: Heinemann.

Adams, M. (2006). 'Colonial Policies and Women's Participation in Public Life: the Case of British Southern Cameroons'. *African Studies Quarterly* 8(3).

Agrosino, M. V., and Kimberly A Mays de Pérez. (2003). 'Rethinking Observation: From Method to Context'. In N. K. Denzin and Y. S. Lincoln (Eds.), *Collecting and Interpreting Qualitative Materials*. London: Sage (pp. 107-144).

Aje-Ori, A. (2003). 'Maintaining Power in the Face of Political, Economic and Social Discrimination: The Tale of Nigerian Women'. *Women and Language,* 26(1).

Aletum, T. (1990). *Bafut Institutions in Modern Politics*. Yaoundé: SOPECAM.

Aletum, T. (2001). *Political Sociology*. Yaoundé: Patoh Publishers.

Althusser, L. (1971). 'Ideology and Ideological State Apparatuses'. In L. Althusser (Ed.) *Lenin and Philosophy and Other Essays*. London: New Left Books.

Antaki, C., Billig, M., Edwards, D. and Potter, J. (2003). 'Discourse Analysis Means Doing Analysis: A Critique of Six Analytical Shortcomings.' *Discourse Analysis Online.* 1(1)

Assie-Lumumba, N. (1997). 'Educating Africa's Girls and Women: A Conceptual and Historical Analysis of Gender Inequality.' In A. M Imam, A. Mama and F. Sow (Eds.), *Engendering African Social Sciences*. Dakar: CODESRIA. 316

Atanga, L. (1996). *The Syntax of Verbs in Bafut. Unpublished* MA Dissertation. Jos: University of Jos, Nigeria.

Atanga, L.L., Ellece, S., Littoselitti, L and Sunderland, J (2010 forthcoming) *Gender and Language in African Contexts*. Edinburgh: Edinburgh University Press.

Awasom, S. (2002). 'A Critical Survey of the Resuscitation, Activation, and Adaptation of Traditional Africa and Female Political Institutions to the Exigencies of Modern Politics in the 1990s: The Case of the Takumbeng Female Society in Cameroon.' CODESRIA 10 General Assembly. Kampala: CODESRIA.

Awasom, S. (2005). 'Towards a Gendered Development Discourse in Africa: Visible Women, Invisible Men.' CODESRIA 11 General Assembly Maputo: CODESRIA.

BAAL (1994). 'Recommendation on Good Practice in Applied Linguistics.' British Association of Applied Linguistics.

http://www.baal.org.uk/about_goodpractice_stud.pdf

Baktin, M. (1981). *The Dialogic Imagination: Four Essays*. Texas: University of Texas.

Bamgbose, A. (1989). 'Issues for a Mode l of Language Planning.' *Language Problems and Language Planning* 13(1).

Bamgbose, A. (Ed.) (2004). *Language Planning and Language Policies: Issues and Prospects*. Amsterdam: John Benjamins.

Baxter, J. (2002). 'Competing Discourses in the Classroom: A Post-Structuralist Discourse Analysis of Girls' and Boys' Speech in Public Contexts.' *Discourse and Society* 13(6), 827-843.

Baxter, J. (2003). '*Positioning Gender in Discourse: A Feminist Post-Structuralist Approach*. Basingstoke: Palgrave.

Baxter, J. (Ed.) (2006). *Speaking Out: The Female Voice in Public Context*. Basingstoke: Palgrave Macmillan.

Baxter, J. (2008). 'Feminist Post-structuralist Discourse Analysis: A New Theoretical and Methodological Approach?' In K. Harrington, L. Litosseliti, H. Sauntson and J. Sunderland (Eds.), *Gender and Language Research Methodologies*. Basingstoke: Palgrave

Bayley, P. (Ed.). (2004). *Cross-cultural Perspectives in Parliamentary Discourse*. Amsterdam: John Benjamins.

Bayley, P. (Analysing Language and Politics. Online Journal of Interdisciplinary Studies on Language and Culture.)

www.mediazionionline.com/arti coli/bayley.htm Accessed 2005

Becker, H. (2000). 'A Concise History of Gender, 'Tradition' and the State in Namibia.' In C. Keulde (Ed.), *State, Society and Democracy. A Reader in Namibian Politics*. Windhoek: Gamsberg Macmillan.

Beetham, D. (1991). *The Legitimation of Power*. London: Macmillan.

Bennett, J. (2006). 'Treating One Another Like Human beings': South African Engendering within the Semantics of Current Feminist Discourse.' *South African Linguistics and Applied Language Studies*, 24(4), 425 - 435.

Bergvall, V. (1999). 'Toward a Comprehensive Theory of Language and Gender.' *Language and Society* 28(2), 273-293.

Bernstein, B. (1990). *The Structuring of Pedagogic Discourse*. London: Routledge.

Billig, M. (1999). "Who's Terms? Whose Ordinariness? Rhetoric and Ideology in Conversational Analysis.' *Discourse and Society,* 10(4), 543-582.

Bing, J., and Bergvall, V. (1998[1996]). 'The Question of Questions: Beyond Binary Thinking.' In J. Coates (Ed.), *Language and Gender: A Reader*. Malden: Blackwell. 318

Blommaert J. and Bulcan C. (2002). 'Critical Discourse Analysis.' *Annual Review of Anthropology* 29, 447-466.

Blommaert, J. (2005). *Discourse*. Cambridge: Cambridge University Press.

Bourdieu, P. (1991). *Language and Symbolic Power*. Cambridge: Polity Press.

Breton, R. and Fohtung, B. (1991). *Atlas Administratif des Langues Nationales du Cameroun*. Yaoundé: CERDOTOLA, CREA-ACCT.

Brown, P. and Levinson, S. (1987). *Politeness: Some Universals in Language Usage*. Cambridge: CUP.

Bucholtz M., Liang A. C., and Sutton, L. (1999). *Reinventing Identities: The Gendered Self in Discourse*. New York: Oxford University Press.

Bucholtz, M. (1999). 'Why Be Normal? Language and Identity Practices in a Community of Nerd Girls.' *Language and Society,* 28(2), 203-223.

Bucholtz, M. (2000). 'The Politics of Transcription.' *Journal of Pragmatics* 32, 1439-1465.

Bucholtz, M. (Ed.). (2004). *Language and Women's Place: Text and Commentaries*. Oxford: Oxford University Press.

Burman, E. (2004). Discourse Analysis Means Analysing Discourse: Some Comments on Antaki, Billig, Edwards and Potter 'Discourse Analysis Means Doing Analysis: A Critique Of Six Analytic Shortcomings'. *Discourse Analysis Online* http://extra.shu.ac.uk/daol/current/

Butler, J. (1999 [1990]). *Gender* Trouble: Feminism and the Subversion of Identities. 2nd edition. New York: Routledge.

Caldas-Coulthard, C. R. and Coulthard, M. (Eds.) (1996). *Texts and Practices*. London: Routledge.

Caldas-Coulthard, C. R. and Iedema R. (Eds.) (2007). *Identity Trouble: Critical Discourse and Contestations of Identification*. Basingstoke: Palgrave Macmillan.

Caldas-Coulthard, C. R. and Van Leeuwen, T. (2002) 'Stunning, Shimmering, Iridescent: Toys as the Representation of Gendered Social Actors.' In L. Litosseleti and J. Sunderland (Eds.) *Gender Identity and Discourse Analysis*. Amsterdam: John Benjamins (pp. 91-110).

Caldas-Coulthard, C. R. (1996). 'Women Who Pay for Sex and Enjoy It': Transgression versus Morality in Women's Magazine s. In C. R. Caldas-Coulthard and M. Coulthard (Eds.), *Texts and Practices*. London: Routledge.

Cameron, D. (1998[1990]). *The Feminist Critique of Language: A Reader* (2nd edition). London: Routledge.

Cameron, D. (1992). 'Not Gender Difference but the Difference Gender Makes: Explanation in Research on Sex and Language.' *International Journal of the Sociology of Language*, 94.

Cameron, D. (1995). 'Rethinking Language and Gender Studies: Some Issues of the 1990s.' In S. Mills (Ed.), *Language and Gender: Interdisciplinary Perspectives* Harlow: Longman (pp. 31-44).

Cameron, D. (1997). 'Performing Gender Identity: Young Men's Talk and the Construction of Heterosexual Masculinity.' In S. Johnson and U. Meinhof (Eds.), *Language and Masculinity*. Malden, MA: Blackwell. (pp. 47-64).

Cameron, D. (1997). Theoretical Debates in Feminist Linguistics: Questions of Sex and Gender'. In R. Wodak (Ed.), *Gender and Discourse* London: Sage. (pp.21-36).

Cameron, D. (1998). 'Gender, Language and Discourse: a Review Essay.' *Signs: Journal of Women and Culture and Society*, 23(4), 945-972.

Cameron, D. (2001). *Working with Spoken Discourse*. London: Sage.

Cameron, D. (2003). 'Gender and Language Ideologies.' In J. Holmes and M. Meyerhoff (Eds.), *Handbook of Language and Gender Research*. Oxford: Blackwell.

Cameron, D. (2003). 'Gender Issues in Language Change.' *Annual Review of Applied Linguistics* 23, 187-201.

Cameron, D. (2006). 'Theorising the Female Voice in Public Contexts.' In J. Baxter (Ed.), *Speaking Out: The Female Voice in Public Contexts*. Basingstoke: Palgrave.

Cameron, D. (2007). 'Unanswered Questions and Unquestioned Assumptions in the Study of Language and Gender: Female Verbal Superiority.' *Gender and Language*, 1(1), 15-25.

Cameron, D., and Kulick, D. (2003). *Language and Sexuality*. Cambridge and New York: Cambridge University Press.

Chambers, E. (2003). 'Applied Ethnography.' In N. K. Denzin and Y. S. Lincoln (Eds.), *Collecting and Interpreting Qualitative Materials*. London: Sage.

Celic, M (2003). 'Teaching Vocabulary through Code Mixing'. *ELT,* 57(4), 361-369.

Chilton, P. and Schaffner, C. (2002). *Politics of Text and Talk: Analytic al Approaches to Political Discourse*. Amsterdam: John Benjamins.

Chilton, P. (2004). *Analysing Political Discourse*. London: Routeledge.

Chouliaraki L. and Fairclough N. (1999). *Discourse in Late Modernity: Rethinking Critical Discourse Analysis*. Edinburgh: Edinburgh University press.

Christie, C. (2003). 'Politeness and Linguistic Construction of Gender in the Parliament: An Analysis of Transgression and Apology Behaviour. Linguistic Politeness and Context.' *Sheffield Hallam University Working Papers on the Web*.

extra.shu.ac.uk/wpw/politeness/Christie

Chumbow, B. S. and Bobda, A. S. (2000). 'French in West Africa: A Sociolinguistic Perspective.' *International Journal of the Sociology of Language*. 141, 9-60.

Chumbow, B.S and Tamanji N. (1994) 'Negation in Bafut.' In Kahrel, P. and van den Berg R. (Eds.), *Typological studies in negation*. Amsterdam: John Benjamins. (p. 211-236).

Chungong, J. (2007). *The Changing Roles of West African Fathers*. Lancaster: Lancaster University.

Cicourel, A. V. (2006). 'The Interaction of Discourse, Cognition and Society.' *Discourse Studies*, 8(1), 25-29.

Clark, J. (2006). 'The Role of Language and Gender in the Naming and Framing of HIV/AIDS in the South African Context.' *South African Linguistics and Applied Language Studies*, 24(4), 461-471.

Clark, L. H. (2000). 'A Matter of Voice: Grace Paley and the Oral Tradition.' *Women and Language*, 23(1), 18-26.

Coates, J. (1993). *Women, Men and Language: A Sociolinguistic Account of Gender Differences in Language*. London: Longman.

Coates, J. (1996). *Women Talk*. Malden, MA: Blackwell.

Coates, J. (1998). *Language and Gender: A Reader*. Oxford: Blackwell.

Coates, J. (2003). *Men Talk*. Malden, MA: Blackwell.

Corbett, G. (1991). *Gender*. Cambridge: Cambridge University Press.

Corson, D. (1993). *Language, Minority Education and Gender: Linking Social Justice and Power*. Cleverdon: Multilingual Matters.

Corson, D. (1997). 'Gender, Discourse and Senior Education: Ligatures for Girls, Options for Boys.' In Wodak, R. (Ed.), *Gender and Discourse*. London: Sage.

Dahl, K. (2006). 'Celebrating' or 'Commemorating' the Lewis and Clark Expedition? Museum Interpretive Text as Text!' *Pacific Northwest American Studies Association Meetings*.

Davies, C. (2002). *Reflexive Ethnography: A Guide to Researching Selves and Others*. London: Routledge.

Davies, S. G. (2005). 'Women in Politics in Post-Beijing Indonesia.' *International Social Sciences Journal*, 57(2), 231-242.

De Celia R., Reisigl M. and Wodak, R. (1999). 'Discursive Construction of National Identities.' *Discourse and Society* , 10(2).

DeFrancisco, L. V. (1991). 'The Sounds of Silence: How Men Silence Women in Marital Relations.' *Discourse and Society*, 2(4), 413-424.

DeMarrais, K. B. and Lapan, S. D. (2004). 'Foundations for Research: Methods of Inquiry in Education and the Social Sciences.' *Inquiry and Pedagogy across Diverse Contexts*. Mahwah: Lawrence Erlbaum Associates.

Denzin, N. K., and Lincoln, Y. S. (2003). 'Methods of Collecting and analysing Empirical Materials.' In Denzin, N. K. and Lincoln, Y. S. (Eds.), *Collecting and Interpreting Qualitative Materials.* London: Sage (pp. 47-61).

Derrida, J. (1987). A Derrida Reader: Between the Blinds. Brighton: Harvester.

Dibattista, D. (2004). 'Legitimising and Informative Discourse in the Kosovo Debates.' In Bayley, P. (Ed.), *Cross-Cultural Perspectives on Parliamentary Discourse.* Amsterdam: John Benjamins. (pp. 151-184).

Duranti, A. (Ed.). (2001). *Linguistic Anthropology: A Reader.* Oxford: Blackwell.

Dutcher, N. (2004). *Expanding Educational Opportunity in Linguistically Diverse Societies* (2nd edition.). Washington, DC: Center for Applied Linguistics http://www.cal.org/resources/pubs/expand.html.

Eades, D. (2000). 'I don't think it's an answer to the question: Silencing Aboriginal Witnesses in Court.' *Language in Society*, 29, 161-195.

Eagleton, T. (1991) *Ideology: an Introduction.* London: Verso.

Echu, G. and Grundstrom, A. W. (Eds.) (1999) *Official Bilingualism and Linguistic Communication in Cameroon.* New York: Peter Lang.

Echu, G. (2003). 'Multilingualism as a Resource: the Lexical Appropriation of Cameroon Indigenous Languages by English and French' (1)

Eckert, P., and McConnel-Ginet, S. (2007). 'Putting Communities of Practice in their Place.' *Gender and Language,* 1(1), 27-37.

Eckert, P., and McConnell-Ginet, S. (1992). 'Think Practically and Look Locally: Language and Gender as Community-based Practice.' *Annual Review of Anthropology,* 21(4), 61-90.

Eckert, P., and McConnell-Ginet, S. (1999). 'New Generalizations and Explanations in Language and Gender Research.' *Language in Society* 28, 185-201.

Eckert, P., and McConnell-Ginet, S. (2003). *Language and Gender.* Cambridge. Cambridge University Press.

Edley, N. (2001). 'Analysing Masculinity: Interpretive Repertoires, Ideological Dilemmas and Subject Positions.' In M. Wetherell, S. Taylor and S. Yates (Eds.), *Discourse as Data.* London: Sage/Open University Press (pp. 189-228).

Elrich, S. (2006). 'Trial Discourse and Judicial Decision-making: Constraining the Boundaries of Gendered Identities.' In B. Judith (Ed.), *Speaking Out: The Female Voice in Public Context.* Basingstoke: Palgrave.

Endeley J., Ardener S., Goodridge R., and Lyonga, N. (Eds.) (2004). *New Gender Studies from Cameroon and the Caribbean*. Buea: University of Buea.

Endeley, J. B. and Ardener, S. (2004). 'Gender-Inclusive Culture on Higher Education: The Case of the University of Buea.' In J. B. Endeley and S. Ardener (Eds.), *New Gender Studies in Cameroon and the Caribbean*. Buea : University of Buea.

ESA (2000). *The Official Report of the FWCW Containing the Beijing Declaration and Platform for Action*. New York: United Nations.

Fairclough, N. and Wodak, R. (1997). 'Critical Discourse Analysis.' In T. van Dijk (Ed.), *Discourse as Social Interaction*. London: Sage.

Fairclough, N. (1992). *Discourse and Social Change*. Cambridge: Polity Press.

Fairclough, N. (1995). *Critical Discourse Analysis*. London: Longman.

Fairclough, N. (2000). *New Labour New Language?* London: Routeledge.

Fairclough, N. (2001). Critical Discourse Analysis as a Method in Social Scientific Research. In Wodak, R. and Meyer M. (Eds.), *Methods of Critical Discourse Analysis*. London: Sage,(pp. 121-139).

Fairclough, N. (2001). *Language and Power* (2nd edition). London: Longman.

Fairclough, N. (2001). 'The Discourse of New Labour: Critical Discourse Analysis.' In M. Wetherell, S., Taylor and Yates S. (Eds.), *Discourse as Data*. London: Sage.

Fairclough, N. (2003). *Analysing Discourse: Textual Analysis for Social Research*. London: Routledge.

Fairclough, N. (2006) *Language and Globalization*. London: Routledge.

Fisher, S. and Todd, D. A. (1988). *Gender and Discourse: The Power of Talk*. Norwood: Abblex Pub. Corp.

Fisher, S., and Todd, D. A. (Eds.). (1986). *Discourse and Institutional Authority: Medicine, Education and Law*. Norwood: Abblex Pub. Corp.

Fishman, P. (1983). 'Interactions: the Work Women Do.' In B. Thorne, C. Kramarae and N. Henley (Eds.), *Language, Gender and Society*. Rowley: Newbury House, (pp.89-101).

Fombe, M. (2005). 'How Women Wield Power in the Traditional Milieu.' Femina.

Fonchingong, C. C. (2005). 'Negotiating Livelihoods beyond Beijing.' *International Social Sciences Journal,* 57(2), 243-253.

Fonchingong, C. C. (2006). 'Expanding Horizons: Women's Voices in Community-driven Development in the Cameroon Grasslands.' *GeoJournal.* 137-149

Fondo, S. (2006). 'Engendering Development: Gender Division of Labour and Women's Decision Making Power in Rural Households: The Case of Cameroon.'

www.codesria.org/Links/conferences/general_assembly11/papers/ sikod.pdf CODESRIA (Vol. 2006).

Fonjong, L. N. (2001). 'Fostering Women's Participation in Development Through Non-Governmental Efforts in Cameroon.' *The Geographical Journal of the Royal Geographical Society* 167(3).

Foucault, M. (1972). The *Archeology of Knowledge.* London: Tailstock Publications.

Foucault, M. (1980). *Power/Knowledge.* Brighton: Harvester Press.

Fowler R., Hodge B., Kress, G. and Trew, T. (1979). *Language and Control.* London: Routledge and Kegan Paul.

Freed, A. (1996). 'Language and Gender Research in an Experimental Setting.' In V. Bergvall and J. Bing (Eds.), *Rethinking Language and Gender Research: Theory and Practice.* Harlow: Longman.

Freed, A. (1999). 'Communities of Practice and Pregnant Women: Is there a Connection?' *Language and Society.* 28(2), 257-271.

Gal, S. and Woodard, K. A. (2001). *Languages and Publics: The Making of Authority.* Manchester: St Jerome Publishers.

Gal, S. (1991). 'Between Speech and Silence: The Problematics of Research on Language and Gender.' In M. D. Leonardo (Ed.), *Gender at the Crossroads of Knowledge: Feminist Anthropology in the Post-Modern Era.* Berkeley: University of California Press (pp. 175-203.).

Gal, S. (1992/1995). 'Language, Gender and Power: An Anthropological View.' In K. Hall K., M. Bucholtz and B. Moonwoman (Eds.), *Gender Articulated: Language and the Constructed Self.* London: Routledge, (pp. 169-182).

Galega, S. and Tumnde, M. (2004). 'Reversing Decades of Gender Injustice in Cameroon.' In J. M. Mbaku and J. Toboggan (Eds.), *Leadership Challenge in Africa: Cameroon under Paul Biya.* Washington: Africa World Press.

Geisler, G. (2000). 'Parliament is Another Terrain of Struggle: Women, Men and Parliament in South Africa.' *Journal of Modern African Studies* 38(4), 605-630.

Gladwin, C. (1991). 'Land in Nso, Cameroon.' In C. Gladwin (Ed.), *Structural Adjustment and African Women Farmers.* Grainesville: University of Florida.

Goheen, M. (1991). 'The Ideology and Political Economy of Gender: Women and Land in Nso, Cameroon.' In C. Gladwin (Ed.), *Structural Adjustment and African Women Farmers.* Gainesville: University of Florida.

Goheen, M. (1996). *Men Own the Fields, Women Own the Crops: Gender and Power in the Cameroon Grassfields.* Madison: University of Wisconsin Press.

Gordon, R. G. J. (2005). *Ethnologue: Languages of the World* (Fifteenth Edition).Dallas: SIL International.

Gramsci, A. (1971). *Selections from the Prison Notebooks.* London: Lawrence and Wishart.

Greenberg, J.(1963). The languages of Africa. Bloomington: Indiana University.

Grillo, E. (Ed.). (2005). *Power without Dominion.* Amsterdam: John Benjamins.

Grimes, B. F. (Ed.). (2000). *Ethnologue: Languages of the world.* Dallas: Summer Institute of Linguistics.

Habermas, J. (1984). *The Theory of Communicative Action.* Vol. 1. London: Heinemann.

Halliday, M. A. K. (1978). *Language as Social Semiotic.* London: Arnold.

Halliday, M. A. K. (2004 [1985/1994]). *An Introduction to Functional Grammar* (1st 2nd and 3rd editions). London: Edward Arnold.

Hammersley, M. and Atkinson, P. (1995). *Ethnography: Principles and Practice.* London: Routledge.

Hammersley, M. (1992). *What Is Wrong with Ethnography.* London: Routledge

Hammersley, M. (1997). *On the Foundation of Critical Discourse Analysis. Language and Communication,* 17(3), 237-248.

Hodge, B., and Kress, G. (1988). *Social Semiotics.* Cambridge: Polity Press.

Holmes, J. (1993). 'Women's Talk: The Question of Sociolinguistic Universals.' *Australian Journal of Communication,* 20(3), 125–49.

Holmes, J. (2005). 'Power and Discourse at Work: Is Gender Relevant?' In M. Lazar (Ed.), *Feminist Critical Discourse Analysis: Gender, Power and Ideology*. Basingstoke: Palgrave.

Holmes, J. (2006). *Gendered Talk at Work*. Oxford: Blackwell.

Holmes, J. (2007). 'Social Constructionism, and Feminist Sociolinguistics.' *Gender and Language*, 1(1), 51-65.

Holmes, J. and Stubbe, M (2003). "Feminine' Workplaces: Stereotypes and Reality.' In J. Holmes and M. Meyerhoff (eds), *The Handbook of Language and Gender*. Oxford: Blackwell (pp. 573-599).

Holmes, J., and Meyerhoff, M. (1999). 'The Community of Practice: Theories and Methodologies in Language and Gender Research.' *Language and Society*, 28(2), 173-183.

Holmes, J., and Meyerhoff, M. (2003). 'Different Voices, Different Views: An Introduction to Current Research in Language and Gender.' In J. Holmes and M. Meyerhoff (Eds.), *The Handbook of Gender and Language*. Oxford: Blackwell, (pp. 1-19).

Holmes, J., and Meyerhoff, M. (Eds.)(2003). *The Handbook of Language and Gender*. Oxford: Malden Blackwell.

Howarth, D. (2000). *Discourse*. Buckingham: Open University Press.

http://www.un.org/esa/gopher-data/conf/fwcw/off/a—20.en

Huntington, S. P. (1993). 'The Clash of Civilizations?' *Foreign Affairs*, 72(3).

Hyman, L. and Katamba, X. F. (1993). A New Approach to Tone in Luganda. *Language* 69 (1), 34-67.

Hyman, L. (2001). *Orthography and Identity in Cameroon*. Pennsylvania. University of Pennsylvania.

Ige, B., and Kadt, E. d. (2002). 'Gendering Politeness: Zulu-speaker Identities at the University of Natal, Durban.' *South African Linguistics and Applied Language Studies*, 20(3), 147-161.

Ilhaam, W. A.-Y. (2003). 'On the Subject of Kings and Queens: "Traditional" African Leadership and The Diasporal Imagination.' *African Studies Quarterly*, 7(1).

Ilie, C. (2006) 'Parliamentary Discourses.' In Keith Brown (ed.) *Encyclopedia of Language and Linguistics*, 2nd Edition, Vol. 9, Oxford: Elsevier, pp.188-197.

Jager, S. (2001). 'Discourse and Knowledge: Theoretical and Methodological Aspects of a Critical Discourse and Dispositive Analysis.' In R. Wodak and M. Meyer (Eds.), *Methods of Critical Discourse Analysis*. London: Sage.

James, D., and Drakich, J. (1993). 'Understanding Gender in Amount of Talk: a Critical Review of Research.' In D. Tannen (Ed.), *Gender and Conversational Interaction*. Oxford: Oxford University Press.

Jaworski, A. (1993). *The Power of Silence: Social and Pragmatic Perspectives*. Newbury Park, CA: Sage

Jaworski, A., and Coupland, N. (1999). *The Discourse Reader*. London: Routeledge.

Jonestone, B. (2000). *Qualitative Methods in Sociolinguistics*. Oxford: Oxford University Press.

Jule, A. (2006). 'Silence as Morality: Lecturing at a Theological College.' In J. Baxter (Ed.), *Speaking Out: The Female Voice in Public Contexts*. Basingstoke: Palgrave.

Kamada, L. (2005). Multi-perspectival Approach within Feminist Poststructuralist Discourse Analysis. BAAL/CUP Seminar: Theoretical and Methodological Approaches to Gender and Language Study. The University of Birmingham, UK.

Kaplan, C. (1998). 'Language and Gender.' In D. Cameron (Ed.), *The Feminist Critique of Language: A Reader* London: Routledge, (pp. 54-64).

Kaur, S. (2005). 'The Performance of Gender in Online Discussion Boards.' *BAAL/CUP Seminar: Theoretical and Methodological Approaches to Gender and Language Study*. The University of Birmingham, UK.

Kendall, S. (2006). 'Positioning the Female Voice within Work and Family.' In J. Baxter (Ed.), *Speaking Out: The Female Voice in Public Contexts*. Basingstoke: Palgrave, (pp. 179-197).

Kennedy, G. (1998). *Comparative Rhetoric: A Historical and Cross-Cultural Introduction*. New York: Oxford University Press.

Kiesling, S. F. (2005). 'Homosocial Desire in Men's Talk: Balancing and Re-creating Cultural Discourses of Masculinity.' *Language in Society*. 34, 695-726.

Kimenyi, A. (1992). 'Why is it that women in Rwanda do not marry?' Paper presented at the 2nd Berkeley Women and Language Conference, Berkeley.

Kitetu, C., and Sunderland, J. (2000). 'Gendered Discourse in the Classroom: the Importance of Cultural Diversity. In Gender Issues in Language Education.' *The Temple University of Japan Working Papers in Applied Linguistics,* 17.

Kitzinger, C. (2000). 'Doing Feminist Conversational Analysis.' Feminism and Psychology, 10(2), 163-193.

Klages, M. (2001). Structuralism/Post-structuralism, http://www.colorado.edu/English/ENGL2012Klages/1997derridaA.html

Konde, E. (2005). *African Women and Politics: Knowledge, Gender and Power in Male-Dominated Cameroon.* Portland: Edwin Mellen Press.

Kosetzi, K. (2007). 'Harnessing a Critical Discourse Analysis of Gender in Television Fiction.' In K. Harrington, L. Litosseliti, H. Sauntson and J. Sunderland (Eds.) *Gender and Language Research Methodologies.* Basingstoke: Palgrave.

Kotthof, H., and Wodak, R. (Eds.). (1997). *Communicating Gender in Context.* Amsterdam: John Benjamins.

Kress, G. (1997). *Before Writing: Rethinking the Paths to Literacy.* London: Routeledge.

Kress, G., and Hodge, B. (1979). *Language as Ideology.* London: Routeledge.

Kress, G., and van Leeuwen, T. (2001). *Multimodal Discourse.* London: Arnold.

Kristeva, J. (1986). 'Word, Dialogue, and the Novel. In T. Moi' (Ed.), *The Kristeva Reader* New York: Columbia University Press, (pp. 35-61).

Krzyanowski, M. and Wodak, R. (2007). 'Multiple Identities, Migration and Belonging: 'Voices of Migrants'. In C. Caldas-Coulthard and R. Iedema (Eds.), *Identity Troubles: Critical Discourse and Contestations of Identification.* Basingstoke: Palgrave

Labov, William (1966). *The Social Stratification of English in New York City.* Center for Applied Linguistics, Washington, DC

Labov, W. (1990). 'The Intersection of Sex and Social Class in the Course of Linguistic Change.' *Language Variation and Change* 2: 205–54.

Lakoff, R. (1975). *Language and Women's Place.* New York: Harper

Lave, J., and Wenger, E. (1991). *Situated Learning: Legitimate Peripheral Participation.* Cambridge and New York: Cambridge University Press.

Lazar, M. (2002). 'Consuming Personal Relationships: Achievement of Feminine Self-identity through Other-centredness.' In L. Litosseliti and J. Sunderland (Eds.), *Gender Identity and Discourse Analysis* Amsterdam: John Benjamins, (pp. 259-272).

Lazar, M. (2005). *Feminist Critical Discourse Analysis: Gender, Power and Ideology.* London: Palgrave.

Leander, M. K. (2002). 'Silencing in Classroom Interaction: Producing and Relating Social Spaces.' *Discourse Processes,* 34(2), 193-235.

Leiter, K. (1980). *A Primer on Ethnomethodology.* London: OUP.

LeMaster, B. (2002). 'What Difference Does Difference Make: Negotiating Gender and Generation in Irish Sign Language?' In S. Benor, M. Rose, D. Sharma, J. Sweetland and Q. Zhang. (Eds.), Gendered *Practices in Language.* CSLI Publications.

Lemke, J. (1995). *Textual Politics: Discourse and Social Dynamics.* London: Taylor and Francis.

Litosseliti, L. (2002). 'Head to Head': Gendered Repertoires in Newspapers Articles. In L. Litosseliti and J. Sunderland (Eds.), *Gender Identity and Discourse Analysis* Amsterdam: John Benjamins, (pp. 129-148).

Litosseliti, L. (2006). Constructing Gender in Public Arguments. In J. Baxter (Ed.), *Speaking Out: The Female Voice in Public Contexts.* Basingstoke: Palgrave.

Litosseliti, L., and Sunderland, J. (Eds.). (2002). *Gender Identity and Discourse Analysis.* Amsterdam: John Benjamins.

Loots, L. (2006). 'Transmission: a South African Choreographer Uses Language to Reflect on the Gendered 'Embodiment' of Writing with and on the Body.' *South African Linguistics and Applied Language Studies,* 24(4), 449 - 460.

Maltz, D., and Borker, R. (1982). 'A Cultural Approach to Male-Female Miscommunication.' In J. J. Gumperz (Ed.), *Language and Social Identity.* Cambridge: Cambridge University Press.

Manuh, T. (1998). 'Women in African Development.' Retrieved 2006

Marra, M., Schnurr, S., and Holmes, J. (2006). 'Effective Leadership in New Zealand Workplaces: Balancing Gender and Role.' In J. Baxter (Ed.), *Speaking Out: The Female Voice in Public Contexts.* Basingstoke: Palgrave.

Martin Rojo, L. (2006). 'Gender and Political Discourse.' In K. Brown (Ed.), *Encyclopedia of Languages and Linguistics.* Elsevier.

Martin Rojo, L. and C. Gomes-Esteban (2003). Discourse at Work: When Women Take on the Role of Managers. In G. Weiss and R. Wodak (Eds.), *Critical Discourse Analysis: Theory and Interdisciplinarity.* London: Palgrave/Macmillan, (pp. 241-271).

Martin, J. (1992). *English Text: System and Structure.* Amsterdam: John Benjamins.

Martinovski, B. (2006). 'A Framework for the Analysis of Mitigation in Courts: Toward a Theory of Mitigation.' *Journal of Pragmatics* 38, 2065–2086.

Mathieu, N. (1989). Identité sexuelle/sexué/desexe?   109-47. Aix-en-Provence:Université de Provence. (D. Leonard and L. Adkins, Trans.). In A.-M. Daune-Richard, et al. (Eds.), 1996 *Catégorisation de sexe et constructions* scientifiques. London: Taylor and Francis, (pp. 42-71).

Mbangwana, P. N. (1996). 'Trends in Female Names in Cameroon: An Expression of Self-affirmation.' *Epasa Moto (Revue bilingue de langue, lettres et de culture),* 1(3), 75- 81.

Mbembe, A. (2001). *On the Postcolony.* Berkeley: University of California Press.

McElhinny, B. (1996). 'Strategic Essentialism in Sociolinguistic Studies of Gender.' In N. Warner, J. Halers, L. Biomes, M. Oliver, S. Wertheim and M. Chen (Eds.), *Gender and Belief Systems: Proceedings of the Fourth Berkeley Conference on Women and Language Berkeley: Berkeley Women and Language Group,* University of California, (pp. 469–480).

McElhinny, B. (1998). 'Genealogies of Gender Theory: Practice Theory and Feminism in Socio-cultural and Linguistic Anthropology.' *Social Analysis* 42(3), 164–189.

McElhinny, B. (2003). 'Theorizing Gender in Sociolinguistics and Linguistic Anthropology' In J. Holmes and M. Meyerhoff (Eds.), *The Handbook of Language and Gender.* Oxford: Backwell.

Meyerhoff, M. (1999). 'Sorry in the Pacific: Defining Communities, Defining Practices.' *Language and Society,* 28(2), 225-238.

Meyerhoff, M. (2003). Claiming a Place: Gender, Knowledge, and Authority as Emergent Properties. In J. Holmes and M. Meyerhoff (Eds.). *The Handbook of Language and Gender.* Oxford: Malden Blackwell, (pp. 302-326).

Mfonyam, J. (1989). *Tone in Orthography: The Case of Bafut and Related Languages.* Yaoundé: SIL Cameroon.

Mills, S. (1997; 2000). *Discourse.* (1st and 2nd editions.). London: Longman.

Mills, S. (2002). 'Third Wave Feminism Linguistics and the Analysis of Sexism and Naming Practices.' *IGALA2.* University of Lancaster, UK.

Milroy, L. (1980). *Language and Social Networks.* Oxford: Blackwell.

Mukama, R. (1994). 'The culturo-linguistic dimension of women's invisibility and silence: an East African perspective.' *Paper presented at the Third Berkeley Women and language Conference,* Berkeley.

Mungwa, A. (2002). Mastering political forces and structures for empowerment: challenges for women in post-independent Cameroon

http://www.codesria.org/Links/Research/Gender/Mungwa.htm

Mutaka, N. M., and Tamanji, P. N. (2000). *An Introduction to African Linguistics.* Muenchen: Lincom Europa.

Mutwii, M. J., and Kioko, A. N. (2004). *New Language Bearings in Africa: A Fresh Quest.* Clevedon: Multilingual Matters.

Myers, G. (2004). 'Matters of Opinion: Talking about Public Issues.' *Studies in Interactional Sociolinguistics,* 19.

Naaum, C. N. (2005). 'Gender Equality and Political Representation: a Nordic Comparison.' *Western European Politics,* 28(4).

Ndongo-Semengue M. A., and Sadembouo, E. (1999). 'L'Atlas linguistique du Cameroun: les langues nationales et leur gestion.' In G. M. Ze (Ed.), *Le français langue africaine: enjeux et atouts pour la Francophonie* Paris: Publisud, (pp.67-79).

Ngo Nsom, J. (2000). *The Convention on the Elimination of all Forms of Discrimination against Women: Cameroon Report.* New York: United Nations.

Ngwang, E. (2004). "Women's Empowerment and Political Change: A Study of Bole Butake's Lake God, The Survivors and And Palm Wine Will Flow.' *Revue ALIZES* 23.

Niba, M. L. (1995). 'Bafut under Colonial Administration 1900-1949' in Perspectives on the State: From Political History to Ethnography in Cameroon.' In I. Fowler and D. Z. Berghahn (Eds.), *Essays for Sally Chilvers.* Oxford.

Nkwi, P., and Warnier, J. P. (1982). *Elements for a History of the Western Grassfields.* Yaoundé: Yaoundé University Press.

Norrick, N. R. (2001). 'Discourse and Semantics.' In D. Schiffrin, D. Tannen and H. E. Hamilton (Eds.), *The Handbook of Discourse Analysis* Oxford: Blackwell, (pp. 76-99).

Norris, P. (2001). 'Cultural Obstacles to Equal Representation.' *Journal of Democracy*, 12(3), 126-140.

Nsamenang, A. B. (2000). *Fathers, Families, and Child Well-Being in Cameroon: A Review of the Literature. National Center on Fathers and Families.* Philadelphia: University of Pennsylvania.

Nyamnjoh, F., and Rowlands, M. (1998). 'Elite Associations and the Politics of Belonging in Cameroon Africa' *Journal of the International African Institute, The Politics of Primary Patriotism.* 68(3), 320-337.

Nyack, P., and Bide, T. (1989). 'La femme camerounaise dans la vie sociale: Plan Socio-politique. MINASCOF: La Femme Camerounaise de Demain'. Paper presented at the *Actes du Symposium*, Yaoundé.

O'Barr, W., and Atkins, B. (1980). "Women's language" or " powerless language"? In S. McConnel-Ginet, R. Boker and N. Furman (Eds.), *Women and Language in Literature and Society.* New York: Praeger.

Ochs, E. (1992). 'Indexing Gender.' In A. Duranti and C. Goodwin (Eds.), *Rethinking Context: Language as an Interactive Phenomenon.* Cambridge: Cambridge University Press.

Parsons, and Shils. (1990 [1951]) 'Toward a General Theory of Action (Harvard University Press),' 53-79. In J. C. Alexander, S. Seidman (Eds.) Culture *and Society.* Cambridge: Cambridge University Press

Pennycook, A. (2001). *Critical Applied Linguistics: A critical approach.* London: Lawrence Eribaum Associates.

Philips, S. (2003). The Power of Gender Ideologies in Discourse. In J. Holmes and M. Meyerhoff (Eds.). *The Handbook of Language and Gender.* (pp. 252-276). Oxford: Malden Blackwell

Pienaar, K. and Bekker, I. (2006). 'Invoking the Feminine Physical Ideal: Bitch-slapping, She-men and Butch Girls.' *South African Linguistics and Applied Language Studies,* 24(4), 437 - 447.

Poggio, B. (2004). Casting the 'Other': Gender Citizenship in Politicians' Narratives.' *Journal of Language and Politics,* 3 (2), 323-343.

Preissle, J., and Grant, L. (2004). 'Fieldwork Traditions: Ethnography and Participant Observation.' In K. B. de Marrais and S. D. Lapan (Eds.), *Foundations for Research: Methods of Inquiry in Education and the Social Sciences.* Earlbaum/TechBooks Associates (pp. 161-180).

Reddy, V. (2002). 'Perverts and Sodomites: Homophobia as Hate Speech in Africa.' *South African Linguistics and Applied Language Studies,* 20(3), 163 - 175.

Reddy, V. and Potgieter, C. (2006). 'Real men stand up for the truth': Discursive Meanings in the Jacob Zuma Rape Trial.' *South African Linguistics and Applied Language Studies,* 24(4), 511 - 521.

Reisigl, M., and Wodak, R. (2001). *Discourse and Discrimination: Rhetoric's of Racism and Anti-Semitism.* London: Routledge.

Remlinger, K. (1999). 'Widening the Lens of Language and Gender Research: Integrating Critical Discourse Analysis and Cultural Practice Theory. *Linguistik Online,* 2(1).

Rich, A. (1978) *Women and Honor: Some Notes on Lying.* Motheroot Publications.

Rich, A. (1980). Compulsory Heterosexuality and Lesbian Existence. *Signs,* 5(4), 631-660.

Romaine, S. (2003). 'Variation in Language and Gender.' In J. Holmes and M. Meyerhoff (Eds.), *The Handbook of Gender and Language.* Oxford: Blackwell.

Ros, J. V. D. (1994). 'The State and Women: A Troubled Relationship in Norway.' In B. J. Nelson and N. Chowdhury (Eds.), *Women and Politics Worldwide.* Yale University Press.

Roseberry, W. (1989). Anthropologies and Histories. New Brunswick: Rutgers

University Press.

Rudwick, S. and Shange, M. (2006). 'Sociolinguistic Oppression or Expression of 'Zuluness'? 'IsiHlonipho' among isiZulu-speaking Females.' *South African Linguistics and Applied Language Studies,* 24(4), 473 - 482.

Sadembouo, E., and Chumbow, B. S. (1990).Standardisation et modernisation de la langue Fefe. *Journal of West African Languages.*

Sadiqi, F. (2003). *Women, Gender and Language in Morocco.* Leiden: Brill.

Said, E. (1985). *Orientalism Reconsidered. Cultural Critique,* 1, 89-107.

Schegloff, E. (1997). 'Who's text? Whose context?' *Discourse and Society,* 8.

Schegloff, E. (1999). 'Schegloff's Text as Billig's Data: a Critical Reply.' *Discourse and Society,* 10.

Schipper, M. (2003) *Never Marry a Woman with Big Feet: Proverbs from around the World.* London: Yale University Press.

Schiffrin, D. (1994). *Approaches to Discourse.* Cambridge: Blackwell.

Schiffrin, D., Tannen, D., and Hamilton, H. (Eds.). (2001). Handbook *of Discourse Analysis.* Oxford: Blackwell.

Scollon, R.; Tsang, W. K.; Li, D.; Yung, V., and Jones, R. (1999). 'Voice, Appropriation and Discourse Representation in a Student Writing Task.' *Linguistic and Education,* 9(3), 227-243.

Sedlack, M. (2000). 'You Really Do Make an Unrespectable Foreigner Policy: Discourse on ethnic issues in the Austrian Parliament.' In R. Wodak and T. van Dijk (Eds.), *Racism at the Top: Parliamentary Discourse on Ethnic Issues in Six European States.* Klagenfurt: Drava Verlag.

Shaw, S. (2000). 'Language, Gender and Floor Apportionment in Political Debates.' *Discourse and Society,* 11(3), 401-418.

Shaw, S. (2006). 'Governed by Rules?: The Female Voice in Parliamentary Debates.' In J. Baxter (Ed.), *Speaking Out: The Female Voice in Public Contexts.* Basingstoke: Palgrave.

Silverman, D. (2001). *Interpreting Qualitative Data: Methods for Analysing Text, Talk, and Interaction.* 2nd Edition. London: Sage

Silverman, D. (2003). 'Analysing Text and Talk.' In N. K. Denzin and Y. S. Lincoln (Eds.), *Collecting and Interpreting Qualitative Materials* London: Sage, (pp. 340-362).

Skeggs, B. (1994). 'Situating the Production of Feminist Ethnography.' In M. Maynard and J. Purvis (Eds.), *Researching Women's Lives.* London: Taylor and Francis, (pp.72-93).

Speers, S. (2002). 'What can conversation analysis contribute to feminist methodology? Putting reflexivity into practice.' *Discourse and Society,* 13(6).

Spertus, E. (1991). 'Why Are There so Few Female Computer Scientists?' *Artificial Intelligence Laboratory.* MIT.

Spivak, G. C. (1996). 'Feminism and Critical Theory.' In G. C. Spivak, D. Landry and G. MacLean (Eds.), *The Spivak Reader.* London: Routledge.

Stevens, P. J. (2006). 'Women's Aggressive Use of Genital Power in Africa.' *Transcultural Psychiatry,* 43 (4), 592–599.

Stoeltje, B., Firmin-Sellers, K. and Okello-Ogwang, E. (2002). 'Introduction to Special Issue: Women, Language, and La w in Africa.' *Africa Today,* 49(1).

Stokoe, E., and Smithson, J. (2001). 'Making Gender Relevant in Conversational Analysis and Gender Categories in Interaction.' *Discourse and Society,* 12(2), 217-244.

Stokoe, E., and Weatherall, A. (2002). 'Gender, Language, Conversational Analysis and Feminism.' *Discourse and Society,* 13(6).

Stone, A. (2004). 'On the Genealogy of Women: Against Essentialism.' In S. Gillis, G. Howie and B. Munford (Eds.). *Third Wave Feminism: A Critical Assessment.* Basingstoke: Palgrave.

Sunderland, J. (1996). 'Gendered Discourse in the Foreign Language Classroom: A Teacher-Student and Student-Teacher Talk, and the Social Constructions of Children's Femininities and Masculinities.' PhD thesis, Lancaster: Lancaster University.

Sunderland, J. (2004). *Gendered Discourses.* Basingstoke: Palgrave.

Sunderland, J. (2006). *Language and Gender: An Advanced Resource Book.* London: Routledge

Swales, J. (1990). *Genre Analysis: English in Academic and Research Settings.* Cambridge: Cambridge University Press

Swales, J. (1998). Other Floors, Other Voices: A Textography of a Small University Building. Mahwah, NJ: Lawrence Erlbaum Associates.

Swann, J. (2000). 'Gender and Language Use.' In R. Mesthrie, Swann, A. Demerit and W. L. Leap (Eds.), *Introducing Sociolinguistics.* Philadelphia: John Benjamins, (pp. 216-248).

Swann, J. (2002). 'Yes, but is it Gender?' In L. Litosseliti and J. Sunderland (Eds.). *Gender Identity and Discourse Analysis.* Amsterdam: John Benjamins, (pp. 43-67).

Tadadjeu, M., and Sadembouo, E. (1984). *General Alphabet of Cameroon Languages.* Yaoundé: University of Yaoundé.

Takougang, J. and Krieger, M (Eds.) (1998). *The African State and Society in the 1990s: Cameroon's Political Crossroads.* Boulder, Colorado: Westview Press.

Talbot, M. (1995). *Fictions at Work: Language and Social Practice in Fiction.* London: Longman.

Talbot, M. (1998). *Language and Gender: An Introduction.* Oxford: Polity Press.

Talbot, M., Atkinson, K., and Atkinson, D. (2003). *Language and Power in the Modern World.* Edinburgh: Edinburgh University Press.

Tannen, D. and Saville-Troike, M. E. (1985). *Perspectives on Silence.* Norwood: Ablex Publishing Corporation.

Tannen, D. (1986). That's not What I Meant. London: Dent.

Tannen, D. (1990). *You Just Don't Understand: Women and Men in Conversation.* New York: William Morrow.

Tannen, D. (1993). *Gender and Conversational Interaction.* New York: Oxford University Press.

Tannen, D. (1998). 'Talk in Intimate Relationships.' In J. Coates (Ed.), *Language and Gender: A Reader.* London: Blackwell.

Tegomoh, E.N. (1999). 'Property, Power and Gender. Women's World conference.' Tromso, Norway.

Temple, B. (1997). 'Watch your Tongue: Issues in Translation and Cross-cultural Research.' *Sociology* 31(3), 607–618.

Thetela, P. H. (2002). 'Sex discourses and gender constructions in Southern Sotho: a case study of police interviews of rape/sexual assault victims.' *South African Linguistics and Applied Language Studies,* 20(3), 177 - 189.

Thetela, P. H. (2006). 'Culture, Voice and the Public Sphere: A Critical Analysis of the Female Voices on Sexuality in Indigenous South African Society.' In J. Baxter (Ed.), *Speaking Out: The Female Voice in Public Contexts.* Basingstoke: Palgrave, (pp. 198-216).

Thiesmeyer, L. (Ed.). (2003). *Discourse and Silencing.* Amsterdam: John Benjamins.

Thompson, J. B. (1984). *Studies in the Theory of Ideology.* Cambridge and Oxford: Polity Press / Basil Blackwell.

Thompson, J. B. (1990). *Ideology and Modern Culture.* Cambridge and Oxford: Polity Press / Basil Blackwell .

Thompson, M. (2006). 'Third Wave Feminism and the Politics of Motherhood.' *Genders Online Journal,* 43.

Titscher, S., Meyer, M., Wodak, R., and Vetter, E. (Eds.). (2000). *Methods of Text and Discourse Analysis.* London: Sage.

Toolan, M. (1997). 'What is Critical Discourse Analysis and why are People Saying such Terrible Things about it?' *Language and Literature.* 6(2) 83-103.

Trudgill, P. (1972). 'Sex, Covert Prestige and Linguistic Change in the Urban British English of Norwich.' *Language in Society.* 1. 179–95.

Uchida, A. (1998). 'Doing Gender and Building Culture: Towards a Model of Women's Intercultural Communication.' *The Howard Journal of Communication*, 8.

Van de Ros, J. and Guldvik, I. (2005). 'Discursive Strategies in Gender Quota Debates in Corporate Norway: Per Gyntian strategies?' Paper presented at the ECPR workshop: Deconstructing Nordic Discourses on Gender Equality, Budapest.

Van Dijk, T. (1993). Editor's forward to Critical Discourse Analysis. *Discourse and Society*, 4(2), 131-132.

Van Dijk, T. (1996). *Discourse, Power and Access*. In C. R. Caldas-Coulthard and M. Coulthard (Eds.), *Texts and Practices*. London: Routeledge, (pp. 84-107).

Van Dijk, T. (1997). *Discourse as Social Interaction*. London: Sage.

Van Dijk, T. (1997). 'What is Political Discourse Analysis?' Paper presented at the Key-note address Congress Political Linguistics, Amsterdam.

Van Dijk, T. (1997). 'What is Political Discourse Analysis?' *Political Linguistics: Belgian Journal of Linguistics*, 11.

Van Dijk, T. (1998). *Ideology: a Multidisciplinary Approach*. London: Sage.

Van Dijk, T. (2000). 'Parliamentary Debates.' In R. Wodak and T. van Dijk (Eds.), *Racism at the Top: Parliamentary Discourses on Ethnic Issues in Six European States*. Klagenfurt: Drava Verlag.

Van Dijk, T. (2001). 'Multidisciplinary CDA: A Plea for Diversity.' In R. Wodak and M. Meyer (Eds.), *Methods of Critical Discourse Analysis*. London: Sage. (pp. 95-120).

Van Dijk, T. (2004). 'Text and Context in Parliamentary Discourse.' In P. Bayley (Ed.), *Cross-Cultural Perspectives on Parliamentary Discourse*. Amsterdam: John Benjamins (pp. 339-372).

Van Dijk, T. (2005). *Racism and Discourse in Spain and Latin America*. Amsterdam: John Benjamins.

Van Dijk, T. (2006). 'Discourse and Manipulation.' *Discourse and Society*, 17(3), 359-383.

Van Dijk, T. (2006). 'Discourse, Context and Cognition.' *Discourse Studies*, 8(1), 159-177.

Van Dijk, T. (2006). 'Introduction: Discourse, Interaction and Cognition.' *Discourse Studies*, 8(1), 5-7.

Van Dijk, T. and Wodak, R. (2000). *Racism at the Top: Parliamentary Discourses on Ethnic Issues in Six European States.* Klagenfurt: Drava Verlag.

Van Eemeren, F., Grootendorst, R. and Kruiger, T. (1987). *Handbook of Argumentation Theory: a Critical Survey of Classical Backgrounds and Modern Studies.* Dordretch: Foris Publications.

Van Leeuwen, T. (1995). 'Representing Social Action.' *Discourse and Society,* 6(1), 81-106.

Van Leeuwen, T. (1996). 'The Representation of Social Actors.' In C. R. Caldas-Coulthard and M. Coulthard (Eds.), *Texts and Practices.* London: Routledge.

Van Leeuwen, T. and Wodak, R. (1999). 'Legitimising Immigration Control: a Discourse – Historical Approach.' *Discourse Studies,* 1(1), 77-122.

Van Lier, Leonardus Arnoldus (1988). *The Classroom and the Language Learner: Ethnography and Second Language Classroom Research.* London: Longman.

Verhelst, T. (1990). *No Life without Roots.* London: Zed Books.

Volosinov, V. N. (1973). *Marxism and the Philosophy of Language.* Translated by Matejka, L. and Titunik, I. R. New York: Seminar Press.

Wagner, I., and Wodak, R. (2006). 'Performing Success: Strategies of Self-Representation in Women's Biographical Narratives.' *Discourse and Society,* 17(3), 385-411.

Walker, C., Gleaves, A., and Navy, D. P. (2003). 'Problems in the Construction of Gender and Professional Identities in a United Kingdom Merchant Navy Training School.' *Research in Post-compulsory Education* 3(8).

Walsh, C. (2001). *Gender and Discourse: Language and Power in Politics, the Church and Organisations.* London: Longman.

Wanitzek, U. (2002). The Power of Language in the Discourse on Women's Rights: Some Examples from Tanzania. *Africa Today,* 49(1).

Warhol, T. (2005). 'Feminist Poststructuralist Discourse Analysis and Biblical Authority.' *BAAL/CUP Seminar: Theoretical and Methodological Approaches to Gender and Language Study.* The University of Birmingham, UK.

Watson-Gegeo, K. (1988). 'Ethnography in ESL: Defining the Essentials.' *TESOL Quarterly,* 22(4), 575- 592.

Watters, J. R. (2003). *Grassfields Bantu.* Yaoundé: SIL.

Weatherall, A., Taylor, S., and Yates, S. (Eds.). (2001). *Discourse as Data.* London: Sage.

Weedon, C. (1996). *Feminist Practice and Post-structuralist Theory* (2nd ed.). Oxford: Basil Blackwell.

Weiss, G. and Wodak, R. (2003). *Critical Discourse Analysis: Theory and Interdisciplinarity.* Basingstoke: Palgrave.

Wenger, E. (1998). *Communities of Practice.* Cambridge: Cambridge University Press.

Wenger, E., McDermott, R., Richard, M., and Snyder, W. (2002). *Cultivating Communities of Practice.* Harvard: Harvard Business School Press.

West, C., and Zimmerman, D. (1977). 'Women's Place in Everyday Talk: Reflections on Parent Child Interaction.' *Social Problems,* 24, 521-529.

West, C., and Zimmerman, D. (1987). 'Doing gender.' *Gender and Society,* 1, 25–51.

Wetherell, M. (1998). Positioning and Interpretative Repertoires: Conversation Analysis and Post-Structuralism in Dialogue. *Discourse and Society,* 9(3).

Wetherell, M., and Potter, J. (1998). 'Discourse and Social Psychology–Silencing Binaries.' *Theory and Psychology,* 8(3), 377-388.

Wetherell, M., Taylor, S., and Yates, S. (Eds.). (2002). *Discourse Theory and Practice: A Reader.* London: Sage/The Open University Press.

Widdowson, H. (1995). 'Discourse Analysis: A Critical View.' *Language and Literature,* 4, 157-172.

Widdowson, H. (1996). 'Reply to Fairclough: Discourse and Interpretation: Conjectures and Refutations.' *Language and Literature,* 5, 57-69.

Wodak, R. (1997). 'I Know, We Won't Revolutionize the World With it, But…' In H. Kotthof and R. Wodak (Eds.), *Communicating Gender in Context.* Amsterdam: John Benjamins (pp. 335- 371).

Wodak, R. (1997). *Gender and Discourse.* London: Sage.

Wodak, R. (2001). 'The Discourse-Historical Approach.' In R. Wodak and M. Meyer (Eds.), *Methods of Critical Discourse Analysis.* London: Sage. (pp. 63-94).

Wodak, R. (2003). Anti-Semitic Discourse in Post-war Austria. In L. Thiesmeyer (Ed.), *Discourse and Silencing.* Amsterdam: John Benjamins.

Wodak, R. (2003). 'Multiple Identities: The Roles of Female Parliamentarians in the EU Parliament.' In J. Holmes and M. Meyerhoff (Eds.), *The Handbook of Gender and Language.* Oxford: Oxford University Press. (pp. 671-698).

Wodak, R. (2005). 'Gender Mainstreaming and the European Union: Interdisciplinarity, Gender and CDA.' In M. Lazar (Ed.), *Feminist Critical Discourse Analysis*. Basingstoke: Palgrave. (pp. 61-89.).

Wodak, R. (2007). 'Controversial Issues in Feminist Critical Discourse Analysis.' In K. Harrington, L. Litosseliti, H. Sauntson and J. Sunderland (Eds.), *Gender and Language Research Methodologies*. Basingstoke: Palgrave.

Wodak, R., and Chilton, P. (2005). *A new Agenda in (Critical) Discourse Analysis: Theory, Methodology and Interdisciplinarity.* Amsterdam: John Benjamins.

Wodak, R., and Cillia, R. d. (2006). 'Politics and Language- Overview.' In K. Brown (Ed.), *Encyclopaedia of Language and Linguistics* (2nd ed.) Oxford: Elsevier Vol. 9, pp. 707-719.

Wodak, R., and Ludwig, C. (1999). *Challenges in a Changing World.* Vienna: Passage Verlag.

Wodak, R., and Meyer, M. (Eds.). (2001). *Methods of Critical Discourse Analysis.* London: Sage.

Wodak, R. and Meyer, M. (2009) 'Critical discourse analysis: history, agenda, theory and methodology.' In Wodak, R. and Meyer, M. (eds.) Methods of Critical Discourse Analysis (2nd edition). Sage. pp. 1-33.

Wodak, R., and Reisigl, M. (2001). *Discourse and Racism.* In D. Schiffrin, D. Tannen and H. Hamilton (Eds.), *The Handbook of Discourse Analysis.* Oxford: Blackwell.

Wodak, R., and van Dijk, T. (Eds.). (2000). *Racism at the Top: Parliamentary Discourses on Ethnic Issues in Six European States.* Klagenfurt: Drava Verlag.

Wodak, R., de Cillia, R., Reisigl, M., and K.Liebhart (1999). *The Discursive Construction of National Identity.* Edinburgh: Edinburgh University Press

Wolf, H.-G. (2001). *English in Cameroon.* Berlin: Mouton de Gruyter.

Post-structuralism www.philosopher.org.uk/poststr.htm

Young, L., and Harrison, C. (Eds.). (2004). *Systemic Functional and Critical Discourse Analysis. Studies in Social Change.* London: Continuum.

Zimmerman, D. H. and West, C. (1975). 'Sex Roles, Interruptions, and Silences in Conversation.' In B. Thorne and N. Henley (Eds.), *Language and Sex: Difference and Dominance.* Rowley, MA: Newbury House, pp. 105–29.

Appendices

Appendix 1

Extract 1: June 12 2004

QUESTION: HONORABLE ETAME FRANCOIS

Merci monsieur le Président de m'avoir donné la parole. Je vais me précipiter
[Laughter].
Cher collègue, question ? Au moment présent me semble engagé sur tous les fronts, pour conquérir l'égalité des sexes le droit d'exercer toutes les activités, l'abolition des sévices de tous genres, l'augmentation du nombre des femmes dans les assemblés etc. Il apparaît de toute évidence que le premier et seul combat gagné jusqu'à lors par la femme camerounaise est le droit de se déshabiller [Laughton] et de marcher nu en public, le droit de boire en public … eh… nous avons vu des exemples dans la fête du 08 mars [hmmm from audience] où les femmes quand elles ont défilé. J'en ai vu a Sangmélima ou les femmes on défilé, les femmes avaient leur pagne du 08 mars. J'ai vu la délégation des femmes de l'ouest qui sont passés avec les pagnes de leurs régions, les femmes du Nord sont passées avec leurs pagnes, les femmes Bamoums sont passées avec leurs pagnes, et dès que le défilé est fini, ces femmes sont rentrées dans leurs maisons, sauf les femmes de Sangmélima [general laughter…] qui sont rentrées dans les bars. Elles ont abandonnées des enfants dans les bars [continued laughter] de ' la radio équatoriale' [name of a bar], (…). [laughter and clapping] Ça c'est donc la journée de la femme.
Je demande au MINCOF, est ce qu'elle peut faire quelque chose pour amener la femme camerounaise à s'exhiber moins et à retrouver sa dignité dans les tenues qui la rend belle et respectable plutôt que sexy et désirable, car de cette tendance à vouloir être attirante a tous prix. La femme fonctionnaire, salarier, étudiante, élève, commerçante, etc., s'expose aux vices qui sont : le harcèlement

sexuel, le …. la prostitution, le pros-élitisme, la pédophilie, etc. Car un adage de chez nous dit ceci : 'qu'il n'est pas toujours nécessaire de copier la mode mais de porter ce qui te va'. [continued comments of support from men] On a toujours dit de la femme : 'ce que femme le veut, Dieu le veut'. On a toujours dit que 'la femme est la mère du monde', la femme accouche l'homme, la femme accouche la femme. Nous sommes chrétien, la femme a accouche Jésus. [comments from audience and renewed laughter] Nous avons perdu notre identité, nous avons perdu nos coutumes.

Je demande à madame la ministre, est ce qu'elle peut faire quelque chose.

Je vous remercie.

Clapping +comments

Appendix 2

FA1 : Minister of Women's Affairs

Président: **Merci monsieur le député, la parole à madame la ministre de la condition féminine.**

Mr le président de l'assemblé national, merci de me passer la parole. Permettez moi, M. le Président de l'assemblé nationale de faire encore sanitage [sic] pour présenter mes chaleureuses félicitations du haut de cette tribune, à l'honorable Eyenga Blandine [clapping] pour sa brillante élection de la loi du 08 Septembre portant à 20 le nombre de député femme à l'assemblé nationale. [clapping] Mr le Président de L'assemblé, honorables députés, l'honorable Etamé François, député du Dja et Lobo, vient de poser une question sur l'accoutrement de la femme camerounaise. Je remercie, à Sangmélima merci, je remercie l'honorable Etamé François pour la question qu'il a bien voulu poser au ministère de la condition féminine, par rapport à l'accoutrement des femmes. En distance, il s'interroge sur que le ministère de la condition féminine peut faire pour amener la femme camerounaise à s'exhiber moins et a retrouver sa dignité dans les tenus qui la rendent belle et responsable plutôt que sexy et désirable.

Je souscris justement à cette question. Permettez-moi, honorable députés à l'assemblé national de formuler des réserves quand à l'affirmation selon laquelle, le premier et seul combat gagné jusqu'à lors par la femme camerounaise est le droit de se déshabiller ou de marcher nu en public, le droit de boire en public.

Il s'agit incontestablement ici d'une appréciation excessive qui occulte des multiples combats mener et gagner tant par les femmes elles mêmes, les élus du peuple que vous êtes, les pouvoir publics ainsi que l'implication direct et personnel du chef de l'état, son excellence Paul Biya dans la promotion et l'amélioration de la vie de la femme camerounaise. A ce titre, faut-il le rappeler, la femme connaît sous le renouveau une évolution ascendante qu'il convient certes de parfaire et d'améliorer mais dont les signes positifs s'observent à travers les actes quotidiens de la vie publique. Le véritable combat de l'heure, qui constitue une préoccupation majeure pour le Président de la République reste bien la lutte contre la pauvreté ; je voudrais dire la pauvreté morale, et la promotion du genre, le partenariat homme/femme, la considération mutuelle, la contribution nécessaire de chaque genre à l'édification de la société, le renforcement des capacités des femmes pour jouer sainement et en responsable leur rôle premier de mère, épouse, de premier éducatrice, de gardienne des valeurs, de gardienne de la paix, les actrices de développement.

L'accoutrement des femmes pour lequel l'honorable Etame François m'interpelle doit donc être relativisé et placer sous son contexte réel, celui d'un phénomène de société qui bien que dans les proportions cernable, l'honorable vient de dire que c'est à Sangmélima et que partout ailleurs les femmes se sont comporté de manière digne. Ce …ce phénomène de société mérite bien d'être cerné, mérite d'être dénoncé, et des mesures d'assainissement en synergie doivent être renforcé. Ainsi, pour revenir a cette question qui concerne une femme citoyenne camerounaise, qui a des droits, et des devoirs reconnu à tout être humain sont une question de paix, de croyance et de religion prévue dans le préambule de la constitution de Janvier 1996, et à d'autres instruments nationaux. Je voudrais effectivement rappeler la manifestation de la volonté politique en matière de la promotion de la femme, instituer le problème de l'accoutrement des femmes dans son contexte, et instituer les interventions multisectorielle engager, ou engager dans le cas du partenariat homme/femme.

Monsieur, pour y faire face.

Premièrement, rappel des manifestations de la volonté politique en matière de promotion de la femme. Sur l'impulsion reître et constante du président de la république, la politique de promotion de la femme est une préoccupation de tout les instances. Celle-ci s'est manifestée une fois de plus quand le chef de l'état créait un ministère autonome et qui confiait les mission d'élaboration et de mise en œuvre des mesures respectives et relative au respect des droit de la femme camerounaise dans la société, à la disparition de toute discrimination à l'égard de la femme, et à l'accroissement des garantis d'égalité dans les domaines politiques, économiques, sociales et culturelles.

Pour la mise en œuvre de ces missions, mon département ministériel s'y emploie, en collaboration avec les partenaires au développement à fin d'engager des femmes comme l'honorable Etame François forte opportunément relever, à conquérir l'égalité des sexes, le droit d'exercer toutes les activités, l'abolition des sévices de tous genres, l'augmentation, et cela nous l'avons vécu encore hier, du nombre de femme dans l'assemblé etc. De ce point de vue, la politique de promotion de la femme interpelle la société toute entière : administrations publiques, privé, parlementaires, associations et ONG, autorités religieuses, sociétés civiles etc. a fin qu'elles soient porteuse d'espoir, pour les hommes et pour les femmes.

Deuxième point : La restitution du problème de l'accoutrement des femmes dans le contexte de la mondialisation L'honorable député relève pour sa part que 'le premier et seul combat gagner jusqu'à lors par la femme camerounaise est le droit de se déshabiller ou de marcher nu en publique, le droit de boire en publique'.

Je réfère Kay Marc Gloire, un écrivain célèbre qui disait que 'le monde est un village planétaire'. Le Cameroun ne saurait déroger à cette exigence par ce qu'il vit et évolue avec la mondialisation dont les contours malheureusement ne sont pas toujours bien maîtriser par tous. Prenons le cas, par exemple des nouvelles technologies de communication et d'information NTIC, outils efficace de lutte contre la pauvreté qui permet aux femmes en particulier de s'inspirer de ce qui se passe ailleurs, d'explorer les opportunités qu'offres les NTIC et d'exporter le cas échéant le savoir faire des femmes. Mais à l'observation, le comportement, l'habillement participe quelque fois de la mauvaise utilisation des NTIC et l'environnement dans lequel les femmes vivent. N'oublions pas que les jeunes filles, ou les garçons enviaient justement les comportements déviants aussi bien des hommes que des femmes. Selon le cas, ce sont nos enfants, nos sœurs, nos futures épouses ou époux qui ont connu une influence de l'environnement ambiant, dynamique et du cadre qui les accueille. Dès lors, il ne s'agit pas en somme, d'un problème de femmes ou hommes mais s'un problème de société qui a des valeurs social positives à préserver et des règles de conduite observer par la société globale pour garantir une société juste, pacifique, harmonieuse et dépouiller de tous les préjugés sceptiques.

Troisièmement, la préservation de la tranquillité et l'ordre publique et valeurs social positive, une affaire de tous. Le problème de l'accoutrement des femmes appelle une intervention multisectorielle. La famille : cellule de base par excellence, cadre d'éducation à la base des enfants, de promotion des valeurs sociales. Nous avons suivi l'honorable tout à l'heure, il a dit ; des femmes de telle région sont rentrées chez elle, et tels autres ne sont pas rentrées chez elle, ce sont les valeurs culturelles positives que doit…doit perpétuer par la famille. Il s'agit donc de la promotion des valeurs sociales et culturelles positives, modernes pour développer le goût de l'effort, le goût du travail bien fait, le goût du respect de l'autre, de l'excellence sur tous les plans.

La famille est donc appeler à se renforcer d'avantage pour que l'éducation et la formation reçu puisse permettre d'avoir un citoyen moderne ou une citoyenne moderne pour faire la fierté du Cameroun. Et c'est à ce fait que le thème de la 14ᵉᵐᵉ édition de la journée de l'Enfant Africain a porté sur « Famille et Enfant ».

Les pouvoirs publics : Le problème de l'accoutrement des femmes rentre dans le cas de la préservation des bonnes mœurs, la décence, et de l'ordre public. Les autorités administratives locale ont ordre d'agir à ce niveau : préservation de l'ordre public, prévention et gestions des mérites sociaux, l'éducation national à travers l'éducation de la citoyenneté, les forces de l'ordre dans les systèmes de maintien de la paix sociale qui jouent un rôle non négligeable, les médias, les services publics et privés à l'instance de l'émission télévisée déviance sont déjà un travail d'éducation et de sensibilisation de l'opinion publique sur les méfaits pervers de tels comportements asociaux. Les déviances aussi bien chez les hommes que les femmes. Le ministère de la condition féminine dans le cadre d'instance de promotion de la femme, institution technique spécialisé de promotion de la femme, implanté dans certains départements et arrondissement, mène au quotidien les actions d'éducation, de sensibilisation et de promotion des valeurs morales et sociales positive ainsi que celle de protection de la femme contre les déviances social. Ces actions se matérialisent par l'éducation morale et physique aussi bien que les jeunes filles des systèmes scolaires que des femmes.

L'éducation sexuel, la maîtrise de la procréation, l'éducation à la vie familiale, rôle de mère, très important, rôle d'épouse également, de gardienne des valeurs social positive et d'agent de développement. L'éducation à la parenté responsable et à ce niveau, nous voulons développer cette éducation dans le cadre du genre, la parenté responsable de l'homme et de la femme. Le renforcement des capacités des femmes en matière de l'utilisation rationnelle optimale et positive des NTIC, en les mettant justement en garde contre les effets néfaste des NTIC. L'éducation de la femme aux droits et devoirs de la femme, dans ce cas effectivement, quels sont les valeurs, quelle est l'éthique dans une société. La lutte contre les IST/VIH/SIDA pour la prévention par l'abstinence, la fidélité et le cas d'échéant ou je dis le cas d'échéant, l'utilisation systématique des préservatifs. En troisième lieu, des partenaires, les représentants du peuple dans le cadre de leurs activités de proximité avec les populations, d'encadrement et d'informations de celle ci. Par le billet des projets de développement, les élus du peuple pourraient ainsi également mener d'autres actions similaires, je vous y invite, ayant trait aux effets de la déviance sociale et de leur corollaires. Les associations et ONG, courroies de transmission entre les pouvoirs publiques et des populations mènent à leur niveau des actions d'éducation et de sensibilisation des femmes. Au total, le maintien de la tranquillité, de la paix et cohésion social ainsi que celui de l'ordre publique, est une exigence fondamentale qui interpelle les hommes, les femmes, les pouvoirs publiques, les partenaires aux développements pour une approche systémique et un partenariat actif, durable, pour le bonheur de nos populations.

Voilà honorable président de l'assemblée nationale, honorable députés, l'essaie de réponse que je voulais apporter à ce problème lié au comportement des femmes.

Je vous remercie.

Merci monsieur le président de l'assemblée nationale.